Strategic Cost Management

A Handbook for Operating Managers

By

John D. Hanson, Ph.D.

in cooperation with the

Supply Chain Management Institute

of the

University of San Diego

ISBNs:
Hardback: 978-1-7372572-0-2
Paperback: 978-1-7372572-1-9
Ebook: 978-1-7372572-2-6

Acknowledgements

A work such as this is never the sole effort of the author whose name appears on the cover, but incorporates contributions from many others who are deserving of acknowledgement. Among these, several are deserving of particular recognition.

This list begins with Dr. David N. Burt who founded the Supply Chain Management Institute at the University of San Diego, and whose dedication to the discipline of strategic cost management resulted in the creation of the courses by that name at both graduate and undergraduate levels.

One of Dr. Burt's students, and a co-author, is Jimmy Anklesaria, who has gone on to create a consultancy business in the field. Jimmy has made numerous contributions to the cost courses at the University of San Diego, both as an instructor and as an employer and mentor for many of our students.

Another individual deserving of special recognition is Raymond P. Hummell, an alumnus of USD and the longest-serving teacher of our cost management courses. Ray has done much of the heavy lifting in developing the course content that is reflected in this book and has served as a valuable reviewer and beta-tester of the contents.

Finally, thanks are due to my employer, the University of San Diego, for providing the support needed to write this book, and to the many students who have passed through our cost courses and given valuable feedback on the material. In recognition of this, all proceeds from this book go to support the activities of the Supply Chain Management Institute to "pay it forward."

Introduction

There are many books about cost, but most are concerned with measuring, predicting or reducing cost. This book addresses the *management* of cost – a more comprehensive activity that requires all of these activities but requires a more strategic view and an expanded tool set. The origins of this book lie in a family of courses called Strategic Cost Management, offered by the University of San Diego at both graduate and undergraduate levels as part of its Supply Chain Management program. This course has been well-received, with numerous students reporting that they found it to be one of the more useful courses in their programs. Over the years, different faculty members have made wide-ranging contributions to the course content, and this book is an effort to capture all of these and preserve them for future use. We think that the content will be valuable to a wider audience – anyone who is charged with managing cost in some way.

Because these courses are part of Supply Chain Management programs, the focus is on those who will work in this field and who will be concerned with the purchasing of goods or contracting for the outside services that are needed to run a business. Since these activities account for somewhere around two thirds of the total turnover of a typical business, there is an acute need to manage these costs. Accordingly, the emphasis will be on managing the costs that are incurred outside the four walls of the firm, although most of the tools can be applied internally as well.

To develop the higher-level view that we call Strategic Cost Management, it is necessary to cut across the fields of Accounting (both managerial and financial), Economics, Finance, Supply Chain Management, Operations Management, Industrial Engineering and New Product Development. It is the integration of these perspectives that makes this book unique and, hopefully, useful.

While achieving a more comprehensive understanding of a subject area is a good thing, more specific learning outcomes are needed if this book is to be useful. There are two high-level learning objectives that will run through the chapters that follow. The first is, fairly obviously, that the reader will have the tools to analyze a wide variety of situations and make the right or appropriate decisions. The second objective may be somewhat less obvious, and that is that the reader will have the tools to convince others that a decision is the right one. This is not a trivial point; far too often a correct evaluation goes nowhere because the analyst is unable to establish sufficient credibility for the result. Operationally-focused managers, particularly those in Purchasing or Manufacturing, often feel that their contributions are not taken seriously at a strategic level. This is often because they have not learned to present their case in a way that is comprehensible, credible, and relevant to an upper management audience. Where numerical examples are used in this book, they are presented according to a template that will be easily grasped by, say, a Chief Financial Officer who may know very little of the operational details involved. To summarize; the goal of this book is that it should help you to make the right decision and convince others that you are right.

Table of Contents

Strategic Cost Management

Part I Introduction

This book is organized in four parts that address the following questions:

I. What is cost and why do we care?
II. How do we measure and model cost?
III. How do we manage (change) costs?
IV. How do we deal with uncertainty?

Each of these sections contains a number of chapters that address the key sub-issues. Many of these chapters also have supplements that serve to provide examples of the concepts at work, or to address material that is somewhat tangential to the main theme.

Part I consists of Chapters 1 through 5 and is concerned with establishing the basic definitions and properties of cost. More importantly, Part I deals with the role of cost in a corporate context and develops the idea that the numbers we need to care about depend on what it is we are trying to accomplish. This also sets the rationale for the remaining sections in which tools are presented for quantifying cost management activities and presenting the results in a manner that is relevant at a corporate level.

Chapter 1 – Defining Cost

We can start with the basic question of "what is cost?" but it turns out that we have to answer another question first: "why do we care?"

These seem like questions that should have simple, obvious answers, but they turn out to be not quite so straightforward when we start digging into them. Take the concept of cost itself; most of us have a pretty good general idea of what it means, but may be surprised by the range of different numbers that can be floated as "cost" in any detailed discussion. As Garrison, Noreen and Brewer[1] put it, there are "different costs for different purposes," and these can be extremely context-specific. Once we have wrapped our minds around the notion that there is no single, unequivocal quantity called cost, we can start to explore the differences between situations and see that the number we calculate depends greatly on why we care about it.

Although some differences of opinion on cost can be attributed to inconsistent or incomplete data, it is more likely that they will result from the parties (tacitly) failing to agree on the purpose of the exercise. Before we can start discussing what constitutes cost and how it should be measured, we have to consider the various reasons we might actually care about it.

Most of us have a good general sense of what cost is, so we can start with a broad definition and move to more specific formulations. In its broadest sense: cost is what you must give up in order to have or to do something. If you want to use this definition to compare alternatives (one of the main reasons we care about cost), you begin to run into various difficulties. Not the least of these is that not all of the things you must "give up" are readily visible or accurately represented by standard measures. Much of our task in managing costs involves uncovering and quantifying these hidden costs. Another major area of difficulty is that not all of the things you must "give up" can be measured in

1 Garrison, R. H., et al. (2010). Managerial Accounting. New York, NY, McGraw-Hill Irwin.

the same units. We will start by expressing as much as we can in monetary terms, while recognizing that there are some things that cannot be readily or reliably converted to currency amounts. We will return to these "intangible" issues later.

There are multiple reasons one might care about cost and we can capture the main ones as follows:

Economic Health of The Enterprise

To survive in the long run, any enterprise must generate a profit or operating surplus. In plain terms this means that there must be more cash coming in than goes out, and this is reflected in the basic equation of business:

$$\textit{Profit} = \textit{Revenue} - \textit{Cost}$$

As a representation of cash flow, this equation is incomplete in that it omits inflows of cash from investors or donors, but the general sense is valid. The "Profit," or operating surplus, can be returned to investors or kept within the enterprise, but it must be positive, at least in the long term, or the enterprise will cease to exist. However, it turns out that what we call profit depends to a large extent on what we call cost, so the definition of profit will depend on what we are seeking to measure.

There are two measures of profit that will come up repeatedly in this book. The more familiar of these is what we call *accounting profit*. This is the figure reported in financial statements and is governed by a strict set of rules that define what counts as revenue and as cost in a given period. Less commonly quoted is *economic profit*; the pricipal difference from accounting profit being the inclusion of the cost of using the assets employed by the business. Although economic profit is arguably the more important measure, the value of the assets in use fluctuates in a marketplace, so it is difficult to pin down a specific value.

That aside, the basic message is clear: anything we can do to reduce total cost in the enterprise is worthwhile. If revenue and cost are independent of each other, there is a 1:1 correspondence between a reduction in cost and an increase in profit. Of course, it is rarely true that the two are totally independent, so this assumption must be made with great care.

While there are plenty of fine details to be worked out, cost is important at the firm or enterprise level, and it is not surprising that every employee of an organization is going to feel constant pressure to reduce whatever costs are within their control. The good thing is that, at an aggregate level, these costs are fairly easy to measure. However, at the departmental or individual level, this is more difficult. This leads us to a second reason to care about cost and how it is measured.

Cost as A Measure of Performance

If cost is important, it is inevitable that management will attempt to measure it, and more importantly, use this information as a tool to motivate appropriate behavior. Many functions within an organization operate as cost centers. That is to say, they are required to perform certain tasks but are not credited with any revenue figure. The costs of performing these activities are tracked, and typically compared to a figure established during a yearly budgeting process. Being below budget supposedly indicates good performance, while being over is considered bad. This budget figure may be adjusted for ups and downs in the business cycle, or not. Often, employee evaluation and compensation are tied to this budget performance.

It is easy to see potential pitfalls in using cost information this way, not the least being how the budget number was set in the first place. There are several established ways of doing this (zero-based, activity-based, value-based, etc.) all of which are subject to error and manipulation by those affected. The more serious problem with using budget as a measure of performance is that the process implicitly assumes that costs in one area are independent of costs in other areas and also of the revenue side of the business, all of which can lead to counter-productive behavior. While protocols do exist to uncover such issues, most firms do not do this very well.

If you are in a position that is measured on cost performance, the definition of cost is simple: it is whatever your controller says it is. In that case it is very important that you understand how your assigned costs are calculated so that you can influence them most effectively either during the budgeting process or in the reporting of actual performance. However, the main point of this book is that you should also understand the cost and revenue implications of your decisions across the firm so that you are in a position to make the argument that you should be rewarded for making the "right" decision, not necessarily the one that minimizes one particular cost. Much of what follows is aimed at providing those tools.

Cost as A Tool for Evaluating Decisions

Any substantive business decision is going to have some impact on costs, often requiring a comprehensive analysis to compare alternatives. The revenue side of the equation may also be involved, increasing the complexity of the analysis somewhat. Some examples of decisions that would require analysis include:

- Should we buy our widgets from supplier A or B?
- Should we buy a new, faster machining center, and if so, from X or Y?
- Should we outsource IT support functions?
- Should we allocate more of our spending to SMWBs (small, minority, and women-owned businesses)?

This short list of examples highlights the concept of *relevance* when talking about costs. This is implicit in our broad definition: what you must give up in order to have or to do something. The point is that the only costs that are relevant are those attached to the decision, not to the thing or the activity. In other words, you must define the alternatives before you can evaluate costs.

In the first example above, we can assume that we must buy widgets – we need them to run our business. Therefore, the only costs we are interested in are those that differ between suppliers A & B. This may be as simple as comparing their prices, but may involve many other factors. If we were to introduce supplier C into the decision, it is entirely possible that these "other factors" may be a completely different list than we considered when choosing between A & B.

In the second example, we actually have three alternatives to consider: business as usual, machine X, or machine Y. While it is possible to do the sum of all relevant costs for all three alternatives, it is often easier to do two separate comparisons. For example, if machines X & Y have similar capabilities, it may easiest to see which one has the lower total cost, then compare that one to business as usual to see if it is justified.

In the third example, there is presumably an outsourcing bid in hand and the real task is in identifying all of the things that will change and assigning costs to them. The complexity of this task is obvious and highlights the need for a comprehensive approach to ensure validity of the analysis and the ultimate decision.

The fourth example introduces intangible costs. Presumably such a move will increase costs, otherwise you should already be doing it! In a philosophical sense, a business incurs social costs (essentially, costs to the public at large that are not reflected in the accounting statements) by operating, and such a move would reduce this social cost burden. If these costs were quantifiable, we could make a decision on that basis, but since they aren't, this will be a rather subjective value judgment. What is important from our perspective is that we do a comprehensive analysis to know exactly what the cost change will be.

The need to be comprehensive extends in two dimensions. One is what we call *cross-sectional*. This means that we must cut across the entire organization to identify everything that is going to change with our decision. These impacts may not be immediately visible, hence the need for careful analysis. For example, as a buyer you purchase a certain component in a particular lot size. The supplier offers you a price discount if you will order larger lots. Since the larger lot size seems well within your usage parameters, this seems like a no-brainer – take the cost reduction, apply it against your performance targets and get your year-end bonus. But wait – larger lot size means higher peak inventory of inbound goods – do you have capacity for that or will you have to use overflow warehousing? It also means higher average inventory, meaning more money tied up in working capital – what will that do to the firm? Higher average inventory also means longer throughput times; if the product is perishable will this affect production availability? There may be other issues as well, but the point is that even apparently simple decisions need to be examined for effects across the entire organization.

The second dimension is *longitudinal*. Many decisions have implications that extend into the future, and the distribution of cash flows in and out may be quite different between alternatives. The purchase of capital equipment is a prime example. Machinery may have a large upfront cost, but it also has a long service life, and small differences in operating or maintenance costs over that life may significantly impact the analysis of which machine is the better buy. The term Life Cycle Costing (LCC) is sometimes used to describe an analysis that captures the total cost of such a decision over its relevant life. The term Total Cost of Ownership (TCO) is now more commonly used for this type of analysis, the word "ownership" suggesting its applicability to the purchase of capital equipment.

The term TCO is now used more broadly in the fields of operations and supply chain management to reflect the fact that a decision involving costs needs to be comprehensive in both dimensions. Interestingly, textbooks in these fields tend to emphasize the longitudinal or life cycle dimension of cost, while academic journal articles tend to focus on the cross-sectional dimension. In this book we address both, in what might be called Total Cost Analysis, or even better: Total Relevant Cost Analysis. However, these terms are not part of the common business vocabulary, so we will use TCO throughout as the blanket term for this activity.

The ultimate expression of a TCO analysis will be a two-dimensional projection showing the total cash flow effects of a decision across the entire organization, both now, and in as many future periods as are relevant. A real-life example of a situation requiring this sort of analysis was in a cabinet-making company that purchased and processed hardwoods such as maple to make kitchen cabinets. The company was nearing capacity and was faced with the need for an expansion. Through analysis, it had previously been determined that the best option for purchasing maple, in terms of cost per usable unit, was in Common 1 grade. However, a comprehensive analysis also showed that by purchasing maple in Select grade (at a cost premium), not only were cutting and processing costs reduced, so was their capacity usage – to the extent that the projected expansion could be deferred for two years. Using both cross-sectional and longitudinal analyses showed that purchasing select grade lumber for those two years was the lower cost option. Actually, it turned out better than that, in a way. The economy took a sharp downturn before the capacity expansion was needed, and it was deferred indefinitely. That outcome illustrates another point, one that wasn't considered in the analysis, and one we won't get to until Chapter 18; that is that there is risk associated with a capital expenditure and therefore an option value attached to the ability to defer it. That value is hard to quantify and doesn't come up that often, so we can put it aside until then.

Cost as A Basis for Pricing

When a transaction for goods or services takes place, unless it is a barter situation, there will be a price involved, expressed in units of currency. That price is of critical importance to both parties. The seller will clearly not wish to sell at a price below its cost, at least not below the costs that are relevant in that particular case. What costs are relevant may change from day to day, but most companies will establish a standard cost figure and mandate that prices must exceed that figure, unless directed otherwise by a responsible executive. Cost is certainly not the only thing that should be considered when setting a price, but it is easy to see why many companies will set prices of many products on the basis of standard cost + x%. This is not quite as simple-minded as it sounds, and it can work quite well in many situations. This subject will be addressed again in much more detail in later chapters.

For the buying company, price is also critical as it determines its own costs. Knowledge of the seller's cost of the good or service allows the buyer to do the same calculation as the seller and to determine the lowest price that the seller might reasonably accept. Other factors can come into play – particularly market prices, if applicable, but that lowest price estimate would represent a target during negotiations. To simplify life, buyers and sellers sometimes agree that the cost calculation will be an open-book between the two and that pricing will be based on a formula that is in turn based on actual cost.

Whichever perspective one takes, we can see that a deep understanding of costs is essential to establishing a transaction price that is acceptable to both parties. Cost may not be the actual determinant of price, but in many situations, one cannot be certain that the price is really right without that information.

Chapter 1 – Key Takeaways

1. Cost is what you must give up in order to have or do something.
2. What you are giving up is defined by your next-best alternative, therefore, cost is not properly attached to the thing or activity itself, but to the decision to acquire it or do it.
3. Many costs are hidden and are not accurately reflected in any records.
4. Some costs are intangible in that there is no generally-accepted way to express them in monetary terms and their value must ultimately be a judgment call.
5. A total cost analysis, or TCO, requires considering the cash flow impacts of a decision across all functions of an organization and across relevant future time periods.
6. Managing (reducing) total costs is important for the economic health of any organization.
7. Costs can be used to measure performance, but must be used with care.
8. Cost analysis is an important part of decision-making.
9. Knowledge of costs is essential to determine pricing, whether buying or selling.

Chapter 2 – Cost at the Aggregated Level

In this chapter we look at costs in a generic way, which is to say we are not trying to associate them with specific products or services, but rather, seeing how they behave in general and establishing some terminology. Many of the sections will refer to each other, as there is no tidy, linear sequence to these points.

Tangible versus Intangible Costs

By convention, we express costs in units of a single currency, as this is how most transactions occur. The currency unit provides a stable and standardized way to quantify what it is that we must give up in order to get whatever benefit we are looking at. However, it is clear that not all elements of cost lend themselves readily to this treatment. There are two ways in which a situation defies easy calculation of cost. One is when the various elements of cost are measurable, but in different units and the other is when the cost impact defies quantification in any generally agreed way.

The first one is the classic "apples and oranges" problem. If alternative A will cost me three apples and alternative B will cost two oranges, which should I prefer? There is simply no way to answer that question unless we establish some cost-equivalence between the two fruits. A more business-like situation could occur when you are adding up the cost of your product in dollars, but one of the components must be purchased in euros. It is not particularly useful to say that the cost of the product is $X + €Y, so we need to find a conversion.

The key point to consider here is that there is absolutely no intrinsic way to calculate a conversion rate between two currencies, just as there is no way to calculate a conversion from oranges to apples. However, that doesn't mean we can't come up with a conversion rate, and the way we do it is to price it in a market. In the case of dollars to euros, millions of people exchange them every day, so there is a pretty good global consensus on their relative worth and it only takes a few mouse clicks to find out what that is. In the case of apples and oranges, we could go to a local market and look at the asking prices. If we can assume that these reflect market values, then we have our answer.

So, when alternatives cannot be measured in the same units, it is not possible to compare them analytically, but it is possible to compare them in a pricing market. This is how we determine the price of a barrel of oil or of a share of stock. It is also possible that there is no market for the things we are trying to compare, in which case we are on our own. It may be necessary for all the stakeholders in a discussion to negotiate and agree upon an "exchange rate" so that the discussion can continue.

The second category of difficulty in comparing costs contains those elements that cannot be quantified. We often call these *intangible* costs in the same way that we talk about the intangible benefits of a situation. Typical cases are those involving human issues such as emotions: "I'm so glad we got rid of that supplier – I couldn't sleep at night worrying about its delivery reliability." Other cases involve unpredictable future outcomes: "We can save a lot by moving our store to a backstreet location, but we will likely lose some business as a result – we just don't know how much."

Several strategies are available for dealing with so-called intangible costs. The first is to be sure that the costs are truly unmeasurable. "Intangible" should not be a convenient tag to hang on things that are simply difficult to measure or predict. Even difficult situations can often be approximated with a reasonable degree of confidence, and this is preferable to just throwing up our hands and saying, "intangible." Needless to say, where approximations are used, you should test the sensitivity of the result to errors in the approximation! A second strategy is to find a proxy for the issue in question. If I am comparing two suppliers, where one is cheaper than the other but has a reputation for unreliable deliveries, it is difficult to translate this into an acceptable price difference. However, I could take the approach of estimating how much additional buffer stock I would need to carry to neutralize that threat, and the cost of that can be calculated with some accuracy. Finally, we sometimes have to admit that an issue is truly intangible. In that case we can take a residual approach by being very comprehensive about calculating the differences stemming from all the other issues, so that we are (hopefully) left with just one intangible issue and a numerical cost difference. We can then ask, "is it worth it?" and while we may not be able to attach a precise value to it, we can often say yes or no to that question with some confidence.

Time Value of Money

An additional difficulty in comparing costs of decision alternatives is that those costs are not always simultaneous, but may be distributed over time. A typical example would be leasing[1] a piece of equipment as opposed to buying it. If we lease it, we pay a certain amount every time period for a fixed period of time, at the end of which we owe nothing and have nothing. If we buy it, we pay a larger amount right now, then at the time when the lease would have ended, we have an asset with some residual value. How are we to compare these alternatives?

This is a classic 'time value of money' problem and is treated in great detail in all Finance textbooks, so we will give only a quick summary here. To analyze situations like this there is a central rule to observe, and that is to follow the actual cash flows, not necessarily the accounting figures. We will discuss the differences in these in more detail later. In the case above, it seems fairly simple – the payments are actually cash flows and are easily observed, and we will assume that any other costs are equal between the alternatives and therefore not relevant. The residual value of the owned equipment at some future date is obviously not a cash flow, but we can conduct an imaginary sale of the equipment and treat the hypothetical proceeds as a cash inflow. Sadly, life is not quite that simple. The lease payments will normally be a reduction in net income for tax purposes, so the actual

---

1   Leases can take on many forms, ranging from a basic rental agreement to a form of financing. They also vary in how they are treated by tax and securities laws, introducing complexity that is beyond the scope of this book. For these examples, think of leases as simple rental agreements.

cash outflow will be less than the lease payment. Similarly, if you own the equipment, most taxing authorities will allow a deduction from profits to represent the depreciation of its value over time. These combined effects must be included in your assessment of the comparative costs. Since they are actually intended to be somewhat equivalent, we will ignore this complication for the moment to show some numerical examples for illustration purposes (see Supplement 2-1).

The central issue behind the time value of money problem is that a unit of income or cost at a future date has a different value to us than the same unit right now. The difference between the two is another of those things that cannot be calculated from basic principles, but can be priced in a market. For example, if you wish to take out a loan, many institutions will advertise competitive rates for what you will be paying back in the future. This is market pricing.

For convenience, we express this difference as a *discount rate*, usually for a period of one year and usually represented as *r*. The way we use it is this: if you owe me $1, due one year from today, and if you ask me what I would accept to pay it off now, the answer is that I would accept $(1-r) \times$ $1. So, if my personal value of *r* is 10% (0.10), then I would accept $0.90 right now to clear the debt – or more precisely, at that point I would be indifferent to accepting the payoff or letting it run its course. If the debt had been due two years from now instead of one, the calculation would be $(1-r)^2 \times$ $1 or in this case $0.81. The general formulation is:

$$PV = (1-r)^n FV$$

Where PV is the present value of this cash flow, r is the discount rate (per period), n is the number of time periods in the future that the cash flow occurs, and FV is the actual numerical of that future cash flow.

There are several points to notice about this calculation. The most obvious one is that a value for *r* has to be chosen. This is actually a very complex issue that we will cover later, so for now we will just assume that we are given a value. A second point to notice is that formulation is indifferent to whether the future cash flow is positive (in) or negative (out). It is possible to have both in- and out-flows in our scenario, and it is typical to use the same value of r for both types, although there is no particular reason that they need to be the same. The final point to observe is that this formulation makes an assumption that any future cash flows occur only at the end of each time period – typically a year. For most situations this will serve as an adequate approximation for decision-making purposes. If cash flows are not uniform throughout a given year, it may be informative to do an analysis by quarter or even by month – being sure to use an appropriately adjusted discount rate.

To compare the costs of different alternatives, we will compute the present values of their lifetime costs and for this the tool of choice is a spreadsheet. In our examples we will use Excel® and its embedded functions.

Sunk versus Relevant Costs

The concept of the *relevance* of costs is central to any effort to manage them. Unfortunately, this concept is not readily grasped or accepted by many people and this lack often results in faulty decisions. The concept should be made clearer by the definition we use for cost: *what you must give up in order to have or do something.* Although something may be labeled as a cost, if it isn't something you are giving up for the specific event of having or doing something, then it doesn't come into play. Put another way, our definition attaches cost to a decision rather than a thing, and if the cost doesn't change with the decision, then it isn't relevant.

Costs that have already been incurred and cannot be recovered by any means are usually referred to as *sunk* costs. This would include future costs that have been irrevocably committed. Although such costs may have been relevant to our situation at some point in the past, that is no longer the case, and they are not relevant to any future decision-making. The important point here is to recognize which costs are relevant to our decision and which are not.

Students of human behavior know that this is not easily done.

There are many classic psychology experiments showing that people attach undue significance to sunk costs. As an example, if you bought an expensive item of clothing and managed to ruin it on first wearing, would you go back and buy another one? Many people would not, even if they could afford it, feeling that the second one would somehow cost double. Rationally of course, the cost of the first one is sunk and therefore irrelevant to the decision to purchase a second, and if you liked it enough to buy it the first time, you should be willing to do so again. In another (real-life) example an individual bought an old sports car from an acquaintance for, let's say, $5,000. Obviously, both parties thought the price was fair. However, the seller made the mistake of leaving a bill of sale in the glove box showing that he had bought the car at a storage garage lien sale for $200. Instead of congratulating the seller on his lucky find, the buyer was irate and felt that he had been cheated. Again, from a rational, third-party perspective, the seller's acquisition price was totally irrelevant to the transaction price, or how either party should have felt about it. Unfortunately, irrational thinking in business about sunk costs is more common than one might wish.

However, that said, there are instances when sunk costs are not totally irrelevant – or at least, where taking them into consideration is not totally irrational. One such circumstance stems from the accounting treatment of assets. When a piece of custom machinery is purchased, its cost is, for the most part, sunk, yet its book value is based on its purchase price. This value is gradually reduced over its expected useful life by a depreciation charge that spreads its cost over time. However, if the machine becomes obsolete or redundant early in its life, the company has a choice – to scrap it out and declare an immediate loss, or to keep it in some sort of limited use to continue to spread this sunk cost over time. At the corporate level, most companies prefer to do the former, but may choose the latter depending on the sort of earnings they want to show the market. At the divisional level, similar thinking may apply and a sudden loss created by a write-off may impact the compensation of a general manager – leading to a rational choice of making a sub-optimal decision.

Another situation where sunk costs may influence decisions comes when a supplier makes certain investments (sunk costs) to supply a customer, in the justified belief that it will be able to recover the investments over time. Suppose the customer then changes the game, perhaps by relaxing a certain specification and thereby making the investment obsolete. While the presence of sunk costs may not change the "right" decision, it will surely figure into the ensuing negotiations and is likely to have some effect on how the money is split up. In an ideal world, this eventuality would have been covered by contractual terms, but in practice it is not possible to anticipate every development, so a certain amount has to be left to the goodwill of the partners and sometimes a sense of moral obligation.

Average versus Marginal Costs

This is one of the most vexatious and unresolvable distinctions in cost analysis. Let's start with the definitions. To begin with, these costs are *per unit costs*, which is almost always the way that costs are defined. The *average* cost to make, buy, or do something is the total cost of that decision divided by the number of units made, bought, or done. The *marginal* cost is the incremental cost incurred to make, buy, or do one more unit of whatever it is.

These two costs are rarely equal, and they serve different purposes in management. For a firm to survive in the long-term, total revenues must exceed total costs, and by extension, the average per unit price received must exceed the average per unit cost incurred to provide it. However, in the short-term, if an additional unit of product can be sold at a price exceeding the incremental or marginal cost of providing it, this would be beneficial to the company.

Let's consider a simple example: the Excel software that we refer to throughout this book. We don't know how much it cost Microsoft to develop this product, but we can safely assume that it was a lot. That number can be divided by the number of licenses sold, or expected to be sold, to get an average value. In contrast, the cost to provide one additional license for its use is very close to zero. So, which is the right cost to use? The answer is that there is no single right answer – it all depends on the actual decision being made. If we are the ones selling, we are most likely to focus on the average cost to tell us whether a price is acceptable or not. On the other hand, if we are buying, we will want to point out that the marginal cost is all that is relevant.

It is this last point that makes the debate so difficult to resolve. In most cases, a calculation of average costs will include some amounts that have already been spent and are therefore sunk. We have already said that sunk costs are not relevant, but while that may be strictly true, they do cast a long shadow. Presumably they were incurred in the expectation that they would be recovered, and to accomplish that, the company must ensure that average selling price exceeds the average cost. If it becomes apparent that the sale cannot be made any other way, and if such a sale does not have any negative effect on other sales, then it might be reasonable to consider marginal cost as the relevant value.

The discussion of whether it is average or marginal costs that are relevant also comes up in make-vs-buy analyses, particularly for products that are currently in production. In making the evaluation, you typically have a supplier's offer on one hand, and your standard cost figure on the other. Previewing Chapter 6, we can know that the latter represents an average cost, and includes amounts that are sunk or previously committed ("period costs"). Suppose you have such a cost figure of $25/unit, and a breakdown shows that, of that, the marginal cost of production (typically just labor and materials) is $15, the balance being various allocations of overheads and depreciation. A supplier offers to sell you the same component for $20/unit – should you accept the offer? The classical recommendation in this situation is "no," on the basis that the costs being allocated are not going away as a result of a decision to purchase, and therefore only $15 per unit is being saved by stopping production.

It should be apparent though, that there is a time dimension to this analysis. In the short-term[1], it may be true that the so-called fixed costs really are fixed – they simply cannot be erased, and there is no immediate possibility of using the excess capacity for other purposes. If that is the case, it is valid to consider the marginal cost as the relevant basis for comparison, and you would continue to produce the component rather than buy it. However, in the longer-term view, it is the average cost that is relevant and it tells you that you are not making competitive use of your assets. Unless you can reduce your costs, you need to buy rather than make, and either shed the excess capacity or find more productive uses for it.

There is an additional cost-related concern embedded in this analysis. Remember that one of the reasons we need to measure cost is that we use it a basis for pricing. In the above case, you have been put on notice that the market price for this component is $20, and presumably your competitors can buy it for that. If you choose to continue making rather than buying, and use the $25 figure as a basis for your own pricing, you risk being uncompetitive. This is one of many cases where the right numbers to use depend on how you intend to use them.

The distinction between average and marginal costs can sometimes appear in unexpected ways. In pursuit of Lean production, many companies have explored the reduction of batch sizes by increasing production cycle frequency and increasing the number of setup changes. The principal benefit is a reduction in average inventory, but what about the costs? Setup changes often require skilled labor and require cutting into the productive time available. If the skilled labor is there anyway and is not fully utilized, and if the facility is not running at capacity, then the marginal cost of a setup change may be zero. This can make Lean production look very attractive, but the logic can only be pushed so far. As you go to ever-smaller batch sizes with more and more frequent setup changes, the point comes

1   Economics textbooks tend to use the expressions short-term and long-term freely, but without being specific about where the dividing line is. For most of our purposes, it is convenient to think of short-term as applying to the current accounting period – typically one year.

where you have to hire an additional skilled tradesperson and/or add a production shift, or buy a new machine. The marginal cost of *that* setup change is very high indeed.

In this case it would be tempting to say that you should pursue more frequent changeovers just up to the point where an additional increment of resources is required, but in practice that is not easily done. In an environment with uncertain production requirements and multiple competing demands for resources it is hard to ensure that a unit of slack capacity will be available when you need it. For that reason, unless you have very precise knowledge about the changes that will be required by your decision, it is generally best to plan on the basis of average costs, even though some part of these will not be strictly relevant.

In summary, we can see that the distinction between average and marginal costs is very closely related to that between sunk and relevant costs. We can also see that there is substantial room for disagreement over which of these is the right cost to use for decision-making purposes. The answer to that is entirely down to context, and while the general message of this book is to focus on relevant costs (usually the same as marginal costs), there are times when it is necessary to take a step back from the specific decision at hand and look at a broader picture.

Opportunity Cost and Discount Rate

A term we encounter frequently in discussions of cost is "*Opportunity Cost.*" In plain terms, this means the value of opportunities that are forgone in order to do whatever it is that we are discussing. If you recall that our operating definition of cost is what you have to give up in order to have or do something, it is apparent that the concept of opportunity cost is embedded in everything we are discussing, and that all costs are, in fact, opportunity costs. This further emphasizes the theme of this book that costs are attached to decisions and not to things.

Although we can generally disregard opportunity costs as a separate category, the concept does emerge in a discussion of discount rates. In the 'Time Value of Money' section we introduced r – the discount rate to be used in present value calculations. We can see that r is also a measure of opportunity cost – in this case it is the cost of forgoing the use of money for a period of time, usually a year. At its core, this is not a value that can be calculated, rather it must be priced in a market, and the values for r (interest rates) for many different situations are published daily.

In the determination of these rates, the concept of opportunity cost looms large. If I ask you to lend me $1 for one year, you will naturally consider the opportunity cost. You could consider the alternative of placing the money in a guaranteed certificate of deposit or a treasury bill, either of which would give you a fixed value for r along with a high level of confidence – approaching 100% – of getting your money back. To lend it to me, you would probably demand some sort of premium above that level, based on your assessment of my riskiness as a borrower. To do this formally, you might check my credit rating and see what rates the market is offering to borrowers in my category. This is more or less how all interest rate markets work and illustrates a fundamental principle that the cost of money (r) is dependent on what it is being used for, not where it comes from.

Now let's examine the personal utility aspect. Suppose you are happy to lend me the money, but you don't have an unlimited supply. Lending to me is going to require you to forgo some other use for the funds. In this case, to receive the loan, I would have to pay a premium large enough to make it more attractive to you than whatever other use you had in mind.

The above pretty much describes how corporate finance works. The main difference is that companies needing cash to run their businesses can not only borrow money, but also receive it as an equity investment. When companies borrow money, they may either borrow it directly from a financial institution or by issuing bonds for sale to the general public. In either case, the interest rate they must commit to paying is determined by their creditworthiness.

Although equity investors generally receive no guarantee of a payback, their thinking is much the same – they want their money back with a premium. The premium or discount rate that they will consider acceptable depends on the perceived riskiness of the business. While bond-holders think of risk in terms of probability of default, equity investors tend to think of it in terms of volatility or uncertainty of business results. The concept of risk and its relationship to cost is something we will consider in more detail later.

The implication of all this for our purposes is that the selection of r is an inexact science, but a cost calculation or comparison that involves the time value of money will be dependent on the value chosen for r. At a minimum, you should know what values your company uses for its cost of capital and for evaluating new investments. These values will normally be exogenous, meaning dictated by corporate, but with knowledge of how these values are derived and used, it may be possible to argue for a different value in a specific case.

Chapter 2 – Key Takeaways

1. Where possible, costs should be measured quantitatively in a unit of currency.

2. When costs cannot be measured directly, it is often possible and necessary to price them in a market.

3. When costs affect future cash flows, Present Value (PV) analysis allows us to evaluate those cash flows in today's currency units.

4. The present value formula, $PV = (1+r)^n\,FV$, requires the use of a discount rate, r, that represents the opportunity cost of forgoing the use of money for a period of time. This value can be difficult to accurately determine, but has a significant effect on the outcome of an analysis.

5. A cost is *relevant* to a particular decision if it can change as a result of that decision. Any cost that will not change with the decision is therefore 'irrelevant' to that decision and does not need to be considered.

6. A sunk cost is one that has already been incurred and cannot be recovered by any means. Sunk costs are irrelevant, by definition.

7. Opportunity costs are the value of opportunities that are forgone in order to do whatever it is that we are currently doing. Since money always has other uses, any monetary cost is an opportunity cost.

8. Marginal cost is the incremental cost of producing one additional unit of a product or service, while average cost is the total cost of providing that product or service divided by the number of units provided. There is substantial room for disagreement over which of these is the "right" cost to use for decision-making purposes.

Supplement 2-1 – Time Value of Money

To illustrate how we will approach cost calculations, we will build a spreadsheet model to evaluate a simple lease vs. buy situation. Let's assume that we need a particular piece of equipment that can be purchased for $20,000. Let's further assume that the manufacturer of the equipment has offered to lease it to us for a five-year period at a cost of $3,500 per year, paid at the beginning of each year. Our task is to evaluate which of these alternatives will cost us less.

The first problem is to put the two scenarios on an equal footing. If we lease the equipment, at the end of the lease the manufacturer will take it back and we will have nothing. On the other hand, if we buy the equipment, at the end of five years we still own an asset with some value. This may be a good thing or not, depending on whether we anticipate an ongoing need for the machine. To equalize the two scenarios, the simplest approach is to assume that if we purchased the machine, at the end of five years we would sell it for its estimated value. This value is typically referred to as the *salvage value*. Although this may not actually be what we would do, it allows us to make a fair comparison. In this example we will assume this to be $10,000.

The next step is to map out the cash flows associated with the two alternatives. In our example this is fairly straightforward[1] and is shown here:

	Year 0	Year 1	Year 2	Year 3	Year 4	Year 5
Purchase	($20,000)	$0	$0	$0	$0	$10,000
Lease	($3,500)	($3,500)	($3,500)	($3,500)	($3,500)	$0

In this example we use negative numbers to show an outflow of cash and positive numbers to show an inflow. As a result, our total cost numbers will be negative values. Sometimes, however, if we are talking solely about costs, we may choose to represent them as positive numbers for convenience. There

---

1   Actually, it's not really quite so straightforward! The tax treatment of these two scenarios may be different, creating differences in the actual realized cash flows. We will ignore that complication for now, but it is an important consideration.

is no harm in doing it either way as long as we maintain consistency.

The second point to notice is the inclusion of a Year 0, meaning the starting point of the analysis period. It is fairly common that business decisions involve some initial cash flow one way or the other, and these are treated a little differently in the analysis. In this example, if we purchase the machine, we obviously pay for it upfront (we may borrow the money to do this, but that is a separate transaction not reflected here). Likewise, if we take the lease option, the first payment will be due at the beginning of the first year.

To decide which alternative is less costly, we need to come up with a discount rate, and in the completed example below, this is arbitrarily set at 15%. From there we use the Excel function '=NPV' to determine the present value of the two different cash flow profiles. Some care is needed in using this function. Obviously, the discount rate chosen should be consistent with the time periods used for analysis – if we want to record our lease payments on a monthly basis, the value of r should be a monthly value as opposed to a yearly one. It is also important to note that the function assumes that all of these cash flows are occurring at the end of each time period. This is not the case for our 'Year 0' outlays, so they cannot be included in the =NPV function, but must be added on separately. From the example, we can see that at $r = 15\%$, leasing is the lower cost option.

	Year 0	Year 1	Year 2	Year 3	Year 4	Year 5
Purchase	($20,000)	$0	$0	$0	$0	$10,000
Lease	($3,500)	($3,500)	($3,500)	($3,500)	($3,500)	$0
Discount Rate (r):	15.0%					
NPV Purchase	($15,028)					
NPV Lease	($13,492)					

Since there may be uncertainty or differences of opinion about the discount rate to use, it may be necessary to do a sensitivity analysis on this. There are two ways of approaching this that are worth knowing how to do. The simplest is just to create a data table (using the Excel Data Table function) to show the effect of changing the discount rate on the relative costs. Such a table is shown below, and from it we can see that the point of indifference is somewhere between 11% and 12%, and we can also see how big a penalty we would pay for making the "wrong" decision at any of the rates listed.

r	NPV Purchase	NPV Lease
10%	(13,791)	(14,595)
11%	(14,065)	(14,359)
12%	(14,326)	(14,131)
13%	(14,572)	(13,911)
14%	(14,806)	(13,698)
15%	(15,028)	(13,492)
16%	(15,239)	(13,294)
17%	(15,439)	(13,101)
18%	(15,629)	(12,915)
19%	(15,810)	(12,735)
20%	(15,981)	(12,561)

This comparison can be a little cumbersome if there is uncertainty or debate about the correct value to use, so sometimes it is more useful to present the analysis in the form of Internal Rate of Return (IRR). Computationally, IRR is the value of r that brings the NPV of the cash flows to zero. This is often used for evaluating capital investments. If the value of IRR for the project is greater than the required hurdle rate, the project is favorable and vice versa. One of the advantages is that you don't have to know in advance what value to use for r – just present the IRR and let the debates begin!

What we want to show now is that IRR can also be used to evaluate cost comparisons. One of the characteristics of IRR is that it cannot be calculated for all situations. In our buy versus lease scenario, there is no value for r that will bring the present value of the costs of either scenario to zero. However, if we view this as a decision between A and B, there is a value that will bring the *difference* between them to zero. This is the point of indifference at which either choice is equally attractive and may be a more useful basis for discussion than a comparison based on a preselected value for *r*.

To make this work, we need to calculate the differences in cash flows between the two scenarios. This concept of differential cash flows will be central to cost comparisons throughout this book, so this is a good time to introduce it. Arithmetically it makes no difference whether we do this in the form of A - B or B - A, as long as we are consistent, the only consideration is in the interpretation of the results. The resulting calculations are shown here:

	Year 0	Year 1	Year 2	Year 3	Year 4	Year 5
Purchase	($20,000)	$0	$0	$0	$0	$10,000
Lease	($3,500)	($3,500)	($3,500)	($3,500)	($3,500)	$0
Difference	($16,500)	$3,500	$3,500	$3,500	$3,500	$10,000
Discount Rate (r):	15.0%					
NPV Purchase	($15,028)					
NPV Lease	($13,492)					
IRR Difference:	11.6%					

All the numbers here are the same as in the previous example except that we have added the 'Difference' row and applied the '=IRR' function to that line. The first conclusion is that at a rate of 11.6%, either alternative is equally costly. From there, we need to be a little bit careful in recognizing that for values of *r* greater than this, leasing is the preferred option. There is always more than one way to do things and the same result could have been obtained by taking the difference between the two values for NPV and using the Excel Goal Seek function to find the value of *r* that brings this to zero.

For anyone interested in replicating these calculations, the same spreadsheet (omitting some columns) is shown below with the actual cell contents (formulas) displayed. Notice that the =IRR function requires an estimate of the discount rate to give it a starting point. Any value in the general vicinity would have worked fine, but in this example, it was convenient to use the value already in cell B6.

	A	B	C	D	H
1			Year 0	Year 1	Year 5
2	Purchase		-$20,000	$0	$10,000
3	Lease		-$3,500	-$3,500	$0
4	Difference		=C2-C3	=D2-D3	=H2-H3
5					
6	Discount Rate (r):	15.0%			
7	NPV Purchase	=NPV(B6,D2:H2)+C2			
8	NPV Lease	=NPV(B6,D3:H3)+C3			
9	IRR Difference:	=IRR(C4:H4,B6)			

Supplement 2-2: The Triple Bottom Line

In Chapter 1 we introduced the concept of economic versus accounting profit, emphasizing that the latter is the real measure of performance as it captures all costs incurred by the organization's owners. It should be emphasized that in all of our discussions, the revenues and costs are *private* benefits or costs. That is to say, they only consider what is experienced by the organization itself. We also know that there are *public* benefits and costs that we are not accounting for. The public benefits are probably incalculable, but we know that there are immense public benefits from the aggregation and investment of private capital to produce goods and services. This side of the equation is beyond the scope of this book, but we are also aware that there are public costs created by private actions, and some of those deserve our attention. Since many of these costs fall into the intangible category, and since we introduced the distinction between tangible and intangible costs in this chapter, this is as good a place as any to have that discussion.

Many readers will have heard of the concept of the Triple Bottom Line; a term reflecting the idea that a private organization must do more than just maximize the first bottom line (profit) and must take into account other effects. These are typically summarized as profit, planet, and people. The latter two are often lumped together under the heading of social and environmental responsibility (SER). Let's first consider environmental responsibility. The main problem here is that our environment represents what economists would call a common good[1]. So, for example, when our manufacturing process releases harmful substances into the environment, we are using this common good for private gain, and devaluing it without any apparent cost to us. Left unchecked, the effects are predictable, and are in fact playing out in many ways and many places. Governments

1   The term derives from medieval times when many towns had a designated pasture called the Common that was the communal property of the inhabitants and the key feature was that all comers were free to graze their sheep there without cost. The result was predictable; the common was often overgrazed to the point of being worthless – an effect referred to by economists as the *tragedy of the commons.*

have attempted to control this by placing limits on certain emissions, but this is clearly a stop-gap approach.

Some proposals have been made to quantify these costs and subject them to market discipline. These include the imposition of a carbon tax and/or the creation of credits (dispensations, in effect) that can be traded in a marketplace. Such concepts are intended to transfer environmental costs to the corporate bottom line. Presumably, this would raise costs, and to achieve breakeven on economic profit, prices would have to rise, albeit not uniformly. As a result, the consuming public would be paying a sort of tax that would result in a public gain. From a global cost management point of view, this seems eminently sensible.

However, these ideas suffer from three critical problems that have so far defied resolution. The first is what to focus on. Currently, the *bête noir* is greenhouse gas emissions, but we know from the field of performance management that if you focus too heavily on a few measures of performance, other measures tend to suffer, and often badly. Numerous studies have sought to demonstrate that electrification of a vehicle fleet is net positive or negative with respect to carbon emissions. That is fine as far as it goes, but there are other issues not included, such as the environmental impacts of increased mining of toxic metals. Ideally, all of these costs would be gathered up into a grand total, but at the moment that seems to be a bridge too far.

The second problem is quantification; what is the cost of emitting a ton of CO_2? We can guess, but that's about it. Alternatively, we could set a cap and let market forces bid for what is now a scarce resource. The problem remains, though: "what should that cap be?" We have some climate models that suggest a range, but there remains substantial room for negotiation. That leads us to the third problem – policing. If countries around the world agree to an emissions cap, they are in effect engaging in cartel bargaining – a worldwide cartel on greenhouse gas emissions. The problem with cartel bargaining, as we have seen with oil and many other products, is that someone always cheats.

What this example means to us as managers charged with managing costs, is that we would have to audit our supply base to be sure that our costs are "right." If our own country sets an emissions cap that causes our cost of production to increase, we may seek out other suppliers. We may find lower-cost suppliers in countries that either have no cap, or do have a cap and claim to enforce it, but we know that they don't. This creates an obvious logistical problem if you want to find the truth, or a moral dilemma if you don't. Companies are increasingly investing resources in finding the truth in the form of cataloging their carbon footprints, but there is still an auditing problem. At the time of writing there is no formal requirement for this, but that could change – as it has for several social responsibility issues.

If translating environmental costs to currency figures is difficult, doing so with social costs is even more so. Many of our choices contain a complex mix of social benefits and costs, and getting agreement on the net value is problematic. However, this is an area where regulatory bodies have intervened, mostly to require disclosure of certain facts rather than to dictate actions. An example of this is the California Transparency in Supply Chains Act of 2010 (S.B. 657) which requires certain businesses to post disclosures about their efforts to combat human trafficking and forced labor (including child labor) in their supply chains. Although the law does not require companies to do anything beyond disclosing what they do (or don't do) it does create pressure to put in place systematic audit procedures to ensure that their suppliers conform to some standard. Similarly, the United States Securities and Exchange Commission (SEC) has, since 2014, required publicly traded firms to disclose their use of "conflict minerals" originating from the Democratic Republic of Congo, which in turn created the need for an extensive audit trail, and certifications (often of dubious validity).

From a cost management perspective, transferring social costs to currency figures in an analysis is not really feasible at this time, but there are issues to be concerned with. Problems are most likely to arise when you go looking for the lowest cost supplier, which is of course what we are trying to do. These are the ones most likely to be using black-market materials and unacceptable employment practices (often through secret subcontracting). While using such suppliers may not violate any law, it creates a substantial risk for your company if these practices are brought into public view – and they often are. A discussion of such risks must accompany any recommendation that might expose the company to them.

Chapter 3 – Cost at a Strategic Level

Impact of Cost on Shareholder Value and Share Price

When we listed the reasons that we should care about cost and its management, the first item was the economic health of the enterprise. We captured this with the simplistic relationship of:

Profit = Revenue – Cost

It is time to explore this relationship in more detail. It is correct as far as it goes, but the relevance to corporate health and performance depends on the details behind the elements of this equation. Revenues and Costs are tracked and reported by (almost) all firms in accordance with accounting standards mandated by securities laws or taxing authorities. These values result in an accounting profit, a figure that may or may not be useful to us as managers.

The accounting figures typically omit several categories of cost that may be relevant to a business decision. One of these categories that is very important to us is the opportunity cost of the assets used to generate the reported profit. While accounting standards generally include a cost reflecting the depreciation of certain physical assets, the cost of using other assets is normally ignored. Remember that when we defined cost as what you must give up to have or to do something, that includes not just the money you must pay out for materials and labor, it also includes the opportunity cost of forgoing other uses for your assets. If you are using land for business purposes, or if you have cash tied up in accounts receivable, you are forgoing the use of those assets for other purposes. If we could properly collect up all of these costs, then our equation would be measuring economic profit, which should be the real goal of the company. Notice that it is possible, even common, to show an accounting profit while at the same time incurring an economic loss. Many bad decisions are made for lack of understanding of this difference.

As a result, we should not be too interested in a profit number in isolation. Instead, we usually try to bring in the cost of assets by measuring return on those assets (ROA). This is simply the accounting profit divided by the total assets of the firm. While this is an improvement, it is still not the whole story. For one thing, the reported "book" value of the assets may not reflect their true value, and some classes of assets (things like intellectual property) are often not recorded at all. We must also know the cost of capital for the company, which is effectively the market's assessment of the opportunity cost of investing in the company. This in turn will be determined by the perceived riskiness of the company and business field it is in. In a rough sense, we can say that if ROA exceeds the cost of capital, the company is making an economic profit.

Since the cost of capital is variable and beyond our control, it is appropriate for managers to focus on improving ROA, since that is somewhat controllable. To understand how changes in cost translate into changes in ROA, a useful tool is the DuPont Profit Model, also frequently referred to as the Strategic Profit Model. Many versions of this model can be found online, along with many descriptions of its use from various managerial perspectives. An example of this model, tailored to our purposes, is illustrated in Supplement 3-1.

From a top management perspective, this model is most useful for understanding the relationships between the high-level performance measures towards the right-hand end of the diagram. Since the focus of this book is more operational, we are more interested in the measures at the left-hand side, and understanding how they impact the high-level results. In our efforts to manage costs, we often face tradeoffs of one sort or another, so the impact of a decision may show up in multiple places in the model. An example of this is described in the supplement.

The reasons for introducing this model in this book are two-fold. The first, more obvious, reason is to allow you to evaluate the impact of any cost management initiative to determine whether it is beneficial or not. The second reason is perhaps even more important, and that is to provide you with a vehicle for arguing for the benefits of your proposals.

By putting the details in the form of this model, they become more relevant for senior management. Where this becomes particularly important is when conventional measures need to be disregarded, as for example, when you wish to argue that buying a more expensive component is the better choice because it reduces other costs or it alters the asset value. Use of this model is not guaranteed to win your case, but it does allow you to present it in terms familiar to non-operating managers. We will explore other ways to do this below, but the DuPont model is an important addition to your toolbox.

Investors are interested in returns on assets as well. If they see a company that is earning a return on assets that is greater than their opportunity cost of investing, they will want to buy shares and will bid the share price up. As the share price goes up, new investors' return on their investment will go down until it reaches the opportunity cost of capital. If returns are below expectations, the reverse will happen – investors will sell their shares, and the price will drop until the return on the investment increases to the opportunity cost level.

Increasing share price is always seen as a good thing, and this illustrates the connection between cost reduction and share price. If we can reduce costs, profits go up, the return on assets goes up and share price goes up. That sounds good, but we have to pay attention to all the elements of the share price valuation. First, we are assuming no change in the revenue component. Second, we are assuming no change to the asset base. And finally, we are assuming no change to the company's risk exposure which would change the true cost of capital. If any of these assumptions are invalid, a more detailed analysis is required to determine whether the change is beneficial or not. The DuPont model is one tool for doing this.

Impact of Cost on Company Performance

Up to this point we have treated cost as part of the inner workings of a company – invisible to the outside world except to the extent that it influences profit and hence ROA. Specifically, we have treated revenue and cost as being independent of each other. This tends to be true in the short term, and most of our cost management efforts and analyses will assume this to be the case. However, if we take a step back and look at the larger picture, we can see that a company's cost situation can influence its approach to the marketplace.

In the absence of regulatory distortions, companies face a market environment that lies on a range from pure competition (commodities) to pure monopoly:

Pure Competition	Monopolistic Competition	Oligopoly	Pure Monopoly

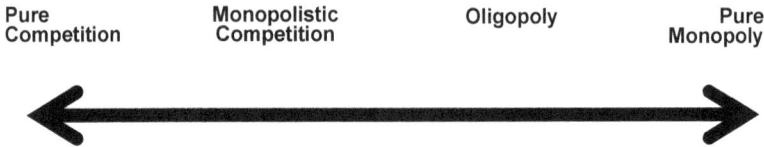

The pure competition (commodity) case is easiest to analyze. This occurs when your product is indistinguishable from anyone else's and the quantities traded are large enough that nothing you do will have any effect on price. Pricing is established in an open market and is known to all players. What we call the demand curve (demand for the product plotted as a function of offering price) is vertical[1]. This means that there would be no point in offering a price less than the market price, because you can sell everything you want at that price. However, if you ask just slightly more than market price, you will find zero demand for your product. In this kind of market, suppliers are said to be price-takers, and the role of cost is very clear. Nothing you do with costs will change the amount of revenue you can generate, so the relationship between cost and profit is very direct – it is the 1:1 relationship implied by the equation of:

$$Profit = Revenue - Cost.$$

Once a company's products have some differentiation from

---

1   Note that economists almost always illustrate price-demand situations with price on the vertical axis, in which case the line would be horizontal, so some care is needed in interpretation. Since we are considering demand to be a function of price as the independent variable, it makes more sense to put demand on the vertical axis.

the competition, it operates in what the economists call *monopolistic competition*. The demand curve is now no longer vertical, but rather, downwards-sloping. This means that you have some freedom to vary pricing, with demand changing in response.

Figure 3.1 The Downward-Sloping Demand Curve

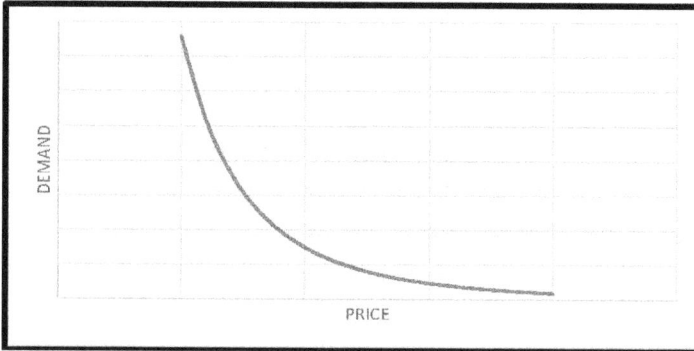

Intuitively we can see that as we increase prices, the revenue per unit will increase, but the total units sold will decrease. This being the case, there is an optimum level for pricing that will yield the maximum possible profit. This optimal price depends on the shape of the demand curve, and on the marginal cost of production.

If the company is able to reduce its marginal cost, the optimal price will also change, resulting in more sales and more profit than if the cost reduction was simply pocketed without changing the selling price. Supplement 3-2 shows a numerical example of this phenomenon at work. From this example we learn several things:

- Except in pure commodity situations, revenue is potentially a function of cost.
- If a company is able to optimize its pricing, the amount of profit that can be gained from reducing costs is always greater than the value of the cost reduction (measured at the original volume level).
- The value of cost reduction is greater when demand is more elastic – meaning when small changes in price result in large changes in demand.

Cost Seen as Opportunity Cost

Returning to the definition of cost as what one has to give up in order to have or to do something, we can see that all costs are, in some sense, opportunity costs. The fact that we can conveniently express most of these costs in currency terms tends to obscure this point. For example, we might say that a donut "costs" a dollar when what we really mean is that if we want to acquire ownership of the donut, we will have to give up a dollar and whatever utility that dollar had for us. This may seem like an overly fine distinction, and in many cases it is, but the point to take away is that the cost of something is defined by the situation, and is therefore properly attached to the decision to acquire it and not the thing itself. To press the example a little further; to someone adhering to a strict diet, the "cost" of that donut would include the 300 calories that would have to be given up somewhere else. Similarly, to someone running to catch a flight, the relevant cost of the donut may include the five minutes it would take to get in line, order it, and pay for it. We can dig deeper yet; if the cash or charge card for the purchase is kept in a wallet with some value and a finite service life, shouldn't some part of the depreciation of the wallet be charged against the transactions that it facilitates? That is how cost accounting works, or would if the numbers were large enough to be material.

This example may be rather contrived, but there are several points to take away from it. The first is that there is a long list of costs that could potentially be associated with an item such as the donut in the example. The second point, and the good news, is that the only costs that matter are those that will change materially with whatever decision is at hand. Happily, this is usually a pretty short list. The third point follows from the second, which is to say that, in order to quantify the cost of a decision, it is necessary to understand precisely what the alternative is to the decision in question.

Conceptually this means that to properly analyze the cost of a decision, it is necessary to map out two scenarios: what would happen with the decision and what would happen without it. These need to be described in sufficient detail to identify all of the things that would change. At this point we can no longer separate costs and benefits since the benefits realized under one scenario become opportunity costs in the other. What we need in the end is the net difference, plus or minus, between two alternatives. The tool that we will use for this is *differential analysis*; simply a fancy term for comparing two scenarios and adding up all of the differences. This analysis is necessarily dyadic (comparing two scenarios at a time), since if a third scenario is introduced, it may require analysis of a completely different set of costs to see where it stands.

The need for a third scenario often occurs when assets are not properly valued – the prime example being real estate. Real estate is typically carried on the books at its acquisition price, and no specific charge is made for its use. If the real estate has appreciated greatly, continuing to use it for current purposes may be incurring a significant cost penalty relative to selling it – the "third alternative" that should be considered. A similar problem can occur in the management of non-profit organizations where people volunteer their time. It is tempting to think of this as free labor and to use it for menial tasks when there are more valuable uses available.

At the corporate level, opportunity cost shows up in the discount rate used for evaluating various initiatives. Companies rarely have unlimited funds available for use. In principle, it should be possible to obtain funds for any project earning greater than the cost of capital, but in practice this is seldom true; issuing new stock is not done readily, and there may be debt covenants that preclude additional borrowing. In these cases, any funds, and particularly capital funds, must come from a fixed budget. When that is the case, companies naturally want to apply their funds to the projects with the highest return. Since it is not feasible to collect up all proposals at once and rank-order them, the usual response is to establish an arbitrary "hurdle rate," or value to be used for r in present value calculations. This value is invariably higher than the average cost of capital, illustrating the presence of opportunity costs.

Non-Monetary or Unquantifiable Elements of Cost

When we start defining costs broadly and looking at things that are different between decision alternatives, we will quickly encounter costs and benefits that are not readily quantified in monetary terms. These are often referred to as intangible items – "intangible" only in the sense that we can't put a number to them. This is no reason to throw up our hands and abandon a rigorous analysis, but it does force us to be creative. There is a difference between things that are impossible to quantify and those that are merely difficult.

A prime example of the latter in business situations is the assumption of risk. As a simple example, it may be possible to buy a component more cheaply from a supplier that is at risk of going out of business without warning – how do we intelligently trade off these different costs? Although we can't simply attach a monetary value to risk, we can often simulate it by pricing certain instruments that will neutralize the risk. We can hypothetically buy an insurance policy or invest in certain derivatives or options – in effect pricing the risk in a marketplace, and while we may not actually do any of these, they provide a monetary estimate of the risk that we are taking on.

Another way to approach this would be to estimate an expected value (cost value multiplied by its probability of occurrence) for the additional overhead costs and possible loss of sales that would result from a supply interruption. This is difficult, and there may be uncertainty about what the values should be, but it can be done and an estimate is better than ignoring the issue. A simpler solution would be to estimate how much additional inventory would be required to provide a buffer against these disruptions and add this figure to the Inventory category, reducing the ROA. The DuPont model shows how this will show up. Although this might not be how you would actually address the issue, it is at least a fairly objective way of quantifying a cost that you are taking on that is not readily quantified by itself.

It may be though, that some costs or benefits are truly

intangible, but there is still value in doing a comprehensive analysis. It is unlikely that there will be more than one serious, intangible factor in a decision analysis and if you have done the rest of the analysis thoroughly, then you have effectively put a price on the intangible part of the difference. While it may not be possible to put an actual value on the intangible factor, it may be a much easier decision to say whether it is or isn't worth the price derived from the analysis.

Establishing a Baseline

A theme that we have been repeating throughout is that cost is a property of a choice between alternatives. This distinction is easily overlooked when one of the alternatives is a zero base, as when something is being done for the first time, or when there is an implied assumption that business-as-usual will continue indefinitely.

This is not always the case. Consider a situation in which production of a certain product is approaching the available production capacity. At the same time, management is considering outsourcing some of the operations. The costs of outsourcing can be added up and compared to the accounting values for internal cost, or we can be more sophisticated as suggested in Chapter 2, and compare outsourcing costs only to the variable component of internal cost. Such an analysis may show that outsourcing is not advantageous, but it fails to take into consideration what will happen if the decision is to keep production in-house. In this case the baseline is not business-as-usual; if the work is not outsourced the firm will have to either limit production (losing sales), or invest capital in a capacity expansion. If these options are taken into account, outsourcing may represent a cost reduction.

Analysis of cost reduction efforts usually focuses on a detailed prediction of the effects of a change. The point to be made here is that a similar level of detail needs to be applied to the alternative, which in many cases is not "business-as-usual" but rather some pending change. This matters, because cost *avoidance* is just as valuable as cost *reduction*, but it tends to be more difficult to document without sufficient analysis.

Chapter 3 – Key Takeaways

1. Cost reductions may result in an increased share price, but attention needs to be paid to any change in asset utilization and to any changes in the risk exposure resulting from the changes.

2. Except in pure commodity markets, cost changes alter the optimum price level.

3. If a company is able to adjust its pricing to the optimum level, the effect of a cost reduction on profit is greater (often much greater) than the actual amount of the cost reduction.

4. The opportunity costs associated with a decision are entirely dependent on the context and the alternatives available.

5. The opportunity cost of discretionary funds to a company is normally higher than its cost of capital.

6. The alternative of doing nothing or the assumption of business-as-usual needs to be analyzed in as much detail as any proposed change.

Supplement 3-1 – The Strategic Profit (DuPont) Model

The financial statements of a company consist of two primary documents[1]: the income statement and the balance sheet. If management of the firm is concerned about return on assets (ROA), then neither of these documents can be evaluated by itself. The 'return' part comes from the income statement, and the 'assets' come from the balance sheet. The two are not independent of each other, and in evaluating any decision, it is important to consider the implications for both numerator and denominator. One tool for doing this is commonly called the DuPont Model, reflecting the fact that it was popularized by its use at that company.

Many variations of this model can be found, but they all follow the same basic structure. The version shown below has been tailored to suit the needs of this book by giving more attention to the operating level details at the left-hand side of the model.

Figure 3-1.1: The Strategic Profit Model

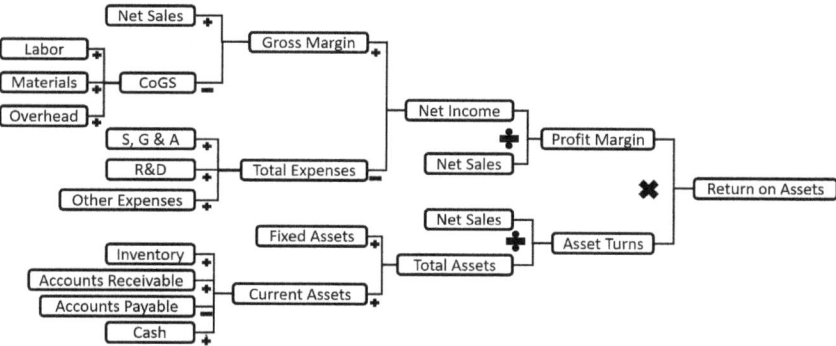

There are several points to note about this model. A basic observation is that the top half of the model is a reconstruction

---

1   There is a third important document called the Statement of Cash Flows. For cost management purposes, we are very interested in cash flows, but only as they relate to operating activities. The Statement of Cash Flows used in financial accounting has as much to do with investing and financing activities as it does operating activities, and as such, it is beyond the scope of this book. We will, in fact, build our own version of an operations cash flow statement in Chapter 10, using what is called the indirect method.

of the income statement, through to the calculation of net income. In this model, we are talking strictly about income from ongoing operations, not from any financing or other activities. Correspondingly, the bottom half represents the asset side of the balance sheet, through to total assets. These are strictly accounting assets, no provision is included for intellectual property, goodwill, etc. To some extent, the last two columns on the right are redundant – we can get ROA just by dividing net income by total assets, but for managerial purposes, margin and turns are familiar and often-used terms.

Digging into the individual items, there are a couple of points to note. The "other expenses" category is a bit of a catchall, but would mostly consist of taxes and interest expense. It would also be an appropriate place to put any overhead costs that are not allocated to specific product because of capacity underutilization. Inventory includes both raw materials and finished goods, and these may be valued differently. Cash in this case would consist only of the cash on hand needed to support current operations, and should be a relatively small number. If the firm has decided to keep some retained earnings in cash in the anticipation of future opportunities, that should not be included here. The rest of the categories should be fairly self-explanatory.

To get a sense of how the model works, consider what happens if (after reading this book!) you are able to achieve a cost reduction on a purchased component. The first effect is a direct reduction in the Materials category under Cost of Goods Sold. This reduction shows up as a corresponding increase in Net Income. So far so good, but if the cost of a component is reduced, so (eventually) is the value of any inventory of that part. So too, is the value of your finished goods inventory, since this is usually based on its cost. This reduces your current assets, and consequently, your total assets. This is a good thing. But there is also a counter-effect; just as the value of inventory is reduced, so is the value of the accounts payable to that supplier, resulting in a slight increase in current assets. Depending on your payment terms, and your factory throughput, the net effect of these adjustments on current assets could be positive (bad) or negative (good). Whichever way it works out, you have influenced both the numerator and the denominator of the ROA calculation.

There is an additional potential effect of this cost reduction that is not discussed here, and that is what would happen if the firm were to lower its prices as a result and make more profit by selling more product. This is a much more complicated calculation since virtually all of the components of the model would be affected. An overview of this case is given in Supplement 3-2 to this chapter, and the actual calculation is described in Chapter 10.

To calculate an actual change in ROA resulting from your activities will require populating the model with company data, but the key point is that if you can explain your actions with this tool, you will be speaking the language that top management understands. That said, it is unlikely that you will want to use a version of this model as your main justification for an initiative. The simple reason is, that when you use total company figures, the effect you are trying to demonstrate will often be little more than a rounding error. As a result, we will use other methods, but the dynamics of this model are still valid.

Supplement 3-2 – Cost and Pricing in Different Markets

Conventional wisdom holds that a dollar saved drops straight to the bottom line as a dollar increase in profit. This example is designed to show that this is not really the case (it's better than that) and that the effect varies according to the market's demand curve.

Consider a company that wishes to produce a seasonal consumer product that will have a one-season life. The total fixed costs to create and produce the product are $100,000 and the variable cost per unit of production is $10.00. These values are assumed to hold true over whatever the quantity of production might be, so we are not worried about capacity constraints, price breaks on purchases, or other such issues. As with all models of this type, the validity of the conclusions depends strictly on the validity of such assumptions, so not only should they be scrutinized; they should also be made explicit in the presentation of results.

Based on past experience with such products, the company expects that it would sell 30,000 units at a price of $15.00. A quick calculation shows that this scenario would result in a profit of $50,000, so the business is probably worth pursuing. But, is this the optimal price to charge? We are ultimately interested in observing the effect of cost reduction on profit, but it is hard to draw useful conclusions unless profits have been optimized.

To know what price to charge, the company must know the shape of the demand curve, not just one point on that curve. This is equivalent to saying that it must know the elasticity of demand as price is changed up or down from the point estimate. Conventionally, this is defined as the percentage change in demand for a percent change in price (and since there are no known examples of demand increasing with price, the negative sign is dropped). The demand elasticity experienced by our example company is made up of two components; one is the willingness of consumers to do without the product altogether and the other is the willingness of consumers to switch to other, similar, brands of the product. Clearly, the more competitors there are and the less differentiated the product, the higher the total effect will be.

While companies often have a good sense of demand elasticity in the immediate vicinity of their historical prices (typically obtained by observing the response to sales promotions or price increases) projecting this elasticity farther out is something of a shot in the dark. This becomes another one of those assumptions that must be scrutinized carefully before acting on the analysis. Economists like to use demand curves that exhibit constant elasticity so that demand quantity (Q) as a function of price (P) and elasticity (a) is given by:

$$Q = kP^{-a}$$

There is no strong theoretical basis for assuming a constant elasticity since it will be different classes of consumers making the decisions to buy or not buy at different points on the curve, but in the absence of actual data, there is no strong reason to assume anything different either.

For convenience, our analysis will assume a constant elasticity curve defined by the above equation. Since we have a point estimate for P and Q, if we know, or can assume, a value for a, we can solve for k. We will use two values for a: 2.0 and 4.0. These span the range from relatively low to relatively high for an individual company's product in a reasonably competitive marketplace.

In the case of low demand elasticity (2.0), we see from Figure 3-2.1 below that $15.00 is not an optimal price. Instead, the company should charge $20.00, at which price it would sell 16,875 units and earn a profit of $68,750. Having established this price, if the company were to achieve a 10% reduction in variable cost to $9.00, and do nothing else, it would show up as a cost reduction of $16,875 and an equal increase in profit to a total of $85,625. However, as shown in Figure 3-2.1, the company could take advantage of this cost reduction to reduce selling price to $18.00, at which price it would sell 20,833 units at a profit (*Profit'* on the chart) of $87,500 – a small but useful improvement over the base case.

Figure 3-2.1: Low Demand Elasticity

Demand Elasticity = 2

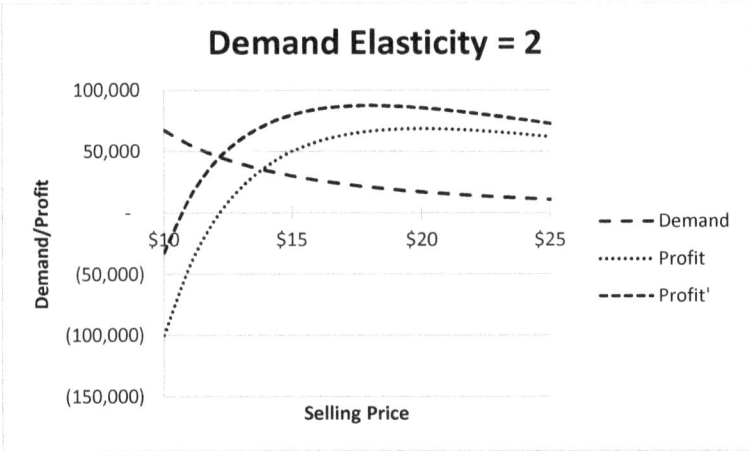

The case of high demand elasticity shows a very different picture. It is characteristic of elastic markets that profits are maximized at lower margins, and we can see this from Figure 3-2.2 below. In the base case, the company should set the price at $13.33, at which price it would sell 48,054 units and earn a profit of $60,181. As before, if the company reduced variable costs by 10% and did nothing else, there would be an increase of profit of $48,054 to $108,235. Also, as before, the company could decrease the selling price to $12.00, at which price it would sell 73,242 units at a profit of $119,727.

Figure 3-2.2: High Demand Elasticity

Demand Elasticity = 4

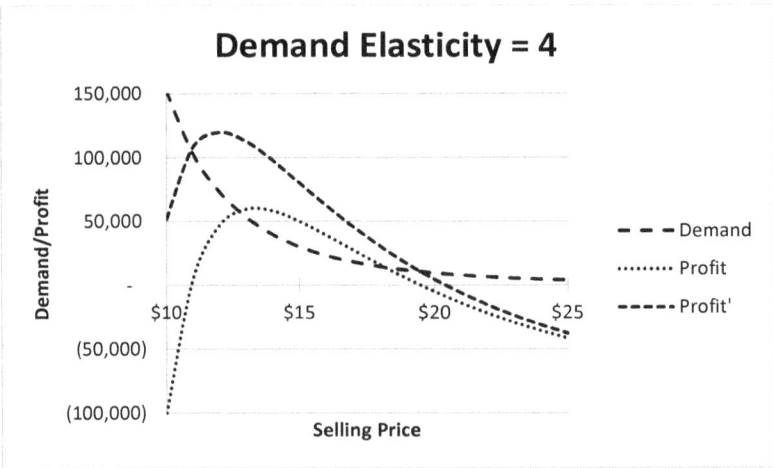

What we learn from this is that cost savings are better than a 1:1 proposition; that a dollar of savings is worth more than a dollar of profit. Most importantly, we see that this effect depends on elasticity of demand, and shows us why cost reduction is more important in competitive markets with little product differentiation.

Chapter 4 – Accounting Treatment of Costs

Distinction Between Financial and Managerial Accounting

All companies have some form of accounting system that takes into account (literally!) the impact of costs. The primary motivation is usually a legal or regulatory requirement, so the systems are designed to comply with those requirements rather than serving any specific managerial purpose. Companies that wish to have their shares listed and traded on an exchange are required to make public a set of statements that are intended to give stockholders and prospective stockholders a clear and factual picture of the company's financial situation. Even privately-held companies usually require the same documents if they are interested in selling partial equity through private placement, or selling the company outright, or, more commonly, if they wish to borrow money, or establish a credit rating. Similarly, taxing authorities are interested in a clear picture of the company's finances to calculate applicable taxes.

Both securities regulators and taxing authorities have fairly rigid requirements for how this financial picture is to be presented, so these requirements form the base of what we call the financial accounting system within a company. There are two key summary documents that underpin this system and these are the income statement and the balance sheet. Because different regulatory bodies have different rules, there may be multiple versions of these documents, but they are all telling the same story. The income statement captures revenues and costs in a defined time period to arrive at a "profit" value, usually referred to as "net income." The balance sheet shows the values and dispositions of the company's assets and liabilities to arrive at what is essentially a net worth statement. In Chapter 3 (Supplement 3-1) we introduced the DuPont (Strategic) Profit Model. If you examine the graphic, you will observe that the top half of the model is a simplified version of the income statement and that the bottom half is a representation of the balance sheet. The lesson is that both of these statements are vital to assessing a company's performance and that neither should be considered in isolation.

The financial accounting system is designed for a specific purpose: to present aggregated historical performance in a consistent and prescribed manner. While this is valuable and necessary, it is of limited use to operating managers, whose interests are in future performance at a much finer level of detail. As a result, all companies use some level of what is called Managerial Accounting. Such use may be very formalized with a standard set of reports used company-wide, or may be very *ad hoc*. In this book we are most interested in the latter as we will frequently be asking "what if?" questions about situations that are not business-as-usual.

The key point about managerial accounting is that it is not mandated by any authority, so there is substantial freedom for companies to use whatever data collection and analysis methods that are useful to them. That is not to imply that anything goes – there are certainly standardized and widely-accepted ways of doing many things. The trick is to recognize when these standard approaches are appropriate and when you need to deviate from them. Similarly, there is a tension between managerial accounting requirements and the established financial accounting system. Both need data, and since financial accounting is a legal requirement, the data collected will be what is needed for reporting purposes. This may or may not be what is needed for operational purposes, and again, the trick is to recognize when you can use the data on file and when you have to collect more.

Basics of Financial Accounting

Let's start this section with a disclaimer. This is not intended to be a reference manual for financial accounting – nothing in this book should be considered as authority or justification for anything that goes into required financial statements. Instead, we are interested in going the opposite way and understanding what financial accountants do, or are likely to do, in order to predict the outcome of managerial decisions.

On any points of uncertainty, you are advised to consult with the professionals; in fact, if you are concerned with cost management, establishing a good working relationship with your accounting personnel should be a high priority.

Financial Accounting: The Income Statement

The purpose of the income statement is to arrive at just that: a net income figure, or what we often refer to as profit. It does this by adding up all the revenues and subtracting all the costs. However, except for the simplest of businesses, it won't do to just add up all the cash inflows and outflows. The income statement tries to match up the costs and revenues associated with specific transactions to give a truer picture of the business, even though some of those cash flows may not have occurred yet, or may have taken place in a prior period. As a result, any income statement you are likely to see is based on the *accrual* of costs and revenues.

What that means is that the revenues and costs associated with a sale are assumed to occur at the time the sale is closed. The fact that you paid for the materials months ago is irrelevant; that wasn't a cost – you were simply converting one form of asset (cash) into another one (raw material). Similarly with the revenue – it is considered to be realized at the moment of sale, even though you may have accepted advance payments or have extended payment terms with your customer. As far as financial accounting is concerned, it doesn't matter whether the revenue was received as cash or another asset class (accounts receivable).

There are several reasons why this matters to us from a cost management perspective, but the main one is that for accrual accounting to work, a cost has to be attached to each unit of product or service that is sold. Now, we have previously argued that costs are not really a property of a "thing" but of a decision to acquire or do the "thing" in question. This means that the cost that the accounting system attaches to a unit of product or service is intended to be the *average cost per unit of the overall decision to make that product or provide that service*. From an operational perspective, it is highly unlikely that this will be the decision you are trying to evaluate, and as a result, the costs that are relevant to you may be quite different from what is found in the accounting records.

A second feature of the accounting data is that financial accounting is really only interested in generating aggregated results for a company or business unit. Consequently, there is little incentive to be overly precise about whether certain costs should be assigned to product A or product B, as long as the totals come out about right at the end of the year. From a managerial perspective, this allocation issue matters a lot, and techniques have been developed to deal with it, but these tend to be used on an as-needed basis. Most companies continue to use relatively simplistic methods for allocating costs, and relying blindly on accounting values for cost can lead to poor decision-making.

Financial Accounting: The Balance Sheet

The balance sheet provides a picture of the net worth of a company by adding up all its assets and subtracting all its liabilities (debts). The difference is supposedly the aggregate worth of what the shareholders actually own. This is a necessary companion to the income statement because we can't know whether a particular figure for net income is good or bad without knowing the value of the assets that were employed to generate it. We typically divide the former by the latter to get an ROA (return on assets) figure, and it is left to investors to decide whether that figure is acceptable or not, given the nature of the business. The fact that the market capitalization (total value of all outstanding shares at today's market price per share) of most companies tends to be considerably higher than the balance sheet value should suggest that "book" values may not be the whole story.

The main reason for this difference is that the intended consumers of balance sheet information are creditors, current and potential. They require that the valuation of assets be conservative, and reflect only that which could be recovered and resold in case of bankruptcy. As a result, the balance sheet is sometimes referred to as an "undertaker's view" of the company, and undervalues many categories of assets. One such category is real estate, which for financial accounting purposes is valued at its acquisition price. The true value can clearly be much higher or lower than this, particularly for companies with a long history. Another such category is what we loosely term "intangibles." This would include the accumulated know-how (intellectual capital) and customer reputation that has been built up over the years – that would presumably allow the company to generate greater profit margins than its competitors. To the extent that these things are the result of the company's own development, they are typically not reflected on the balance sheet at all, because this is not seen as an asset that liquidators could readily convert to cash. However, if the company acquires another one, the price paid is normally higher than the book value of the acquired company, so the accountants have to find a place to record this. They do this by creating an asset called "goodwill" that is shown on the balance sheet. Interestingly, while a company's own goodwill is normally undervalued (by not reporting it at all), acquired goodwill is almost always overvalued.

Of the remaining classes of assets on the balance sheet, one that we want to draw attention to is that called depreciable assets. Typically, this consists of buildings and equipment that wear out with use. To allow for that, their value is reduced every year on the balance sheet until they ultimately have zero value. The reduction amount is called *depreciation* and requires a corresponding entry on the income statement, even though no cash flow occurs. This is done by charging a depreciation cost to each unit of sales that makes use of the depreciable asset. This is an example of those costs whose allocation to specific products is not particularly critical for aggregate reporting, but may be of great importance for managerial decision-making.

Basics of Managerial Accounting

Although financial accounting as discussed above does an excellent job of presenting financial reality to creditors, prospective investors, and taxing authorities, it has multiple shortcomings from the perspective of managerial decision-making. As a result, managerial accounting has evolved to support the decision-making functions. Because managerial accounting is not subject to regulatory oversight, there is considerable freedom to tailor the analyses to the specific problem at hand, although there is a well-established body of knowledge to provide standardized and widely recognized methods.

The problems addressed by managerial accounting differ in two main ways from those addressed by financial accounting. Financial accounting is primarily backwards-looking, recording what actually happened, while managerial decisions are almost invariably forward-looking, requiring projections of what might happen. Secondly, financial accounting is primarily designed to generate aggregated values and bulk averages, while managerial decisions are made at a much more granular level of detail. Managerial accounting has evolved to address these and other issues from the perspective of decision-making and has a well-established set of techniques. This standardization is facilitated by professional societies such as the Institute of Management Accountants (www.imanet.org) which offers a certification called the CMA (certified management accountant). One of the topics covered in their certification exam is cost management, so there is clear relevance to our subject matter. We will draw heavily on the content of managerial accounting, and the reader is encouraged to acquire expertise in this area whenever the opportunity presents itself.

There is a lot more to managerial accounting than cost management, but it makes two main contributions that are important to us. One is the explicit distinction between relevant and non-relevant costs – a point we have already discussed. The other is addressing the problem of cost allocation at the product or activity level to better inform decision-making at that level. This is an important theme, that will keep recurring.

However, this is not a book for management accountants, it is a book for operating managers. We will use the tools of managerial accounting, specifically those relating to cost allocation and capital budgeting, but our interests are a bit different. At the risk of generalizing, those formally engaged in managerial accounting tend to be interested in planning, control, and standardized reporting for executive decision-making. Our interest is in making operating decisions that are net-beneficial to the firm, regardless of how they may appear in the reporting system. To do this, we need to understand that reporting system well enough to be able to argue when and why it should be modified for evaluation of a particular decision. A good analogy is a baseball game: the umpires (accountants) are expected to know the rules and enforce them consistently. However, a good manager (you) will know the rules even better than the umpires do, to be able to argue why certain interpretations are appropriate in a particular situation.

Accounting for Economic Profit

In Chapter 3 we briefly discussed the difference between accounting and economic profit and the need to understand the latter, even though it is not normally a reported, or even a calculated, value. Both are versions of the basic 'Revenue - Cost' calculation, but the difference is in what costs are counted. In the accounting model, costs include all outlays except capital investments. The cost of using a capital asset is approximated by use of a depreciation charge. The cost of using non-depreciating assets such as land, working capital, and intellectual property, is ignored. Economic profit on the other hand, includes the opportunity cost of all assets employed. Since not all assets are readily valued, and since the opportunity cost of their use is priced in a fluctuating market, economic profit is more of a theoretical construct than a calculable number. However, if we can make reasonable estimates, economic profit is a better way of measuring our performance. On this scale, zero is the midpoint – if you are making zero economic profit, you are holding your own and doing OK (it takes a bit of getting used to, to see zero profit as being OK!). Some different accounting schemes have been developed to do this.

The significance of the difference is best illustrated by

examples. Suppose two farmers buy adjacent plots of land at the same price and set about to grow wheat. Farmer A is favored by fate and turns out to have a plot with above-average growing conditions, such that, while the costs of planting and harvesting are the same, the crop yield is greater. Farmer B has average growing conditions. If both farmers sell their crop at market price, Farmer A will show higher accounting profit than Farmer B. But, what about economic profit? With its productivity now demonstrated, plot A is clearly more valuable than plot B, so Farmer A is actually using more assets to produce wheat than is Farmer B. How much more depends of the market value of the land, and in a perfect market its premium in value over that of Farmer B should exactly cancel out the present value of all future profit gains due to the productivity difference. If both farmers are farming with equal skill, then chances are they are making equal economic profit. (The discovery of above-average growing conditions represents a windfall profit related to the land and has nothing to do with actually growing wheat.) Similar situations can occur with things like inventory. Two factory managers, running similar operations, may approach things differently. Manager A keeps a lot of inventory on hand – raw materials, work in process, and finished goods. As a result, production schedules can be smoothed out, overtime avoided, capacities reduced, etc. Manager B runs lean, with minimal inventory at every stage and relies on quick response with larger capacities and use of overtime and flexible labor. Since the cost of inventory doesn't show up (directly) in accounting profit, Manager A may be seen to be running the lower-cost operation. When the cost of the assets is counted, the story may be different.

One managerial accounting "fix" for this is the *residual income* approach. For this it is necessary to assign an asset value to each business unit. That number is then multiplied by the required rate of return to arrive at a cost figure to be charged annually to the business unit for the use of those assets. The income generated by the unit after subtracting this cost is called the residual income. While this is sound in principle, assigning the asset value is far from simple. What is important for managerial purposes in a residual-income system is that any changes to the asset value must be captured by the accounting system.

More comprehensive versions of this approach are referred to as Economic Value-Added models[1]. At its heart, this is still a residual-income approach, with a cost-of-capital charge for the use of assets. However, to properly measure economic profit, there is a multitude of adjustments required to accounting figures to capture the true economic impact. Most of these are best left to the accountants if a company wishes to report a standardized figure, but some are of interest to operating managers. The biggest of these is the treatment of R&D, or any investment in new product or technology development that is not just maintenance of current product. From an economic perspective, these are investments in future business, and conceptually no different than investments in plants or equipment. This suggests that they should be treated similarly to capital, and amortized over their useful life, and this is what is done under Economic Value-Added accounting. The financial accounting treatment is quite the opposite; they are treated as expenses to be charged against current revenue. It is easy to see how this would cause R&D spending to be evaluated by the wrong criteria.

The promise of Economic Value-Added accounting is that it motivates managers to make decisions as if they were investors and that this, in turn, will lead to higher company valuation and share price. Although this seems to be a reasonable hypothesis, empirical evidence is mixed and not totally conclusive. The use of these techniques experienced an initial flurry of interest when they were first formalized, but this seems to have subsided, and this equivocality of outcomes may be one of the reasons. There are other reasons that reporting values for Economic Value-Added may not be too popular. The calculation depends on knowing a value for the cost of capital, which is hard enough by itself. (The author, at one time employed by a Fortune 50 corporation, asked the corporate economist for a value to use in these types of calculations. The response was a five-page document, plus

1   Although the acronym for this, EVA, is widely-used in business conversations, the term is actually trademarked by the accounting firm of Stern, Stewart & Co. In recognition of this, we will use the full name throughout.

appendices, explaining the difficulties with the calculation and offering three different values to choose from.) The true cost of capital is determined in a marketplace, based on average performances across multiple industry segments. As a result, we would expect the average Economic Value-Added to be close to zero, with many companies falling below that figure. Very few companies want to report a figure that tells the world that their management reduced the value of the company over the past year! Much better just to report net income and total assets, and let investors draw their own conclusions.

In a sense, the stock market is constantly assessing this, but the asset base it is considering is not the book value of the company – it is what we call the market capitalization of the company: the value that investors have attached to the company. If the market thinks that you are making a positive economic profit, your stock price will go up and vice versa. In a perfect market, it will go up or down until the Economic Value-Added is zero, when using the market capitalization as the asset base.

Chapter 4 – Key Takeaways

1. All companies maintain a set of "books" reflecting their financial situation and past performance.

2. These records are primarily intended for creditors, investors and taxing agencies, and not for operating managers.

3. Most companies use an accrual method of accounting which requires that a per-unit cost be attached to their products and services.

4. These per-unit costs suffer from two major deficiencies:

   a. The method by which shared costs are allocated to specific products or services may not be appropriate or useful for managerial purposes.

   b. These costs do not capture the cost of the assets used to create the products or services, and as a result, Accounting Profit is not the same as Economic Profit.

5. Managerial Accounting systems usually try to address the cost allocation issue more usefully than do Financial Accounting systems.

6. Some Managerial Accounting systems also try to calculate economic profit by addressing the cost of the assets used, but these systems are often not readily understood and are not widely-used.

Chapter 5 – Total Cost of Ownership (TCO)

Evolution of Current Practice

The idea that decisions should be evaluated using all relevant costs has been with us forever, but the development of robust procedures to implement that idea has been comparatively recent. The need became most critical in the purchasing function as it evolved from simple procurement of raw materials to increasingly complex acquisitions of components and services. There are two main categories of purchases that require comprehensive analysis: the acquisition of capital equipment for long-term use, and the procurement of products or services to support current business. These two situations have different perspectives on the issue and as a result they have historically had different types of analysis and different terminology applied to them. Increasingly, these perspectives are being merged, as most decision situations have elements of both, the difference being only one of emphasis. As a result, some of the terminology has become separated from its historical roots.

The first example, long-term ownership of a piece of equipment, is easily seen to be a time-value-of-money problem as illustrated in Chapter 2. In comparing even superficially similar alternatives (say, machine A compared to machine B) it is necessary to analyze carefully the actual cash flows over time, corresponding to things like different maintenance schedules or training needs. There was recognition that some of the same thinking needed to be applied to other categories of procurement as well, and one of the first formalized approaches to analysis where a time component is involved was called Life Cycle Costing (LCC)[1] in which it was recognized that costs and benefits are not constant over time and that the entire life cycle needs to be analyzed, applying a time value of money approach to get a true picture. This thinking is not limited to capital expenditures; any decision

---

1   Jackson, D. W. and L. L. Ostrom (1980). "Life Cycle Costing in Industrial Purchasing." Journal of Purchasing and Materials Management 16(4): 8-12.

having long-term consequences deserves to be analyzed this way. For example, the decision to launch a product should not be based simply on the estimated per-unit profitability at launch – there should be a projection of how sales, costs and prices will evolve over time. This kind of analysis is what we call a *longitudinal* approach in which costs are tabulated chronologically, often under headings such as: acquisition costs, ownership costs and post-ownership costs. These models are seen in the premier purchasing textbooks such as: Monczka, Handfield et al. (2009) and Burt, Petcavage et al. (2010).

The second example, the purchase of materials for immediate use, doesn't typically have a significant time dimension to consider, but still requires careful analysis to make the best decision. This is what we call a *cross-sectional* approach, collecting cost impact information across all affected activities – not necessarily all in the same company. The term Total Cost of Ownership (TCO) first appeared in this context, but is now broadly-used for both cross-sectional and longitudinal analysis. Collecting the costs of cross-sectional effects is actually quite tricky because of the allocation problem. As explained in Chapter 4, financial accounting systems have no real incentive to distinguish costs at this level of granularity, so the information that is available is often misleading. Managerial accounting has stepped in to at least partially address the allocation problem, with the best-known technique being Activity-Based Costing (ABC) – a topic we will explore in more detail later. We say "partially" here because while accounting systems can do a good job of characterizing what is happening now, they are rarely well-equipped to project what *might* be if you were to make changes. Academic articles describing (or recommending) industry practices tend to emphasize cross-sectional issues, and operate on the assumption that ABC data is readily available. Ironically, there is substantial evidence that this assumption is faulty!

Acceptance of these methods (LCC & TCO) is sufficiently broad that every textbook on supply management contains a discussion of one or both terms. The approaches differ only in emphasis and for many purposes the terms have evolved to be largely interchangeable. In keeping with general industry practice, this book will use the term TCO broadly to cover both longitudinal and cross-sectional approaches.

In spite of the widespread acceptance of the principles and familiarity with the terms, research has repeatedly shown that actual understanding and use of these techniques is at a low level. As an example, in the USA, federal funding of transportation infrastructure projects typically requires life cycle cost analyses, yet 30% of state transportation agencies surveyed did not use any form of this at all[1].

A similar pattern holds true in private industry, where it is found that attempts to implement some form of TCO analysis on a formal, ongoing basis are not only cumbersome but still do not adequately answer the questions at hand. For one thing, as reported in the articles mentioned above, they tend to focus only on the cross-sectional data. Additionally, they rarely have any capability for modification to address new circumstances.

Approaches and Techniques

Clearly, both longitudinal and cross-sectional perspectives are potentially necessary in an analysis, yet relatively few attempts have been made to combine them in any formalized way. The result is that TCO analyses are most often performed on an *ad hoc* basis, an approach with two major drawbacks. One is the room for skepticism that the analysis was done comprehensively and accurately. The other is that starting anew each time can be a lot of work.

We will address the first drawback by building our cost analyses in the form of a business case. Many companies have a somewhat standardized format for these, but the templates provided in this book will be readily intelligible to a wide audience. The advantage of this format is that it provides the framework for both longitudinal and cross-sectional data in one document.

---

1   Harbuck, R. H. (2009). Life Cycle Cost Analysis for Transportation Projects. AACE International Transactions, AACE International.

The second drawback is mitigated by the recognition that cost (or TCO) is attached to a decision, not to a thing. This means that only relevant costs need to be considered. The length of that list will depend on the complexity of the decision at hand, but is typically fairly short.

For those unfamiliar with the business case format, such documents normally start with a multi-period (typically five years but sometimes more or less) pro forma income statement. This statement looks like a financial accounting document for a couple of reasons. The first is familiarity – the target audience will understand immediately what they are looking at. The second reason is that while our decision will not necessarily be based on the yearly net income values, the firm's taxes will be, and these are a necessary part of a comprehensive analysis.

Once the impact of taxes is determined, the resulting net income line can be converted to a cash flow line. This is called the indirect method and is done by adding back the depreciation cost that was used to calculate taxable net income, since the depreciation is not a cash flow. It is also necessary to add in the net in- and out-flows of both fixed and working capital, since these are actual cash flows, but are not treated as costs or revenues in the income statement. The resulting multi-period cash flow statement can then be discounted at the appropriate rate to get a net present value (NPV) as illustrated in Chapter 2.

The trick with this, or any, analysis is what to include and what to leave out. After all, calculating the NPV of the entire firm's future business prospects may be a valuable exercise, but it is probably not what we are evaluating. Remember that we are evaluating the total cost impact (or TCO) of a decision; in other words, we are interested in the cost *difference* between business under alternative A and under alternative B. We can do two (or more) separate NPV calculations, but we would quickly see that most of the data was common to both or all alternatives. The common data is not relevant, so we can leave it out – we don't even need to know what it is. The result will normally be a pretty streamlined analysis, and while the actual data are unlikely to be found in the existing records, the data collection will be reduced to a minimum.

Once the focus is on relevant costs only, there are still some options. We can do multiple separate NPV calculations and compare the differences, but we need to be careful if we have more than two. Costs that are relevant when comparing A to B may not be relevant when comparing B to C and vice versa. Thus, if we are going to take this approach (comparing more than two alternatives at a time), costs that are relevant to any comparison of alternatives within the sample set must be included. If this starts to become cumbersome, the problem can be avoided by doing only pair-wise comparisons. If this is done, the analysis can be presented on a single document by using differential values as illustrated in Chapter 11. While this can further streamline the presentation, you do have to be careful to get the ± symbols correct!

Chapter 5 – Key Takeaways

1. The term TCO (Total Cost of Ownership) is a widely-used term that emphasizes the need to consider all relevant cost differences associated with a decision.

2. Costs may differ between alternatives over time, requiring what is called a longitudinal analysis and a time-value-of-money (NPV) calculation.

3. Cost impacts of a decision may vary across different functions and activities, requiring what is called a cross-sectional analysis.

4. The task of conducting a TCO analysis is simplified by focusing only on relevant costs – costs that will change with the decision.

Part II – Introduction

If we want to manage costs in an active way, we have to be able to answer questions of the "what if?" type, as in: "what if we were to outsource our plating functions?", or what if we were to blow-mold our own bottles as needed instead of buying them? Whether we realize it or not, the analysis needed to answer questions of this sort requires the creation of a model – essentially a set of formulas that predicts the cost effects of the changes we are contemplating.

In most companies, such a model already exists in the form of a standard cost calculation, often referred to as a *cost file*. This cost calculation attempts to represent the average cost per unit of production over its lifespan, and serves several purposes. These include the matching of costs to revenues for accounting purposes, managerial control through the tracking of variances from standard, and the setting of selling prices.

For cost management purposes, the information in the cost file is of obvious interest, but it is unlikely that the data, or the calculations used, will be exactly relevant to any particular case. We will have to build our own models, but an important first step is to understand in detail what is in the cost file and how it was arrived at. That is where we will start this section before progressing to actual modeling.

Chapter 6 – Standard Costs

How Costs Are Calculated

For any product or service sold at a set price there will be some estimate of its cost. Unless it is a one-time event, this cost is intended to represent the average per-unit cost of the product or service over its lifetime. This cost serves many purposes, the main one being to determine the accrual of costs for financial statements, as discussed in Chapter 4. However, another principal use for this information is as the basis for an acceptable selling price.

These cost estimates, usually referred to as cost files because of the inclusion of backup documentation, will normally follow the outline shown in Figure 6.1.

Figure 6.1: Product Cost File

Sample Product Cost File	
Direct Costs:	
Net Purchases	$2.00
Direct Labor ($20x5/125)	$0.80
Total Direct Cost	$2.80
Overhead:	
Specific Depreciation	$0.40
General Overhead (@250% of DL)	$2.00
Total Overhead	$2.40
Total Factory Cost:	$5.20
Sales and administrative expenses (10% of Factory Cost)	$0.52
Total Cost:	$5.72
Target profit (10% of total cost)	$0.57
Target Selling Price:	$6.29

There will of course be a great deal of detail below these

headings that will vary greatly from industry to industry, but the top-level categories are fairly consistent. The actual numbers that make up this detail may come from a variety of sources. In the case of purchased materials, it may be from a supplier quotation. For the labor content, the number may be based on an engineering analysis or actual time measurements. The overhead categories are typically based on budgets approved for various departments. In all cases, estimates may be used in the absence of any better information, although this is generally resisted.

There are several key features of this cost formulation that we should observe. One is at the bottom where the information is used to calculate a standard selling price. The margin percentage used is a management decision, and is presumably calculated to generate the sort of return that earns at least the company's cost of capital as discussed in Part I. In reality it is more apt to be a rule of thumb, and is often based on industry averages. The question of what this number should be in any particular situation is a contentious one. In this book we are not looking at what our own company's selling prices should be, but we do look very closely at what our suppliers' selling prices (to us) should be, and this is where we will look at what margins are appropriate. A second feature of note is the seemingly arbitrary distinction between "factory costs" and the administrative overhead costs. In the case of a remote, actual factory reporting to a central head office, this distinction makes sense, but if a business is more self-contained, it may be difficult to identify what is the "factory" and what is the "front office." Nonetheless, the distinction is important because of the different nature of the costs incurred in each. The components of factory costs are direct *consequences* of production – things you have to have in order to do the job at hand. The non-factory costs, on the other hand, are more typically the results of management decisions. For example, money spent on R&D for future products is a management decision that has very little connection to current business, but it must be paid for out of current revenues. As a result, management imposes a "tax" on current products or services to fund this necessary activity. At least, it is necessary from the company perspective

– customers may have a different view about funding future development!

Notice too that this cost file outline is snapshot at one point in time, implying that costs will remain constant over the life of the product. This is frequently an unrealistic assumption, and more sophisticated cost files will include life cycle costing. Certain costs can be projected to change over time, either by market forces or by management intervention. This is not the place to try to forecast the price swings in basic commodities, but some categories, such as computer chips, have a reasonably well-defined trajectory that can be incorporated in a cost model.

A more important category is that of active cost reduction efforts, which is actually where we come in. The base cost file may represent costs as they exist right now. The problem may be that if you add a reasonable margin to that cost, your price will be too high and you won't get the business. If you want the job, you will have to bid lower, and if you want to make money on the job, you will have to reduce your costs over time. Accordingly, many cost files used for pricing purposes will bake in a year-over-year cost reduction target of X%. This target is then handed off to the operations managers to make it happen. Clearly this reduction target cannot be applied to all categories of cost – good luck getting a year-over-year reduction in your property taxes! However, direct materials and labor are generally seen to be addressable costs and would be included in this kind of analysis.

In the following sections we will look at each of the headings in more detail.

Purchased Materials

Broadly speaking, this category is everything that you purchase to make the product or deliver the service in question, however, only direct costs are listed here. Direct means that that there is a linear relationship between the quantity of the product produced and the quantity of the material or service purchased. The list is normally obtained by taking the Bill of Materials (BOM) and indenting it or breaking it down until everything gets back to purchased parts or materials. Some companies prefer to distinguish between components and raw materials, but this distinction is not normally important for our purposes. This breakdown is not quite complete, as there may be purchased services along the way, such as when you send your stamped parts out to be electroplated. These will not necessarily show up in the BOM, but they will in the material control file called the routing, and should be in the cost file as a result.

Conceptually, this should be the easiest category to analyze as all the purchased items have a specified quantity and price, but there are some wrinkles to watch out for. The first one is the price itself. For the costlier, more strategic components this is not generally an issue as the company will likely be relying on one or two strategic suppliers and price will have been established with a formal quotation and a long-term contract. However, there is often a host of lesser, more commodity items where suppliers are interchangeable and prices fluctuate with market conditions.

Within this category, there is plenty of room for inaccuracy and some outright mischief. This matters from a cost management perspective because we need to be able to predict the cost impact of proposed changes, both in absolute terms and also in comparison to a baseline. If the baseline is incorrect or if the method of calculating certain costs is not appropriate for what we are doing, we won't be able to do this. When looking at standard cost numbers, one thing we need to be aware of is the role of incentives and how they serve to distort what we are seeing. In particular, remember that buyers are usually evaluated and rewarded for their ability to achieve cost reductions.

Starting with the price itself, consider how the number got there in the first place. When the cost file is originated, it will typically come to the buyer in the form of a bill of materials and specifications for the individual components to be purchased. A good buyer will usually know of several suitable suppliers, and will probably have a pretty good idea of what the item should cost. Most companies strongly oppose the use of estimates and insist that the "standard" cost be based on supplier quotations. So, our buyer will send out several requests for quote (RFQs). The actual number that goes into the file may not be the lowest quote received. There are good reasons for this, typically revolving around the suppliers' reputations for quality and delivery reliability, but including other factors, such as the existence of long-term relationships. However, there are also less benign reasons for this. Remember that the buyer is evaluated on an ability to achieve cost reductions, and so might keep a lower quote "in the pocket" so to speak for a future cost reduction. It is actually in the buyer's best interests to have the initial price as high as possible without drawing unwanted attention. Now, most buyers are professional enough not to play this game, at least to extremes, but the point is that the number in the cost file may not represent what is actually being paid – or what should be paid.

From an accounting perspective it is too cumbersome to adjust the standard every time the actual price changes, so any over or under values are posted to what is called a variance account that can be settled up at the end of the year. For purchased parts, this is called a Purchase Price Variance (PPV) account, and this number is often used as a measure of performance for the purchasing function. Hopefully the reader is already starting to see the potential pitfalls in this! Ideally the cost file information should be updated periodically to reflect true values, but whether that is done or not depends on the individual company. The take-away from all this is that the official number may not be the true number, and any cost modeling effort that depends on this value as a baseline may require further digging before decisions are taken.

A significant portion of the cost of some purchased materials is the cost of transport. Ideally the standard cost number should reflect that actual cost of that material at the buyer's point of use. This can be facilitated if the suppliers are asked to quote prices on a delivered basis[1] but many companies

---

1   Such quotes are frequently referred to as "FOB: buyer's place of business" but this is actually a misuse of the term FOB. Under international INCOTERMS, a more appropriate designation would be CIP or CIF, but these tend not to be as readily understood in everyday conversation.

prefer to manage their own in-bound freight. However it is handled, freight is an inescapable part of the cost of the decision to buy from a particular supplier and needs to be attached to that decision. Most companies do this in one way or another, and the results may or may not be accurate. Some companies use a flat percentage added to the cost of purchased goods, which is clearly not accurate, but may be perfectly adequate from a financial accounting perspective. Again, any cost modeling that we do that involves the cost of purchased goods must accurately capture the true cost of shipping as applied to the alternatives under consideration.

Closely related to the cost of shipping is the cost of handling once the product arrives at its point of use. Most companies do not bother with trying to assess the specific handling costs associated with each component and instead lump these into a general overhead category rather than under purchased materials. Alternatively, it may show up, but as a flat rate – usually a percentage of cost. Neither of these are useful for cost modeling; for example, if you were considering paying a supplier more to package its parts differently to reduce your handling costs, the effect would not be visible under either method, so you would have to create your own model.

There is more! Unfortunately, not all of the material that is received makes its way to production. We are not talking here about defective product which would normally be charged back to the supplier or carrier. Rather, a certain percentage of material received is damaged, lost, stolen, or otherwise becomes unavailable for use. This should be a small number, although in retail businesses, the "shrinkage" factor can be significant. Frequently, a small percentage will be added to the cost of purchased materials to allow for scrap, and once again, such flat rate measures are not useful for cost modeling as they may not capture an effect that you are trying to modify.

Finally, scrap can have more than one meaning in production environments. The nature of production processes is such that you can't always use all the material you purchase. The simplest example is to imagine a stamping operation that stamps out pieces from a sheet or strip of material. The material left behind (sometimes referred to as offal) is of no further use to you, so the material cost that shows up in the cost file is normally the cost of the full blank even though only a part of it goes into the product. However, the remainder may have substantial value if reclaimed, particularly if generated in sufficient quantity to be commercially interesting. It has the advantage of being "pure" in the sense of having a known composition, so it is more valuable than mixed scrap. Management accounting and control systems have frequently not done a good job of tracking this potential revenue stream with the result that more than a few plant managers have been found to be playing games with it. A classic example would be paying a favored contractor to haul away such scrap, which looks legitimate enough on the surface to those lacking detailed knowledge. The contractor would then be able to sell this material, and some of the revenue might find its way back to the person authorizing the contract, by means left to the reader's imagination. Ideally, the cost of material shown in the cost file should be the net cost after recovery of scrap value, but in our experience, this is the exception rather than the rule. Any cost modeling that deals with the cost of materials may need to take this into consideration. How this can play out in practice is illustrated by an example provided by the Copper Development Association, Inc.[1]

Direct Labor

As with the cost of materials, adding up the cost of direct labor seems relatively straightforward, but has many of the same issues. Unlike materials, it is not always that obvious whether labor is direct or indirect. Different companies may use different categorizations, which is perfectly fine as long as they are consistent. For our purposes, labor is direct if it is unambiguously linked to the product or service (hands touching the work) and if the quantity of labor consumed varies linearly with the quantity of production[2]. At one time, direct labor may have been the largest single category of cost, but in the modern industrial economy this is much reduced and is often less than 10% of total costs. This would suggest

---

1 https://www.copper.org/applications/rodbar/alloy360/whybrass.html
2 This is actually a tricky point – see the supplement to this chapter: Is Labor Really a Direct Cost?

that we do not need to be too concerned about extreme precision in our measurements, except for one big factor. Direct labor is still widely-used as a baseline for allocating indirect costs to products, and as its percentage of total costs decreases, the multiplier effect increases, meaning that small errors or changes may have outsized effects on the accounting picture. For modeling purposes, we will try to sidestep this issue as much as possible by not using labor as the baseline, but there is still plenty of reason to be precise about our labor cost.

Labor costs are expressed as a number of hours per piece, which is the inverse of what we call the standard – the number of pieces per hour. The number of hours per piece is multiplied by the average cost per hour of labor to get the cost per unit.

The cost per hour figure is what we call a *fully loaded* cost, meaning that all the costs attributable to labor above and beyond the basic wage rate are included. Primarily this consists of payroll taxes and benefits. Bear in mind too that not all paid hours are productive hours. Meal and rest breaks, and washup time need to be paid for as well, so there will be a multiplication factor to get from hours worked to hours paid. The result of all this tends to be a figure much higher than the wage rate that the employee sees, and explains why we see what seem like really high values quoted in the press when the subject of labor costs comes up. This fully loaded rate is a bit of a black box, and as an operating manager you are not going to have much ability to look into it. You will be given a number and that is about it. One exception that you might be able to argue is if your company has a two-tier wage structure, as is present in some union contracts. If the distribution of high and low-wage employees is not uniform, it might be possible to argue that a certain product has a higher or lower wage rate than the average.

When looking at the labor standard, it is like the case with material cost: there are incentive issues to deal with. The actual standard may be determined by engineering analysis (particularly for new products), by actual measurement, or in some cases, by negotiation. Upper management would like the standard to be as high as is feasible, but those involved in setting it would like the opposite. Manufacturing likes to see a relatively low standard for several reasons: one, it takes some pressure off for when slipups occur, and two: like buyers, they are rewarded for improvement – in this case raising the standard. Starting off from a low point makes life a lot easier.

Similarly, direct labor personnel, perhaps as represented by a union, like a low standard as it makes work less stressful and, more commonly, allows the workers to meet schedule ahead of time and go home early. When doing their analyses, industrial engineering personnel tend to be pretty neutral on this, but they are subject to pushback from the constituents mentioned. Setting standards by actual measurement is also fraught. Unions in particular react very negatively to this, and going out into a factory with a stopwatch and clipboard can be an eye-opening experience. When you do actually try to measure work, the workers know they are being watched and will tend to work as slowly as they credibly can.

Just as with purchased materials, most people involved are not going to play these games to the extreme, but in the presence of strong incentives, we need to be aware of it. With purchased materials, while the numbers in the cost file may not reflect reality, the differences are mostly not all that great. With direct labor it is not unusual for workers to be able to beat standard by 50% or more when they put their minds to it. This is not to imply that the standards are wrong by that amount, just that they tend to be pretty conservative. As long as they are consistently conservative across the company, there is only a little harm done, but if they are not consistent, the multiplier effect on overhead mentioned above can lead to some poor decision-making. In the same vein, a proposed process improvement may look a lot less attractive when compared to actual rather than standard, so again, it is important to know the baseline you are starting from.

Overheads

If the allocation of direct costs (labor and materials) to

a product has a few stumbling blocks along the way, the allocation of overhead presents a minefield. Overhead is the general term for all those costs that are necessary to support production, but are not clearly tied to any one unit of product. Examples would be heat, light, depreciation of the building, maintenance, taxes, and so on. As operations and their supply chains have gotten more complex, the category of overhead represents an ever-larger share of total cost.

From an aggregate accounting perspective, this is not a problem – it is just a matter of adding up the totals. However, for the purposes of setting prices and matching costs to revenues, it is necessary to allocate these overhead costs to individual units of production. We know that these overhead costs are necessary, and we know that our products must be priced at a level that allows them to be recovered or we will go out of business. The problem is to know what that level is for any particular product.

The key word in the previous paragraph is 'allocate'. If the costs cannot be clearly identified as belonging to a particular unit of product, then some way must be found to allocate them. There are many ways to do this, none of which are strictly correct, and all of which are ultimately somewhat arbitrary. The methods also vary considerably in their usefulness for modeling and decision-making.

It is fairly common to separate the overhead category into direct and indirect components. The distinction is far from clear-cut, as costs span a range from those that vary in direct proportion to production volume to those that don't vary at all. Costs that are classified as direct overheads are those that would be charged to a single product, or family of products, and not to any others. This can be a bit confusing as some of these are variable costs, and some are fixed, so they behave differently. Examples of the variable type would be materials or services used specifically for the product, such as electricity, or grease, or special handling. These would be expected to vary somewhat proportionally with production volume and, really, the only reason they are not itemized as direct costs is that it is too much work for too little benefit. Examples of the fixed type might include the depreciation or lease costs for any equipment used specifically for a certain product. Although clearly tied to specific units of production, these costs are fixed over a time period, so the per-unit cost impact will vary inversely with the volume of production. This means that any number you see in the cost file is based on a forecast of that volume.

Indirect overheads, on the other hand, are those costs that cannot be assigned to specific products, and must be allocated on some basis. The way allocation is done in practice is that accounting gathers up all the budget numbers for the coming year from all of the cost-generating functions in the operation. Then we select one or more class of activities that can be identified for all products and designate those as *cost drivers*, meaning that we think they have some role to play in determining total costs. We have already stated that direct labor hours is a widely used measure for this purpose, but other examples might include floor space used, machine run-time (in a highly-automated environment), number of shipments per period, and so on.

The next step is to obtain a forecast of the quantity of those driver activities that are expected in the coming year – as in total labor hours, or total floor space used, etc. The indirect costs are then divided up and assigned to their most relevant cost drivers. Dividing the totals gives a cost per unit for each activity that can be applied to each product. The total indirect cost per unit of product is the sum of these values multiplied by the amount of each driver used or generated by each unit of product.

As an example, suppose we decide that labor content and floor space usage were our main cost drivers. We would take the forecast of total indirect costs for the coming year and divide them into two bins according to which category seems most relevant. Heat, light, property taxes, etc. would probably go in the floor space category, while benefits, material handling, etc. would go in the labor hours bin. We would then have to decide what percentage of available floor space would be used by each product category over the year, and assign this percentage of the "floor space" cost bin to that product. We would divide that figure by the forecast number of units to be produced in the coming year to get a per-unit cost allocation. The labor time bin would be treated similarly – a forecast would be made of the total number of labor hours to be used in the coming year, and the corresponding indirect cost bin would be divided by this to get a cost per-hour allocation of indirect cost. This would be divided by each product's labor hour standard (remember, the standard is in pieces per hour) to get a per unit allocation.

When the process is described this way, it is not hard to see some of the weaknesses. A big one is the reliance on forecast information, both for the overhead costs themselves, and for the amount of cost driver activity – which is another way of saying the sales forecast. We also see that the cost calculation rapidly increases in complexity as we go beyond one cost driver. Another weakness is the reliance on standard information, particularly for labor hours – a problem discussed above. If all costs are allocated on the basis of direct labor hours, even a small error in the standard can have a large effect. A somewhat less obvious weakness but an important one for cost management, is the fact that once the overhead costs are rolled up into a total, some transparency is lost. As a result, overhead costs are sometimes not subjected to the same level of scrutiny as are direct labor and materials. Consequently, overheads are fertile hunting grounds for cost reductions, but the problem is that the results may not show up very explicitly in the accounting records, making it hard to claim credit or justify the effort.

Our discussion so far had been mostly about how we allocate these aggregated overhead costs to individual products. There is another issue lurking here that we need to highlight, and that is capacity utilization. If we imagine a facility that has low level of utilization, perhaps because of economic conditions, then we will forecast that we will only use a fraction of the available capacity. If we add up all the costs as we described, and parcel them out to the actual production, we see that each piece is "paying" for some amount of idle capacity. From an accounting perspective, there is nothing wrong with this, and for taxation purposes it may be correct, but in this case, using this allocation of costs as a basis for pricing would be a serious mistake. A product burdened with the overhead of unused capacity is apt to be uncompetitively priced which will just make the problem worse.

Ideally the allocation of overheads should be based on "full" capacity utilization. The quote marks are used to signify that "full" is a matter of definition. Just as "full employment" in the economy doesn't mean zero unemployment, full capacity won't mean 100% utilization of all available assets. There is a certain amount of unavoidable downtime as when old products are phased out and new ones set up. There are also peaks and valleys in demand and it is a matter of management policy how these will be dealt with. In a product business, inventory can be used to smooth these out, but that is not always possible, and in a service business it is not an option. If management wants to meet a high percentage of demand using production capacity, and if that demand fluctuates a great deal, then there will be a lot of unused capacity – by design. Therefore, full capacity – the denominator used to calculate the cost per unit of cost driver – will depend on the nature of the business and management policy. There is plenty of room for disagreement about what it should be.

For accounting purposes, the ideal is to use a single cost driver that is broadly representative of all products being produced and one that is stable and readily forecasted. Traditionally, direct labor time has been this driver, and many companies continue to use it exclusively. As long as the products of the operation are relatively homogeneous in terms of their demand for overhead services as a function of labor hours worked, and as long as the labor content per unit of production is not changing, this is actually a pretty good driver to use. When this is not true, substantial errors can result – at least from a managerial and pricing perspective. An actual example of this was a fully-automated production cell that used zero direct labor, in a plant where this was not the norm. Clearly the allocation of indirect costs to this product should not have been zero!

However, while the use of simple cost drivers may be good enough for determining the long run average cost per unit of a product, it is not very useful as a cost model for projecting the impact of changes. This is illustrated in Supplement 6-2 on the role of "mix" and will be discussed in more detail in Chapters 7 & 16.

A major focus of managerial accounting has been to develop cost formulations that serve better as cost models. The basic approach has been to add more cost drivers to the calculation so that changes to any of the product's attributes result in a truer representation of the impact. The umbrella term for this approach is Activity-Based Costing (ABC), a term popularized by Robin Cooper and Robert Kaplan[1].

There is a substantial literature addressing the justification and implementation of ABC, and the reader is encouraged to become familiar with at least the basics. The rationale for using multiple cost drivers is compelling, particularly for decision-making in non-homogeneous production environments, and many companies use some version of it in their normal accounting. That said, there are problems too. The real question is, how far do you want to go? Developing overhead rates for multiple cost drivers and keeping them updated is a significant amount of work, but unless you go to an extremely fine level of detail, the chances are good that you won't have captured all of the relevant cost effects for any particular decision anyway. As a result, we find that formal use of multiple cost drivers for routine accounting purposes is much less common than one might expect. Or, to put it more bluntly, the detailed information you need to model a particular change is probably not going to be found in the accounting records.

Sales, General and Administrative Expenses (SG&A)

The naming of this category varies a bit by company, and is often expanded to include engineering; at least, the part of engineering that is dedicated to R&D or the development of new products. Some of the costs in the SG&A category are somewhat related to the volume of business, such as the accounting and financial reporting functions. The majority however, are reflective of management policy. It is

---

1   See for example: R. Cooper, R. Kaplan: *Measure Costs Right, Make the Right Decisions,* Harvard Business Review, September-October, 1988

management that decides how much to spend on R&D, on advertising, on charitable activities, on investor relations, on lobbying, etc. As a result, these costs have little to do with actual production of current product and are imposed as a sort of corporate tax on the operation. The basis for this tax could be almost anything, but it is normal to use factory cost for this purpose.

If you are an operating manager subject to this tax, there is probably not much you can do but live with it, although the appropriateness of the numbers may come up during pricing discussions. On the flip side of this, if you are purchasing materials, it is worth getting an understanding of what sort of corporate tax your suppliers are paying and whether or not it is appropriate for that type of business.

Since the SG&A category represents a cost to the business, it is appropriate to apply cost management practices here as well, but the logic tends to be reversed. For basic things, like printing of annual reports for example, we can act conventionally and shop around for the lowest price that will meet our requirements. However, for things like advertising or R&D, the decision of how much to spend has already been made, and the focus is on how to get the most result from that value. The mindset of value improvement is a bit different from conventional cost reduction, but in truth, when we talk about cost management, all of our efforts should really be about value improvement in one way or another.

Chapter 6 – Key Takeaways

1. Products or services normally have a "standard cost."

2. For accounting purposes this cost will be a snapshot in time and is needed to develop financial statements.

3. Another major use of the cost information is to determine an acceptable selling price, and for this analysis, the cost information may use Life Cycle Costing.

4. The figures that make up the standard cost may not be very accurate and need to be checked before using them as a baseline for changes.

5. The manner in which indirect costs are allocated needs to be understood in detail to determine whether the allocations are appropriate, and also how they will change with changing circumstances.

Supplement 6-1 – Is Labor Really a Direct Cost?

When we talk about direct labor, it has been conventionally assumed that it varies proportionally with the amount of end product required. Although there are certain efficiencies of scale that might come into play, it is generally true that the actual time spent working does vary proportionally with the quantity of output. However, for our purposes, we are actually more concerned with the labor time that is actually paid for, and this varies according to quite different rules. Labor has two characteristics – and yes, these are technical terms – it is *lumpy* and it is *sticky*.

Lumpy means that you can't purchase labor in infinitely small increments as needed. You have to hire the whole person, and there is usually some minimum block of time that you have to commit to. If the setup of your production is such that you need a person, but that person is only actually busy thirty minutes out of each hour, you generally have to pay for the whole hour, although there are some situations where it is possible to pay on a piecework basis. The amount of labor recorded in the cost file will usually be for the whole person that you have to pay. However, if production volumes go up or down, so will the actual busy time, but the cost will not change, up to the point where you have to add another whole person (or can eliminate the job, perhaps by rolling what remains into someone else's).

So, rather than being a straight line, the relationship between production volume and labor cost may be a stairstep. As long as the steps are small relative to the scale of the operation, we can generally ignore this issue, but that is not always true. It is also worth noticing that the effect of labor laws, as they attempt to protect the interests of workers, have tended to make the steps bigger, as employers find it more attractive to use overtime rather than add headcount.

Labor also tends to be sticky, meaning that once you take on a worker it is not necessarily that easy to let them go, or to dial back their hours paid. Again, labor laws in the world's more advanced industrial countries have tended to increase the stickiness of labor. As a result, it is increasingly more useful to think of labor the same way we think of salaried personnel – as a period cost, or fixed overhead. The implications of this have to be thought through as you build cost models, and focus on what *actually* changes in responses to decisions you make.

An interesting footnote to this is that the relative lack of lumpiness and stickiness of labor in so-called low-cost countries is actually as big a part of their cost advantage as is the basic wage rate. The ability to rapidly ramp production up and down in response to market conditions allows substantial savings, not only in wages paid, but in inventory as well. This is one of the main reasons why electronics production is unlikely to return to the US or EU in the foreseeable future[1].

---

1   https://money.cnn.com/2012/10/17/technology/apple-china-jobs/

Supplement 6-2 – The role of Mix

When we set budgets for the coming year, we forecast sales volumes by product. As actual sales unfold over the year, we can map unit sales against the forecast to see any variances that are developing. We can then track costs and revenues the same way, to see where they are compared to what is expected, given the level of unit sales.

In an operating review, the first look will be to see if unit sales are on target. If they are ahead of forecast, there is usually a nod of satisfaction, but if they are short, the responsible manager will be asked to explain. Absent any specific issues, the explanation may rest on economic conditions beyond the manager's control. Revenues are then scrutinized to see if they are above or below what is expected, given the unit sales. A shortfall may reflect pricing issues, or it may be attributed to a thing called "mix." An example would be that we sold as many units as projected, but customers opted for lower-priced versions than we expected. Hence, a shortfall in sales revenue due to mix - presumably something beyond our control.

The same analysis applies to costs. There may be actual cost overruns that need to be explained, but the operations manager may also invoke the explanation of mix, particularly with respect to indirect costs. If actual indirect costs do not vary as the chosen cost drivers suggest that they should, the actual cost incurred may vary from what is projected, even though everything is operating appropriately. The variance may be over or under, and while it is only the bad variances that get attention, both cases are distorting the true picture.

Finally, the net income may vary from forecast for all the reasons given above, but also because demand may shift to products that are more or less profitable than forecast. In other words, mix. Since operating reviews tend to focus on who to blame for unsatisfactory results, it should not be surprising that the word 'mix' comes up a lot in these reviews!

Chapter 7 – Cost-Volume Modeling

One of the commonest, and most contentious issues in cost management is what happens to costs as production/sales volumes change. The goal of that discussion is usually to determine what should happen to a selling price, either from a seller's or a buyer's perspective. The analysis would be somewhat simpler if we were able to talk about only about total costs over a period, but prices, and hence costs, are more commonly expressed in per-unit terms at a point in time. This is needed for accounting purposes, but also allows for the reality that total volume may be uncertain at the time a price is set.

If we look at the standard cost file model, we will find that there is nowhere to input volume directly to see its effect. The allocation of indirect costs is determined by an aggregate forecast of all economic activity in the operation. If we revise the forecast number for an individual product, we would have to change the allocation for all products of the operation – something that is obviously not going to happen. So, the standards don't change, and accounting keeps track of the under- or over-allocation by using variance accounts. But, costs do change as a result, and we need to calculate the effect in order to evaluate pricing. This evaluation helps both the buyer and the seller in the setting of prices and it is likely that both will be performing some calculation or estimation of this.

The basic model is based on the distinction between fixed and variable costs. The definitions of these terms are fairly self-evident. Fixed costs are normally expressed with respect to a period of time, such as a year, so are sometimes referred to as period costs. The defining characteristic of such costs is that they do not change as the volume of activity changes. Some are obvious – lease costs on a facility tend to be the same no matter how much or how little is produced. Variable costs, on the other hand, are those that vary in direct proportion to the volume of activity. The categories of purchased materials and direct labor are generally considered to be truly variable costs in that the total of each category for a given period will be a constant multiplier times the total units produced – in other words, a straight-line relationship with a zero intercept. When fixed and variable costs are discussed on a per-unit basis in the context of changing volumes, this leads to the seemingly paradoxical situation that variable costs are fixed and fixed costs are variable! These relationships are illustrated in Figures 7.1 – 7.4.

Fixed versus Variable Costs

We will use the following numeric data for these examples:

- Fixed costs: $10,000/yr.
- Variable Cost: $2.00/unit
- Volume 0 - 50,000 pieces per year

Since fixed costs are, well, fixed, they remain the same over a year as shown in Figure 7.1.

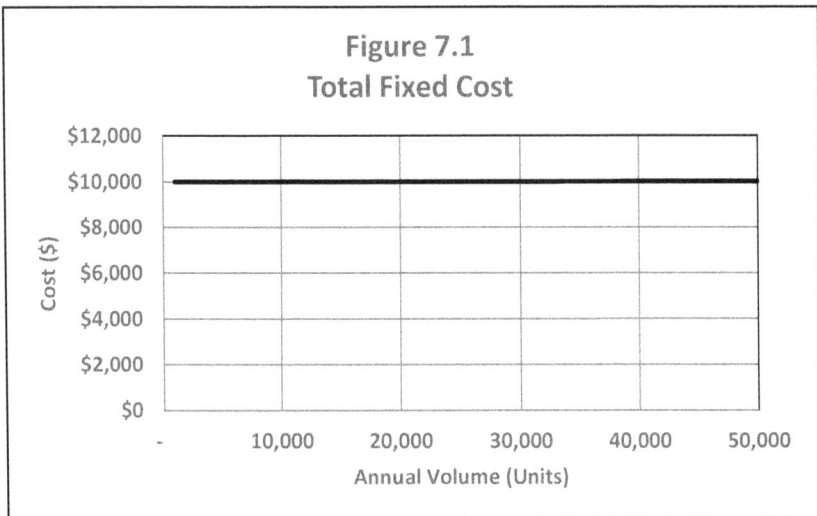

Figure 7.1
Total Fixed Cost

Variable costs on the other hand are fixed on a per-unit basis, so the total variable cost over the year will depend on the actual volume produced. This is assumed to be a straight-line relationship over the whole range as shown in Figure 7.2.

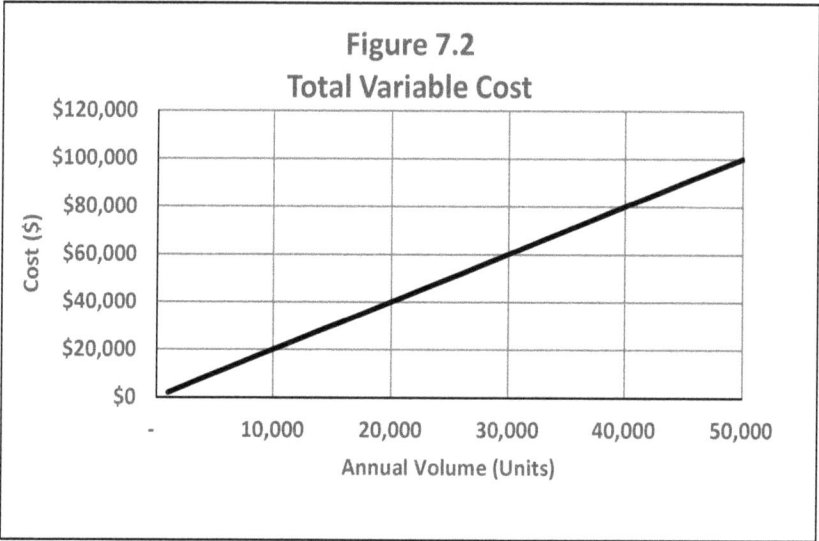

Figure 7.2
Total Variable Cost

We can simply add these curves together to get the total cost of production over the year as a function of volume produced. This is shown in Figure 7.3.

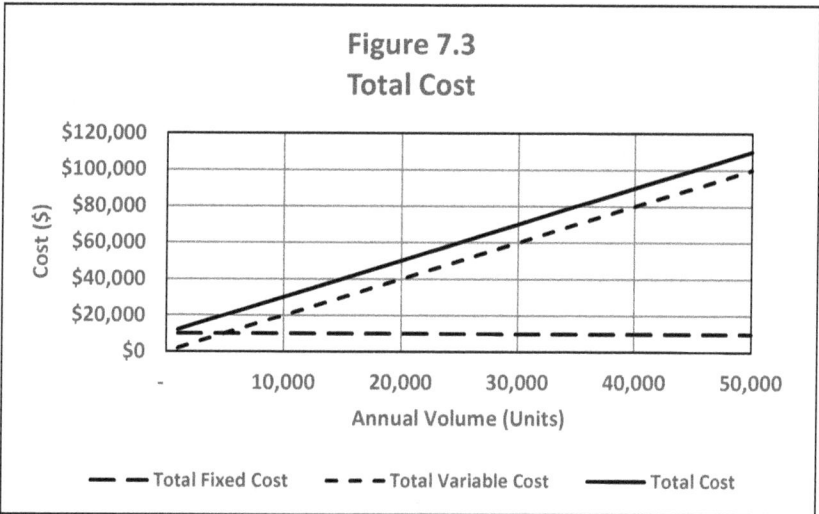

Figure 7.3
Total Cost

The result of interest in all of this is the per-unit cost of production at these various volume levels. We get this by dividing total cost by volume produced to get the curve in Figure 7.4. Notice that the variable cost component is constant throughout, but the amount of fixed cost that has to be allocated to each part varies non-linearly with volume.

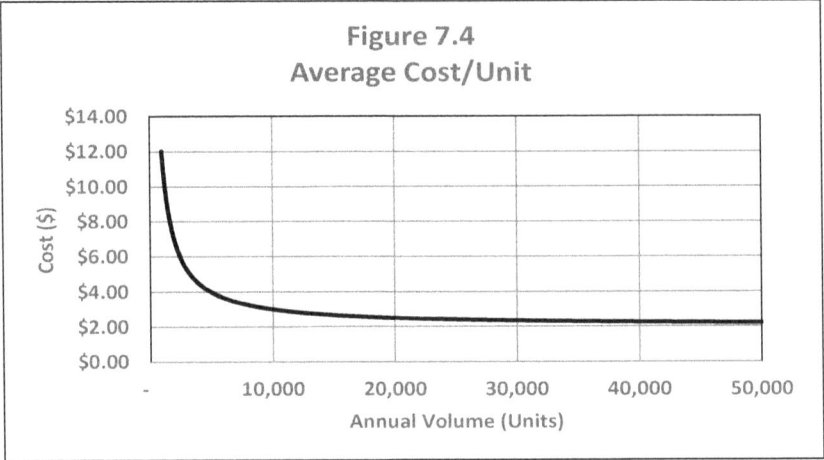

Figure 7.4
Average Cost/Unit

Cost/Volume Modeling with "Lumpy" Costs

The values for both fixed and variable costs are only valid over some range. For example, the cost of leasing a warehouse doesn't change – up to the point where you have to lease an additional increment of space and the cost takes a jump. This characteristic is called "lumpiness" and the following example shows the effect of volume changes on per unit price where fixed costs are lumpy. We will use the same numbers as before except that the fixed cost of $10,000 is the cost of owning (or leasing) a machine, and that one machine has

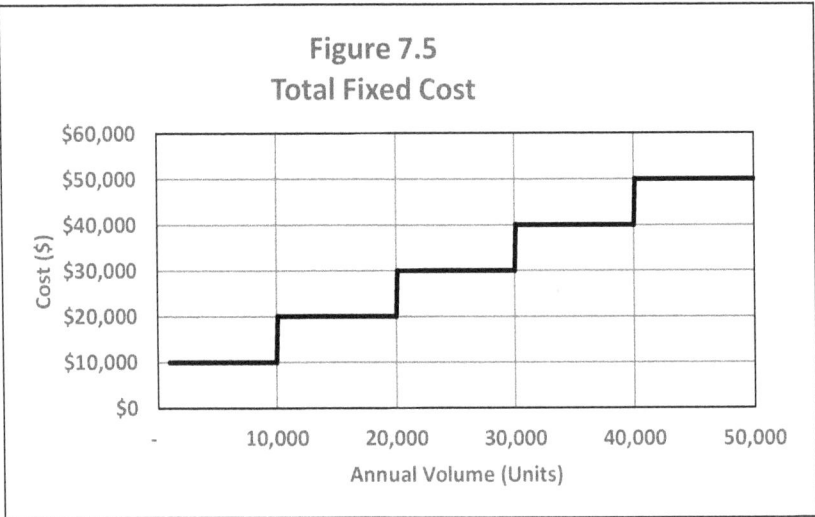

Figure 7.5
Total Fixed Cost

a capacity of 10,000 pieces per year. Higher volumes will require multiple machines. In Figure 7.5, we can see that total fixed cost for the year is now a stairstep function of volume produced. As before, when we add together the fixed and variable components, we get total cost for the year as a function of units produced. This is shown in Figure 7.6.

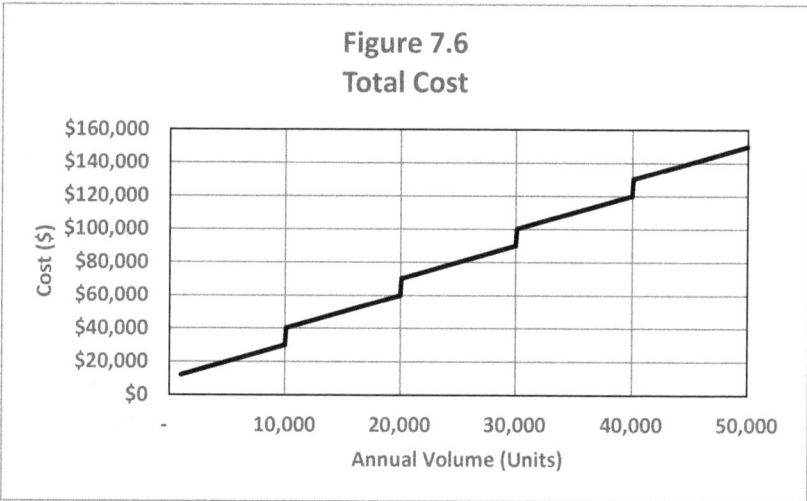

Figure 7.6
Total Cost

Again, the quantity of interest is often the per-unit cost at the different volume levels, and again, we can divide total cost by volume to get this. The result is a somewhat jagged curve as shown in Figure 7.7.

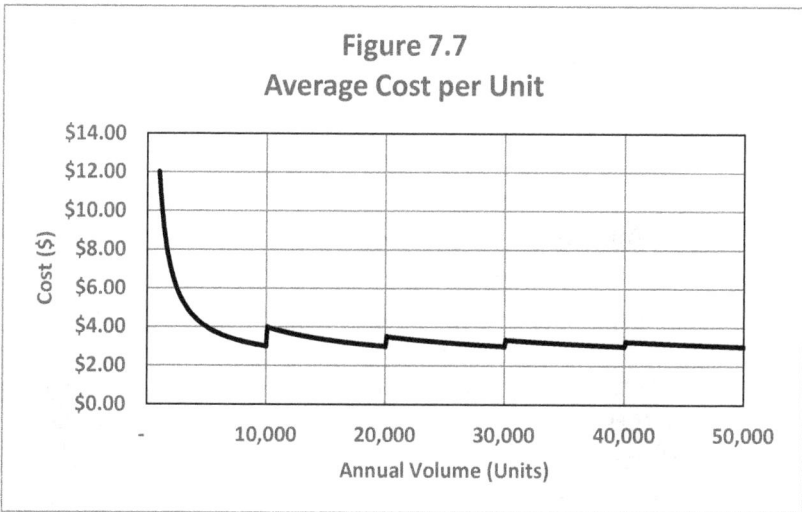

Figure 7.7
Average Cost per Unit

This suggests that we need to exercise care when doing cost analyses in the vicinity of capacity increments, meaning that you have to know where these are. Unfortunately, that is not always easy, especially when the resource in question is shared with other products or operations and you are not privy to their forecasts.

To summarize the above examples: to model the effects of volume changes, we need to separate total costs into fixed and variable components. Cost files typically do not do this for you directly, but they may give you the overhead category divided into fixed and variable components. In the latter case, you can usually add together the purchased materials, direct labor and variable overhead to get a per-unit variable cost. You may, however, want to look into how the overhead costs were divided. If a division is not given, you will have to estimate it from the categories of overhead in the breakdown. The problem is that several categories of overhead are somewhat variable, but not in a directly proportional way with volume. Things like utilities, shop supplies, material handling, and such will change with volume, but not in a strictly linear fashion. These may be referred to as semi-variable costs. We could break each category down further to get a clearer separation, but we need to be mindful of the value in doing so. At some point it is sufficient to make an estimate and be satisfied with being approximately correct. The data problem is even more severe when attempting to model suppliers' costs to evaluate pricing. If cost breakdowns are not available from suppliers, it is sometimes possible to estimate the fixed/variable split by observing how prices are quoted at different volumes.

There are several reasons to want to model cost as a function of volume. As stated at the beginning of the chapter, the commonest is to evaluate the appropriateness of pricing as volumes change – either the buyer would like to get a price reduction in exchange for an increase in orders, or the seller wants a higher per unit price to compensate for lower-than-expected orders. Understanding the effects of lumpy costs is very important in this context. We see from Figure 7.7 that there are situations where an increase in volumes results in an increase in per-unit cost – something that would need to be justified in negotiations!

A second important, but not so obvious, reason for cost

modeling as a function of volume is to establish a baseline of business-as-usual, or more precisely: business as planned. Cost reduction efforts must always be measured against what would happen without them. If an increase in variable cost allows the avoidance of an incremental "lump" of fixed cost, it may be well-justified – but you wouldn't know that without modeling the baseline. As can be seen above, the calculations are not complicated, but obtaining the necessary data may be the hard part.

Lumpiness is one problem in dealing with per-unit costs, but another is stickiness, as mentioned in Supplement 6-1. It is expected that as volumes go up, so will costs, as in adding additional personnel or another machine. The problem is that if volumes go back down again, it's not so easy to make those costs go away. This is more of a management problem than a modeling problem, but we need to be aware of it. From a cost management perspective, we want to avoid costs that persist, hence a preference for overtime rather than new hires and for general purpose equipment (easily re-sold) over specialized machines. If these preferences incur extra costs that need to be justified, the models shown here can be modified to show a baseline that incorporates stickiness as costs evolve over time. Since these choices are actually introducing an option into the calculation, a fuller discussion is reserved until Chapter 18.

Chapter 7 – Key Takeaways

1. Costs change with volume, and since changes in volumes can occur for many reasons, it is necessary to be able to model the impact.

2. The results of this modeling are important for price negotiations and for evaluating cost avoidance activities.

3. The key task is to separate total costs into those that change linearly with volume and those that don't. This separation can be difficult and may need to be an approximation.

4. When discussing per-unit prices in the context of changing volumes – variable costs are fixed (constant on a per-unit basis) and fixed costs are variable (again, on a per-unit basis).

5. Particular care must be taken when the cost/volume relationship in the vicinity of capacity increments. The larger these increments are, the more important the analysis becomes.

Chapter 8 – Modeling Using Cost Drivers

In Chapter 6 we introduced the concept of a *cost driver* as a basis for the allocation of indirect costs. The term reflects the fact that costs don't just happen, they are the result of decisions and activities. At the factory cost level at least, these are decisions about the configuration of the product and about the process by which it is made and sold. Conceptually at least, every element of the total cost of a product or service can be broken down into discrete activities that have price tags on them, all of which added together give us our total cost. This notion of 'activities' is the basis of the term Activity-Based Costing (ABC), previously mentioned. It is easy to get lost in the details of this sort of breakdown, so it helps to define the purpose for doing it.

Why Do We Need to Identify Cost Drivers?

Using cost drivers can help us to address three different problems, either individually or in combination. The first problem is that of allocation as discussed in Chapter 6. On one side of the ledger, we have the order book of products being produced, and on the other side we have the total add-up of all the costs incurred by the facility. For a variety of reasons, we want to allocate these costs as accurately as possible to individual units of production. This is really only an issue with indirect costs as the allocation of direct costs is pretty straightforward[1].

A second problem we need to address is to discover where and why costs are actually being incurred. For direct costs that is usually obvious enough, but it may not be apparent that certain indirect costs are being disproportionately caused by one product. This is where ABC is an asset: if we have a comprehensive catalog of cost drivers for our products, it

---

1   Of course, nothing is ever totally straightforward! There is such a thing as joint production, where one process results in more than one product. This is most common in chemical process industries, but can show up elsewhere. This creates an allocation problem similar to that with indirect costs, with no really right answer.

can provide us with a priority list of where to focus our cost reduction efforts.

The third problem is actually the subject of this chapter, and that is the modeling of costs. By that we mean developing a model such that if we set out to make some change to product or process, we will be able to predict what the effect will be. To do so accurately we must identify the linkage between the proposed changes and ultimate cost. This is actually a very different problem than the one of allocation as it is going in the opposite direction. For allocation purposes, we know the costs and want to figure out where they came from. For modeling purposes, we know the change we want to make and want to know how the effects will ripple through the system. To do that, we may be able to use some of the cost drivers already in place, but more often we will have to develop our own.

There is a companion problem that arises when attempting to model changes. If we change something that is being used as a cost driver for allocation purposes, it is likely that the accounting version of the cost effect will be wrong, and lead to an inappropriate evaluation. In these cases, we will have to build our own model and be able to defend it. This is discussed in more detail in Chapter 16.

How Do Cost Drivers Work?

The mechanics of using cost drivers for allocation purposes has been discussed in Chapter 6. The basic computations are pretty simple, but they require a logical pattern of thinking to formulate them correctly. However, for modeling purposes, it is a bit different and not quite so simple. The trick is to identify every category of cost that will be affected by a change, and write a formula for that effect, such that the before and after values can be compared.

Let's start with a simple example: suppose we are looking at the number of bolts on a flange, and the bill of materials specifies six bolts. We are wondering if four or even three might do the job as well. For our purposes, the number of bolts becomes the cost driver. It starts off simply enough; we can look up the price of an individual bolt and multiply it by the driver to get the unit cost impact (recognizing of course that the price per bolt might change if larger ones would be needed). However, a little thought suggests that there is labor associated with installing the bolts, so we need to look up (or estimate) the cost per bolt for installation and add this to the calculation. What about the holes the bolts go into? Do they have to be drilled and tapped? If so, we need to work out a cost per hole and add that into the mix.

Now we come to the indirect costs, where cost drivers are more typically applied. Notice that our decision about the number of bolts affects direct labor, possibly in more than one area. If direct labor is used in this company to allocate indirect costs, there will be an apparent change in overhead costs that is most certainly not real. However, there will be some real changes and the trick is to decide whether they are material enough to be included in the cost model. If we reduce the number of bolts per unit, we will reduce the quantity and weight of material that has to be delivered to the assembly point. Most likely this will not result in any real change to the cost of material handling, but it is a question that should be asked. We will also see a reduction in inventory level of bolts, which may result in reduced storage costs and also in reduced working capital. A reduction in working capital will result in a one-time cash inflow to the company that may be significant. The end result is that there will be a number of cost items that can be expressed as a function of the number of bolts specified. The sum of these functions gives us the answer we are looking for. For this simple example, these effects may not be material enough to bother with, but they are questions that need to be explored. The template we will introduce in Chapter 10 provides a framework for incorporating them.

Let's look at another example that deals more specifically with indirect costs. There are some basic costs of operating a facility that don't relate directly to production volumes, but still have to be allocated to products. Examples would be building depreciation, maintenance, property taxes, landscaping, heating, lighting, etc. Some companies allocate this on the basis of standard direct labor, while others find it more appropriate to allocate it on the basis of floor space utilization (and there are probably many other ways to do it). Now suppose that we are considering rearranging a product assembly area to reduce the floor space used. In this case we would want to treat the space utilization as the cost driver, but how do we compute the cost savings?

If the company already uses a figure for the cost per unit of floor space, then that is probably as good a number as we are going to get, although it is always worth digging into it a bit to understand what is in it and what isn't. If the company doesn't do this already, then it will be necessary to compute a value if we want to be able to argue for the benefits of the rearrangement. Accounting already has the numbers we need, and with their cooperation we can get a reasonable approximation. But what is the true value of a space reduction?

This is an example of a marginal versus average cost situation. If we simply move some machines closer together to take up less floor space, and nothing else changes in the plant, then the total cost of the operation won't change even a little bit. It can be argued that the marginal value of the rearrangement is zero and that it is not worth doing. On the other hand, it can be argued that floor space has been freed up that can and should be used for something else, and that the computed value of the savings is valid. In most cases, the latter argument will be more appropriate even if no other use of the space is made and there is no actual reduction in total cost. What *should* happen is that the overhead allocated to the unused space should be charged to an unabsorbed overhead account and not to the product in question. This is particularly true if the cost information is being used to evaluate pricing.

Cost modeling using drivers can be used to explore the origins of cost, and sometimes runs into linkages that are not quantifiable, but the logic is still valuable. Suppose your company makes consumer technology products and you are concerned about the cost of product returns. Looking for cost drivers here can be more difficult. Quality defects would be one obvious choice, so using a defect rate, the resulting model would be:

Product sales (units) x % defective x cost per return = cost of returns attributable to product quality.

But, the majority of returns may not be due to specific defects, so we need to analyze this further. We might identify consumer propensity to return product (C.P.R. as a % of sales) as a cost driver, and write:

Product sales (units) x C.P.R. x cost per return = cost of returns attributable to product.

If we just want to allocate costs, that is sufficient, but for cost reduction purposes we would probably want to work on reducing the % returned. Clearly this is related in some way to the product characteristics but it may not be possible to discover exactly how. That doesn't mean that we can't build hypothetical models to argue that better quality control, better product literature, better tech support, etc. might serve to reduce the return percentage. While quantification might not be feasible, the use of cost drivers in modeling still provides a "what-if" framework for exploring the potential impact of changes.

Cost Drivers as "What-If" Tools

This last example highlights the use of cost drivers that is most central to the goal of this book – as predictive tools to understand how costs will change with proposed improvements. It also shows why this chapter is comparatively short: cost modeling is an ad hoc exercise – you are not going to find all the information you need in the company's records, and you will have to build your own model. The concept is simple enough, but the range of applications is endless so it is not feasible to offer a comprehensive guide. Even in the unlikely event that the company uses a very detailed level of activity-based costing, it will probably still not be detailed enough to capture what you need. To some extent, this explains why use of ABC is not that detailed or widespread – it is too much work for too little gain. Since we pretty much have to build a new model every time, in Chapters 10 & 11 we will introduce a template to provide some structure to the process. The key trick is to think things through thoroughly to be sure that your evaluation is comprehensive – this is more important than absolute accuracy.

Chapter 8 – Key Takeaways

1. Cost drivers are intended to reflect attributes of product or process that are in some way causal for costs.

2. The commonest use of cost drivers is for allocation of indirect costs in the accounting model.

3. Cost drivers can also be used in the reverse direction to identify the origin of costs of interest.

4. Properly used, cost drivers form the basis of models that allow us to answer "what-if" questions about product or process changes.

Chapter 9 – Modeling Cost Over Time

Many of our decisions regarding costs have implications that extend beyond the current period. Capital investments are an obvious example, but the list is far longer. A proper comparison of costs between scenarios requires consideration of the time value of money as discussed in Part I. But it is not sufficient to simply project the current state ahead into the future; costs can, do, and should change over time. Several forces come into play on this, so it may be necessary to combine multiple effects to achieve a valid cost model. At the same time, it is important to realize that all of this applies not just to a proposed initiative, but to the baseline as well. The do-nothing option does not necessarily have static costs, and a major theme of cost management is cost avoidance – sidestepping costs that would otherwise have been incurred. Costs can change for many reasons, and in the following sections we will examine some of the more important ones.

Inflation

Inflation is simply an erosion of the purchasing power of a currency, which, in theory, should apply uniformly to all of a firm's costs. It won't of course; the prices of goods purchased from a foreign country may follow a different pattern, and in any case, price adjustments do not occur smoothly and continuously. However, in the longer-term we can assume that inflation will be experienced across the board. At the time of writing, Western economies are experiencing a period of historically low inflation, so there has not been a lot of recent discussion about the role of inflation in pricing and business planning. That simplifies life, but it is possible that higher inflation rates will return, and there are economies in the world where inflation is still high.

For modeling purposes, the question really comes down to this: if you are projecting costs into the future, say five years out, should you put in the numbers that you expect to see after inflation, or use the current numbers without adjustment? As always, the answer is that you can do it either way and get a valid result, but the recommendation here is to do the former.

There are two main reasons for this. The first one is that the discount rate we use, r, is normally built on a base of a risk-free rate of return – typically as available through government-backed treasury bills. This risk-free rate is a good proxy for the expected rate of inflation; in other words, the inflation rate is already baked into the analysis. If you were to use non-inflated values, you would appropriately use a different value of r, but this would be unusual and probably not well understood.

The second reason is that cost management strategies may include either taking on or avoiding the risk of inflation. For example, you could agree to a higher price for a component in exchange for a commitment to hold that price for a period of time – in effect, paying someone else to take the risk of inflation. To evaluate the worth of such a strategy, your baseline for comparison would need to show the expected after-inflation values. Otherwise, the impact of your strategy would not be visible in the comparison.

Technology/Market Evolution

It is well-known that technology improves year over year, with the result that the real prices of many products and functions decline over time. Certain industries, most notably semiconductor manufacturing, have developed expectations of how performance and cost should evolve[1] and while these don't always translate neatly to pricing, industry experts tend to have quite consistent views on how prices should evolve. To evaluate the impact of decisions in these areas – a technology choice for example – these expert opinions should be consulted for inclusion in your model. For example, the decision of when or if to switch over to a new battery technology would be strongly influenced by projections about the future costs of the competing technologies.

Unfortunately, beyond these generalizations, it is difficult to

1   The best-known examples are Moore's first and second laws: the first states that the density of transistors on a chip doubles every two years, and the second says that the capital cost of a semiconductor fabrication facility doubles every four years.

give any specific guidance. The progression curves will be different for different technologies, so it is important to be expert in the technologies you use to be able to model your choices appropriately. This anticipates a point that we will make later – that decisions at the product design stage have a huge impact on the future costs of a product and hence, its profitability. Make friends with your product development people!

Just as technology evolves, so do markets, and the effects are often intertwined. When a product or technology is in a market entry phase, production volumes are increasing rapidly and we expect costs and prices to be declining as a result of this volume increase. Much of this will come from the amortization of startup costs, but there will also be indirect effects such as increased competition, and development of an industry infrastructure.

The propagation of a new technology into a market place, whether it is something totally new or a replacement for an existing technology, follows what is called a *diffusion curve*. Differently-shaped curves have been developed for different market situations, and the best-known is the Bass or Logistic diffusion curve. These curves are generally S-shaped from initial market entry up to market saturation. If the market size at saturation can be estimated, and if there are at least two good data points on the progression to date, then it is possible to solve for the parameters of the curve and predict market size at any point in the future. Clearly, these numbers will have wide error bands, and it may be difficult to translate the market-size numbers into costs, but at least they can form the basis of an estimate that may be better than ignoring the phenomenon.

While it is the front side of the diffusion curve, the ramp-up phase, that gets the most attention, from a cost management standpoint, the back-side or phaseout period may be every bit as important. As a technology gets superseded and is phased out, the volumes will drop – often dramatically. This may produce a period of low prices as manufacturers try to get as much revenue as they can out of a dying technology with surplus capacity. That's the good news for a buyer, but the bad news is that once the capacity has shrunk, there will be a period of poor availability and probably higher prices. At some point it may not be possible to buy certain products at all any more.

This situation tends to occur in industries that have low clockspeed[1] relative to their supply bases. For example, a military aircraft design may be in production for twenty years or more, but the state-of-the-art electronics in the operating systems rely on an industry where products become obsolete every 18 months or so. Failing to design around these issues can result in substantially increased costs down the road.

Continuous Improvement – Learning Curves

Production costs can also change as a result of improvements made by those doing the production. In fact, they should change (decrease of course!), if for no other reason than to keep up with competition that is doing the same thing. These improvements are really improvements in knowledge – knowledge of how best to do something. This knowledge can reside in many "places," ranging from the muscle memory of a line operator to the design of the entire production facility and we refer to the improvements in knowledge over time as *learning*. This term will be familiar as most people have heard the term *learning curve*, a term suggesting that one's knowledge of how to do something improves with experience.

There is room for debate as to whether this learning is *autonomous*, meaning that it is a natural result of repetition, or *induced*, meaning that deliberate actions were taken to improve a process. In truth, both may come into play in varying proportions. The supplement to this chapter elaborates the classical view of a learning curve and how to use it for calculation purposes. This formulation has the implicit assumption that learning is a function of experience and therefore autonomous. Induced learning, better known as continuous improvement is a deliberate approach to cost reduction and may take on quite a different pattern, but in general there will still be a relationship between cumulative

---

1   "Clockspeed" is a term coined by Charles Fine to describe the frequency with which major design changes occur within an industry.

experience and cost regardless of which causes which.

For cost management purposes, some sort of learning or progression curve may be used to predict costs, but is more commonly used to set a performance target when writing a contract or evaluating personnel. It is important to realize that learning only applies to addressable costs. Direct labor is an obvious target for improvement and purchased materials are also addressable as we expect our suppliers to engage in their own continuous improvement. The variable components of overhead such as indirect labor or utilities can be considered addressable, but fixed overheads generally are not. Calculating the effect of learning on total costs requires breaking out these components, assigning curve to each and adding up the total. Truly addressable costs may be a relatively small component of that total.

Trying to assign a particular learning curve to any activity has serious limitations and plenty of room for error. As noted in Supplement 9-1, there is no theoretical basis for any particular value of the learning coefficient, so applying say a 90% or an 80% learning curve to a process is really just a rule of thumb based on similar situations. Process design and management philosophy will affect whether a particular coefficient is applicable or not. Highly automated processes will have very little labor content in the first place, but we would not expect much learning to take place since there is very little freedom for the operators to vary their techniques. "Automated" does not just mean machine-based; a process that has been carefully thought out in advance, perhaps prototyped, and tightly-scripted, will have a similar characteristic in that very little improvement can be expected. In effect, such a process is not starting from Job 1.

This highlights a philosophical issue, and a way in which the Toyota Production System (TPS) diverged from much of the thinking of the day. In the TPS view, trying to get the process perfect out of the gate is a waste of resources – better results are achieved by getting something that is adequate, and then working continuously to improve it. Notice, though, that the ability to continuously reduce costs requires the avoidance of fixed (sunk) costs. This is one of the hidden costs of automation, and if you are trying to model the difference between more or less automated approaches, you would assign different learning curves to the labor content involved.

Just as the choice of learning coefficient (*b* in the supplement) is complex, so is the determination of what actually constitutes cumulative experience (X). Most companies produce families of related products, and when a new product is introduced, it shares many of the existing processes, and benefits from whatever learning has taken place. In effect, it is already some way down the learning curve, so that a doubling of its volume is not really a doubling in the total cumulative volume of relevant products, and the learning improvement will be much less than the curve might predict. This can be adjusted by assigning an X-value greater than unity to the first unit produced, but there is no realistic way to calculate what that value should be.

All of the above should suggest that, while learning curves are real and important, they are of limited value in cost modeling. They do have their applications, but most companies take a more direct approach to cost improvement over time. Notice that the base here is time, not cumulative experience as in the learning curve formulation. It is simply stated that certain costs are expected to decrease by some percentage, year over year. This can be used for modeling purposes, but is more commonly used as a performance target for employees and suppliers alike. The theoretical basis for this is at least as strong as that for a cumulative volume approach, and it is easier to use. The actual percentage chosen will be specific to an industry or a product and may be the result of a negotiation.

Chapter 9 – Key Takeaways

1. Some costs can be predicted to evolve in certain ways over time.

2. Incorporating this information is important for both proposed initiatives and for the business-as-usual case.

3. Inflation can be modeled and should be included in numerical values if it is also a component of the discount rate (which it usually is).

4. The cost of emerging technologies may be changing rapidly and can be approximated by extrapolation.

5. Market shares of new products and technologies are modeled with diffusion curves.

6. Learning curves can be used to approximate the effects of continuous improvement efforts, but in many cases a fixed %/yr. approximation is just as valid.

Supplement 9-1 – Learning Curves, Theory and Practice

The concept of the learning curve is based on the common-sense notion that if you do something repetitively, you tend to get better at it. This is normally quantified by the time it takes to complete a task, and has an obvious, direct relationship to the cost of doing it – hence our interest in the subject. Although the concept has been known since the dawn of time, it was only in the last century that people started to observe that this improvement seems to follow a predictable pattern that persists across all types of activities. This pattern can be expressed either as the measure of the time/cost required to complete one unit, or as the cumulative average of time/cost to that point. The former is more useful in trying to predict what something should cost in the future, and may be combined with a diffusion curve analysis of volume to achieve that. The latter is more useful when contracting for a batch of product – to know the effect of batch size on price. These are both handy pieces of information whether you are buying or selling, but one must always be questioning whether they are valid or not.

This regular pattern of learning can be expressed in a couple of different ways, the simplest being a power function that projects the per unit cost (time to complete task) as a function of cumulative units produced:

$$Y = aX^b$$

Where:

Y is the average cost or time over quantity X,

a is the cost or time required for the first unit,

X is cumulative total of units produced,

b is a constant describing the learning rate, and is the slope of the curve in log-log form.

The notable feature of this equation is that for every doubling of cumulative experience (X), the average cost (Y) drops by a constant percentage. It also true that the per-unit cost drops by a constant (but different) percentage, and that the cumulative total cost increases by a constant percentage. Many studies have found that this relationship matches actual field measurements with reasonable fidelity.

The computation and use of learning curve values is not totally straightforward, and requires attention to the terminology and definitions being used. It is common to speak of learning curves in terms of percentages, such as a "90% learning curve" which would mean that that for every doubling of experience, the average cost or time drops by 10%, or, expressing Y as a function of X:

$$Y(2X)/Y(X) = 0.90$$

Again, the Y-value is the *average* unit cost or time over the total production. If we want make use of the above formula to calculate specific values, we need to solve for b, which in this case (skipping a few steps in the algebra) would work out to:

$$b = log(.90)/log(2) = -0.152$$

The 0.90 can be replaced with whatever learning curve rate you want to use. Armed with the value of b, we can calculate the average per-unit cost or time at any level of production. If we want to know the total cost or time required for a batch, we can just multiply the batch size times the average over the total quantity. For example, if we think a 90% learning curve is valid, and the first item of a batch takes one hour to process, the average per-unit processing time for a batch of 1,000 would be:

$$Y=1\times1000^{-0.152}= 0.350 \; hrs.$$

and the total time to produce the batch would be 350 hours. Notice that if the batch size is doubled, the equation reads:

$$Y=1\times2000^{-0.152}=0.315 \; hrs.$$

and the total time taken would be 630 hours. As expected, 0.315 is 90% of 0.350.

Now, if we want to know the time or cost for unit #X, what

we want is the slope of the cumulative function at point X:

$$\textbf{\textit{Cumulative Time (X)}} = X \times Y = XaX^b = aX^{b+1}$$

and therefore:

$$\textbf{\textit{d(XY)/d(X)}} = a(b+1)X^b$$

So, if you know a and b, then you can calculate the time taken per unit at some point in the future.

The above formulation, and others, were developed to model actual observed behavior, highlighting an important point: this is strictly an empirical relationship – there is no definitive theory of learning curves! Not that there haven't been many attempts to develop theories that explain observed behavior[1], but none have emerged that can tell us what we really want to know, which is what rate of learning should be expected in a given situation. The best we can do is to say that in similar situations, certain values have been observed to apply.

The implication of the learning curve model is that practice or experience actually causes the improvement, and there would seem to be some truth in that. When you do something for the second time, you can avoid some of the mistakes you made the first time – if you remember them. Realistically, it would seem more likely that your efforts at improvement would be much more dependent on how many times you are expecting to perform the task in the future, rather than what is in the past. The more you expect to do something, the more attention you will give to doing it efficiently, with the result that when you look at the results in hindsight it may look as though the improvement was the result of experience, when in fact it may have been the result of anticipation of experience. It is virtually impossible to disentangle these effects in empirical data, so we are left with learning curves as an empirical rule of thumb, to be used with care.

We should not leave the subject of learning curves without noting that there is also an unlearning (or forgetting) curve. While we may gain experience with practice, we also lose it

---

1   For the author's own take on this, see: Hanson, J. D. (2011). "Cost Modelling Based on Experience; Do We Have It Backwards? " International Journal of Procurement Management 4(5)

with time unless rigorous measures are taken to preserve it. We can expect gaps in production to at least partially reset the learning curve, with the amount of re-setting depending on the duration of the gap, and also the expectations about whether production would be resumed or not.

Chapter 10 – TCO and Differential Analysis

Frameworks for TCO

The term TCO (Total Cost of Ownership) has become widely used to mean taking into account all of the costs that apply in a situation, not just the obvious ones. The realization of this need is a good first step towards cost management, but like many other techniques, it tends to break down a bit when you actually try to apply it. The use of the word 'ownership' suggests that the concept evolved to address the acquisition of assets such as capital equipment where there is an extended lifetime involved and where the actual purchase price may be a small portion of the total.

The format usually suggested for such a calculation derives from the capital budgeting model that we examined in Part I when we looked at time value of money. If we consider an asset that has an acquisition cost (A), yearly upkeep costs (Y), an expected service life of k years, and some salvage value at its end of life (S), the formulation would be:

$$TCO = A + \sum_{n=1}^{k} Y \times (1 - r)^n - S \times (1 - r)^k$$

where r is our ever-present discount rate – subject to all the debates about its appropriate value! All of these categories need to be analyzed in some detail, and this is where it sometimes becomes difficult to know what should be included.

Acquisition cost will obviously include the purchase price of the asset, but also includes taxes, duties, shipping costs, installation costs, operator initial training costs, setup and tryout cost, and possibly some other categories, depending on the nature of the asset. It is also useful in many cases to incorporate the effect of income taxes on the acquisition. The actual price of the asset will normally be booked as a capital asset, meaning that the purchase price doesn't enter the calculation of net income, which is the basis of corporate income tax. Most of the other charges will likely be billed as expenses and deducted from net income, so the true cost of those items to the company is really the expense amount times one minus the tax rate.

Why is this important? Different decisions may have different distributions of expense and capital items over time, and these differences may be significant. The effect becomes clearer when we look at annual costs. Most assets require some sort of maintenance and upkeep, and you may want to include utility use, insurance, ongoing training, and other categories as appropriate. What we don't include in the formulation above is a charge for the depreciation of the capital asset since the full value was included in the acquisition cost. However, a charge for depreciation does go against the calculation of net income for tax purposes. In effect, the firm receives a rebate every year for the amount of depreciation times the tax rate. This is actual money (cash flow) so we need to include it because it may vary according to the decision alternatives available to us. Determining the actual amount of the depreciation charge is beyond the scope of this book as it is defined by tax laws in different jurisdictions. In the absence of better information, it would make sense to use a straight-line method – for example, if a machine had an estimated life of ten years, use one tenth of the value every year. However, most taxing authorities try to encourage businesses to invest in capital assets, so they typically allow a faster, non-linear depreciation curve. Consult with your accounting contacts on the values to use – they should be your friends by now; you need to work with them!

End-of-life values are more hypothetical and can be positive or negative. It is not normally a given that an asset will be disposed of at the theoretical end of its life, but that is usually the best way to model it. Other decisions, such as whether to keep it in operation, can be evaluated at that time. Other terminology may be encountered in this area. *Salvage Value* is often used to describe any potential gain from the sale of the asset. There is a tax implication to this as well. If we assume the asset to be fully depreciated at that point, it will have zero book value, so any money received from salvage will be treated as income and therefore taxed. Salvage value can also be negative if you have to pay for disposal and cleanup. These costs would be expenses, deductible from income.

The term *residual* is also used, as in residual value, with a similar meaning to salvage value. The term residual is also used to capture any ongoing gains or losses past the end-of-life date. Usually there won't be, but if there were any such values, they would be reduced to a single value at the end-of-life date for inclusion in the formula above.

The TCO formulation seems most applicable to the acquisition of capital equipment, but similar logic can and should be applied to the purchase of production materials or supplies. Many such purchases have no significant time dimension, so the analysis can be condensed to a single time period. However, other purchase decisions do have a lifetime, either by way of long-term contracts, or simply because switching costs are high, and it can be assumed that there will be a more lasting relationship. As with capital equipment, acquisition costs include more than just the purchase price. Production materials often have setup costs, or NRE (Non-Recurring Expense) charges to start production. There may also be tooling, which you may choose to own, in which case there is a capital asset to account for. There may also be significant one-time costs to qualify the part – for example, if it has to be certified for aviation or medical use, or perhaps to certify a new supplier to your quality standards. In such situations, a multi-year cost model makes sense. In this case, the purchase price of the unit would be under annual costs, along with all the extra costs described in Chapter 6. If tooling is purchased as part of the decision, the tax rebate on depreciation would go here as well. Production materials won't usually have an end-of-life value, unless tooling is involved. However, it may be appropriate to include a residual term to capture things like anticipated liability or warranty claims.

Differential Analysis

As we start to dig into the different categories that make up TCO, we start to discover some of the limitations of the process. Specifically, what do we include and where do we stop? We can illustrate the problem with a simple example[1]. Imagine a small woodworking company that specializes in maple furniture. The company is clearly interested in the cost of the wood it buys and it might seem sensible to ask: "what is the real total cost (TCO) of the maple we buy?" What we find is that, framed this way, the question is impossible to answer in any meaningful way. What costs should we include? Clearly purchase price would be included, along with shipping and perhaps handling and sorting. Storage and drying costs should probably be considered since maple must be bought seasonally to avoid staining. But, should we include the costs of cutting, routing, sanding, and varnishing? Are those relevant? They may be – there are purchasing decisions that could have an impact on these downstream functions. The point is that we cannot decide what costs are relevant until we know what alternatives are under consideration. Otherwise, we could conclude that all of the costs incurred by the company are in some way related to the purchase of maple and therefore potentially relevant. Now some might argue that since all those costs are in the records, it should be a simple matter to pull out the necessary data. However, we showed above (Chapter 4) that the numbers in the records are based on a cost model that may not be relevant to decisions that we want to evaluate. It is also the case that the records contain no information about hypothetical alternative states that we may be considering. Building a universal TCO model for each item is not only a lot of work, it is also not very useful.

What we observe is, that when we frame the question as the total cost relative to a defined alternative, the list of relevant cost factors is substantially reduced. In the example company above, if the question was really about whether to continue buying lumber from Supplier X or switching to

1   A version of this discussion can be found in the author's article: Hanson, J. D. (2011). "Differential Method for TCO Modelling: An Analysis and Tutorial," International Journal of Procurement Management 4(6).

Supplier Y, the analysis is much simpler. As long as the product is otherwise indistinguishable, we only have to look at supplier-related costs. To be thorough, we might consider the following:

- Purchase price, typically per board-foot.
- Shipping costs (including duties if foreign-sourced)
- Payment terms
- Order quantities (trade units)
- Delivery lead times
- Delivery reliability
- Quality levels (cost of quality)
- Handling costs (related to order quantities)
- Supplier relationship costs (site visits, quality audits, etc.)
- Inventory value (for purposes of taxes and insurance, and effect on working capital)
- Any other terms and conditions that vary between the two suppliers

As we can see, the list is much more manageable, but still potentially quite lengthy. Now, if we were to attribute a cost to each of these items for each supplier and add them up, we would get totals, but those totals wouldn't be meaningful numbers on their own – they would only serve as a basis for comparison to each other. This then, is the basis for differential analysis – the idea that the only numbers that are meaningful are those that differ between choices – which is actually the definition of what costs are *relevant*. As an example, we don't care what the total handling costs are for wood bought from X or from Y, we only care about the difference between them – if any. To further illustrate the concept of relevance, let's now suppose that the person asking the question had a different choice in mind. If the company had been buying maple in Common 1 grade, it might be worthwhile to buy Select grade instead. The difference is that Select would have fewer defects and hence more usable lumber per unit of measure. The price per unit will be higher, but you will have to buy (and handle, and store, and process) less of it. How much less is the critical question, and the answer will depend on the products being made. If the requirements are only for small pieces, it may be quite efficient to get those out of Common 1 with only minimal increase in yield by switching to Select. However, if the product requires large areas of clear wood, there may be substantial wastage with Common 1 and a significant improvement by switching. This is something that would have to be analyzed, and should be revisited if the product mix changes. Assuming that a yield factor can be agreed upon for the different grades, the list of costs to consider might now look like this:

- Purchase price per unit, typically per board-foot.
- Quantity required (based on yield)
- Shipping costs
- Handling costs
- Storage costs
- Inventory value (for purposes of taxes and insurance, and effect on working capital)
- Sorting and cutting costs
- Recovery value of scrap
- Capital equipment required

As we can see, the lists overlap somewhat, but only partly. The categories of interest are determined by the alternatives being considered. One key difference in the second example is that the decision has potential downstream consequences – in this case the amount of labor and machine time required to cut the raw lumber down into production components. When we start talking about assigning costs to these elements, we are faced with the choice between average and marginal costs. This is one of those unresolvable issues as discussed in Chapters 2 & 8, and there are arguments to be made either way.

The general recommendation here is to use marginal costs in the comparison – but only if they can be reliably determined and are believed to be stable over time. The reason is that we want to keep our focus on what will actually change as a result of a decision. It is all too easy to redesign a work process, and on the basis of average costs, claim to have achieved a certain value of cost reduction. However, if you test that claim by asking which person will be paid less, or will not be employed after the change is implemented, it often turns out that there is no such person, and actual labor costs will not change at all. The problem with using marginal costs is that they are not uniform with volume, but lumpy. They are also not uniform over time as the break points will shift as other demands on resources come and go. This means that in many cases, especially those with longer time horizons, the marginal cost of an activity cannot be reliably reduced to a single number. In those cases, it will be necessary, and more appropriate, to use average costs.

However, if your decision will involve crossing a capacity break-point, up or down, the marginal cost can become very significant. It is important to capture this effect as it may influence the decision. The above example is loosely based on a real situation where a cabinetry company was faced with growing demand but was constrained by the capacity of some of its equipment. And it wasn't simply a matter of buying a new machine as there was no room for it, and a plant expansion would be required as well. Analysis determined that switching to a higher grade of lumber would reduce the processing requirements sufficiently to defer the capital investment by two years. This has real value that can be calculated with a discounted cash flow analysis in the form we will introduce here.

These are the arguments in favor of using marginal costs and focusing on what will actually change with a decision. But, you must know with some certainty what those marginal costs will be. This can be quite difficult in a large operation with shared resources where you don't know what plans other departments are making for those resources. In those cases, it is more sensible to use average costs, at least for labor, since the lumpiness tends to get smoothed out in larger operations.

We can do one more extension to the example: suppose we are considering substituting birch for maple as a possible cost reduction. This introduces a new dimension to the analysis since the end product changes. Customers may notice and/ or care, with the result that there will likely be changes to prices and quantities sold, and the latter will affect most of the cost categories of the income statement. The analysis of this kind of situation would normally be called a business case analysis rather than a cost analysis, however we can use the same framework for both. This is not normally a concern for the cost management issues we are discussing, and it does complicate the calculations. For that reason, we will leave out any volume effects in the examples that follow, but for completeness, a description of how to deal with them is given in a supplement to the chapter (Supplement 10-3).

Continuing with our example; if we imagine that our decision to switch to birch involves a change in supplier as well, the list of things that might change incorporates all of the above categories, and then some:

- Purchase price, typically per board-foot.
- Shipping costs (including duties if foreign-sourced)
- Number of units required
- Handling costs
- Storage costs
- Inventory value (for purposes of taxes and insurance, and effect on working capital)
- Sorting and cutting costs
- Assembly and finishing costs
- Recovery value of scrap
- Payment terms
- Order quantities (trade units)
- Delivery lead times
- Delivery reliability
- Quality levels (cost of quality)
- Supplier relationship costs (site visits, quality audits, etc.)
- Any other terms and conditions that vary between the two suppliers
- Price effect on revenue
- Volume effect on revenue and on cost of goods sold
- Capital equipment required

As we can see, doing a thorough analysis of a change of this sort can be quite complex and requires that the entire process be thought through. Notice the inclusion of assembly and finishing costs in this list – a change of this sort may have significant downstream effects that must be taken into account. In practice, the way to do this is to identify the person responsible for each cost category and get their concurrence on the cost changes that will result. Fortunately, it is usually much easier to agree on and quantify what will change rather than trying to add up total costs for each case.

This discussion highlights the need for a cost analysis to be both comprehensive and transparent. By transparent, we mean that anyone looking at the analysis can see that it was comprehensive, so that you don't get any questions of the sort; "well, what about....?" Ideally, any category that might be discussed will have a clear and obvious place in the analysis, and a number that was agreed to by the responsible person (especially when that number is zero). While people may disagree with some of the numbers, having a transparent analysis will allow you to test different sets of assumptions to see whether they are material or not. To do that systematically, it helps to have a template, so we offer a universal framework that can be adapted to most situations.

TCO Template

To create this template, we begin with one of the better-known financial accounting documents, the income statement. We do this for two reasons: one is that most audiences will be familiar with the format and therefore will be better able to follow the logic, and the second is that we actually need the net income effect as part of the analysis. Companies may present their income statements in a variety of ways, but in general they will follow the format of Figure 10.1. Students of accounting will notice that there are many categories missing compared to what companies publish in their annual reports, and this is because we are only interested in the net income effect from continuing operations. Other adjustments such as acquiring or divesting business units, financing decisions (such as stock re-purchases, retirement of debt, etc.), extraordinary items, changes in inventory policy, and so on, are considered beyond the scope of what we are doing and therefore not relevant.

Figure 10.1: Outline Income Statement

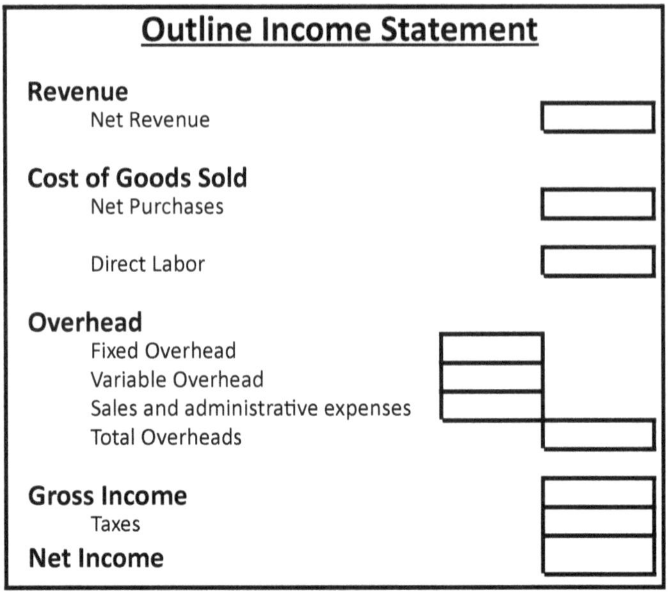

The income statement is by its very nature a summary document, so to get to the level of detail we need for our purposes, we need to expand the categories. How far to go on this depends on the questions being asked. We need to expand the categories to cover all the things that will change, per the example lists given above. In the case of the second example (buying wood in a different grade), an expanded income statement might look like Figure 10.2. You will notice that not all of the categories are represented, because not all of the changes resulting from our decision actually show up on the income statement, so we aren't finished at this point. Also notice that a category of Depreciation has been added, to reflect what would change if we have to buy new equipment or are able to dispose of existing machines.

Figure 10.2: Expanded Outline Income Statement

Expanded Outline Income Statement

Revenue
    Net Revenue

Cost of Goods Sold
    Purchased Materials
    Shipping
    Storage Costs
    Less recovery on scrap
    Net Purchases

    Direct Labor

Overhead
    Depreciation
    Other Fixed Overhead
    Material Handling Costs
    Other Variable Overhead
    Sales and administrative expenses
    Total Overheads

Other Income
    Gain (Loss) on disposal of capital assets

Gross Income
    Taxes
Net Income

The depreciation charge is not a cash flow item, but it does reduce gross income for tax purposes, so it is important to us for that reason. There is also a category for gain or loss associated with disposal of capital equipment. This too, is not a cash flow item and is only relevant for calculation of taxes, which are a cash flow item. See Supplement 10-1 for a discussion of depreciation and book values. The actual changes in cash flow associated with the decision do not all show up on an income statement, so we will need to deal with those below the line, so to speak.

The next issue to deal with is the time frame. The formal income statement is a backwards-looking document that deals with the past, one period at a time. We need to project into the future, so we need what is often called a *pro forma*[1] income statement, covering as many time periods as are relevant. If the total effects of whatever change we are considering will play out in the course of one year, then a single-period analysis is justified. Otherwise, as for example, when you incur a one-time cost to qualify a new supplier on a part that will be in production for some years, then a multi-period analysis is called for. There is no magic number for the number of periods to use, although five years is very common. If a product or its production machinery has a foreseeable end-of-life, that time span might make the most sense. Similarly, if a long-term contract is in effect for some key aspect, then the duration of that would be a good choice. Figure 10.3 shows the previous income statement example expanded to a five-year analysis.

The impact on net income is important, but it is not sufficient to determine which alternative is better. For that we need a discounted cash flow analysis as outlined in Chapter 2. Obviously, this requires knowing the year-over-year cash flows, and we emphasize again that net income is not a cash flow number. The easiest way to get to a cash flow projection is to build a bridge from the income statement, since much of the information we need is already there.

The first step is to reverse the entries that are not cash flows. In our example, these items are depreciation, and gain or loss on disposition of assets. We can simply add and subtract these items respectively to get an adjusted income line. Then we must account for the cash flow items that do not appear on the income statement. The main one is the cash that goes out to buy a capital asset or that comes in from its sale. We can capture this on one line, with negative values for the acquisitions and positive values for the dispositions, or you can use separate lines if you prefer.

---

1   "pro forma" in this context means forecast values based on our standard operating assumptions. What that means in practice is that the effects of any decision alternative must not be compared to today's values, but rather to the values that we project to be in effect in future periods.

Figure 10.3: Pro Forma Income Statement

Pro Forma Income Statement

	Year 0	Year 1	Year 2	Year 3	Year 4	Year 5
Net Revenue:						
Cost of Goods Sold						
Purchased Materials						
Shipping						
Other Items (duties, storage, etc.)						
Total Purchased Goods						
Direct Labor (by category)						
Overhead						
Depreciation						
Other Overhead Categories (itemize)						
Sales and administrative expenses						
Total Overheads						
Other Income						
Gain (Loss) on disposal of assets						
Gross Income						
Taxes (at effective tax rate)						
Net Income						

There is one more item, and it is one that many people overlook; the change in working capital. This can be seen in the strategic profit model in Supplement 3-1, and for our purposes working capital consists of the value of inventory, plus accounts receivable, minus accounts payable. Accounts receivable will not usually be of interest to us in the context of cost management. Inventory is the product of the average amount of inventory held multiplied by its acquisition cost per unit[1]. Anything that changes this, or the amount owed to our suppliers will result in a one-time flow of cash as the values increase or decrease. Specifically, an increase in the value of inventory represents a negative (outflow) cash flow and vice versa. Changes in accounts payable terms work the same way, with an increase in amounts payable representing an inflow of cash and vice versa.

---

1   Some companies choose to value their inventory on its replacement cost rather than its acquisition cost. This may give a truer picture of its value, but for our purposes, the difference is unlikely to be material.

This results in the complete template as shown in Figure 10.4. The bottom line of this template is a profile of cash flows relevant to the decision in question, on which we can perform a present value analysis as described in Chapter 2. Since the present value calculation (with the Excel function PV, or NPV) assumes that the cash flows take place at the end of each period, and since many of our decisions will have an upfront cash flow impact, it is convenient and appropriate to add a Year 0 column to the template.

Figure 10.4: Complete TCO Template

TCO Template

	Year 0	Year 1	Year 2	Year 3	Year 4	Year 5
Change in Net Revenue:						
Changes in Cost of Goods Sold						
Purchased Materials						
Shipping						
Other Items (duties, storage, etc.)						
Net Change in Purchased Goods						
Changes in Direct Labor (by category)						
Changes in Overhead						
Depreciation						
Other Overhead Categories (itemize)						
Sales and administrative expenses						
Total Overheads						
Changes in Other Income						
Gain (Loss) on disposal of assets						
Changes in Gross Income						
Change in Taxes (at effective tax rate)						
Changes in Net Income						
Plus Depreciation						
Less Gain (loss) on disposal of assets						
Adjusted Net Income						
Less capital expenditures						
Less Increase in working capital						
Changes to Net Cash Flow						

However, before we do any calculations, we should address the differential aspect of this analysis. As we have emphasized repeatedly, what we are calculating is the cost of a decision, which is to say the difference in cost between two alternatives, one of which may be a base case of business-as-usual. The categories we chose to itemize were those that were relevant to that particular decision and are not a complete list of all cost items. As a result, simply adding them up doesn't necessarily give us a useful number – we are only interested in the differences between the cases. This is fortunate in many ways because it is often much easier to quantify what is different between scenarios than it is to come up with accurate totals for each.

As we saw in the calculation of standard costs, the totals we arrive at depend on a number of assumptions, including production volume and basis of allocation. Many of these details have nothing to do with the decision at hand, but if we want to work with totals, we have to be sure to maintain consistency of the assumptions behind the totals being used, which sounds simple enough, but can easily become a burden[1], and worse, it introduces a threat to the credibility of the analysis. On the other hand, if we focus on the differences, we can state in detail what will actually change and, by agreement with those responsible, attach a cost to them. So, the intent of the template is that all of the entries are actually the differences between two scenarios.

To illustrate the use of differential information, let's look at the example where we considered changing the grade of lumber purchased. A critical parameter is the change in volume of lumber purchased (up or down). A yield factor for each grade would have to be worked out and agreed to by the shop foreman or equivalent. Suppose it is agreed that by buying a higher grade, the quantity purchased can be reduced by 15%. Considering only the pricing, it is simple enough to calculate the total cost of purchases either way, and to take the difference. However, there are other impacts – handling for example. You could attempt to calculate the

---

1   It is the nature of plans, budgets, and analyses that they are being continually revised and updated. Unless the updates are kept current across all of your analyses, it is very easy to lose consistency and consequently the validity of your analysis. Focusing on the differences between scenarios allows you to avoid dealing with any changes that apply across the board.

total handling costs attributable to this material, identify what part of that total is variable, and apply the 15% factor to that. This is not only a lot of work, but also depends on the assumption that the "variable" portion is strictly linear with volume; in other words, it uses *average* costs.

Consider the alternative of looking at *marginal* costs: go to the yard foreman and ask, "if we were to get 15% smaller (or fewer) shipments of this material every month, what would that do to you?" You might get a variety of answers, such as, "Well, nothing really. It wouldn't reduce the load enough to allow me to lay anyone off." Or, the answer might be, "That would help; I'm running about 20% overtime in that area right now, and that could bring it down to 10%." Or, you might get additional information: "You know, we don't buy every month, we buy seasonally, and I have to bring on temporary labor during the season. I could probably get away with one fewer worker for four months of the year." All of these answers are quantifiable in terms of the difference between the scenarios, without having to make reference to any total handling costs. The result is also much more credible, as it goes directly to the changes resulting from the decision.

There is the ever-present tension between using average or marginal costs to quantify the differences between decision alternatives, and one should be careful not to simply select whichever one gives the most favorable results! If a cost item is purely linear with volume, then marginal and average costs are the same thing; it is the non-linearities that cause the difference. In the above example, overtime costs introduce a non-linearity, as does the lumpiness of labor cost in adding or subtracting personnel. Marginal cost tells the true story of a particular change at a given moment, but whether it is an appropriate basis for a decision depends on whether or not those conditions apply for time horizon of the decision. For example, reduced overtime costs may be a valid cost savings in the near term, but might not be a factor six months from now if the overall level of business goes up or down. Judgment will have to be your guide here.

A step-by-step guide to the use of the template is given in

Supplement 10-2, but from an overview perspective, there are some additional points to be made about differential analysis. The principal feature of differential analysis is that it focuses our attention on the costs that are relevant to a particular decision, but it also allows some other options in presenting the results. As discussed in Chapter 2, if you have streams of cash flows with different patterns over time, attributable to different alternatives, you can calculate the present value of each one and compare them to see which is best. Equivalently, you can calculate the present value of the differences to see whether it is positive or negative. However, this comparison is only valid for a particular cost of capital (discount rate). If there is uncertainty or disagreement about what rate to use (and there often is), then the calculations will have to be done for each value of discount rate we wish to consider. This is easily enough done with a spreadsheet data table, but it tends to draw discussion away from the key factors. With differential analysis it is often (but not always) possible to use the internal rate of return (IRR) function to show the difference between alternatives. This changes the decision question from: "at a discount rate of X%, what is the best decision?" to: "the return from this decision is Y%; is that sufficient for our purposes?" The latter is frequently an easier discussion and doesn't require committing to a particular discount rate in advance.

There are some apparent drawbacks to differential analysis. One is that it is dyadic by nature, meaning that it only compares alternatives two at a time. If you want to compare more than one alternative to the base case, you will have to do separate calculations for each. This is actually not as onerous as it sounds, and in fact allows you to avoid some calculations that are not relevant for a particular pairing. For example, if you are over capacity for a certain operation and are currently doing half yourself and outsourcing half, you may wish to compare the current state to either outsourcing all of it, or expanding capacity to do it all yourself. This will need two separate analyses since the cost categories involved are quite different. A useful fact is that the present values add, so it is not necessary to analyze every pairing: if the outsourcing alternative shows an NPV advantage over the current state of $10M, and the expansion shows a $20M advantage over the base case, then it would be true that capacity expansion would have a $10M (20 – 10) advantage over outsourcing; if that question were to come up.

Chapter 10 – Key Takeaways

1. Total Cost of Ownership (TCO) is a blanket term referring to the need to take into account <u>all</u> costs relevant to a decision.

2. This analysis may need to be done over a period of time, and across all affected activities within a firm.

3. A TCO analysis is only meaningful in the context of decision alternatives under consideration. Sometimes these are implicit in the situation description, but it is always preferable to define them.

4. When decision alternatives are defined, costs can be evaluated on a differential basis without the need to calculate totals. This is often much easier and more accurate.

5. To properly evaluate alternatives, it is necessary to compute the differences in actual cash flows over time, and the best way to do this is to develop a pro-forma income statement and then make adjustments for the cash and non-cash items.

6. Differential analysis implies pair-wise comparison of alternatives which may seem like extra work but in most cases actually saves work.

Supplement 10-1 – Depreciation and Book Value

The acquisition and divestiture of capital assets will sometimes enter into our calculations of TCO for a specific decision alternative. Since our ultimate goal is to provide a discounted cash flow analysis of these decision alternatives, we are naturally interested in the cash amounts spent to acquire assets or received from their disposition. The accounting world treats this a little differently and we have to know how to make the transition.

What accounting is trying to do is to match the cost of the asset with the revenues generated from its use, while recognizing that certain assets have a finite lifespan. The initial purchase is basically not counted as it is really just a conversion of one asset (cash) to another (equipment). However, when an asset diminishes in value over time, that reduction in value is treated as a cost to be charged against income. The charge is called depreciation and shows up on the income statement, but it does not represent an actual cash flow. The intent is to spread the cost over the useful life of the asset; normally on a time basis.

The amount of depreciation to be charged each period can be calculated in a number of ways. The simplest approach, and a reasonable assumption in the absence of any other information, is the straight-line method, taking an equal charge each year of the projected life. The actual method used may be determined primarily by tax laws, and since taxation authorities usually want to encourage investment in new equipment, they allow non-linear schedules of depreciation. In the U.S., this is referred to as MACRS (Modified Accelerated Cost Recovery System), and IRS publications describe how it is to be applied. The best advice we can give is to consult with your accounting department on the lifespan and depreciation schedule that are appropriate for the equipment in question. If that information is not available, making a reasonable estimate of life and applying a straight-line schedule will be close enough for most purposes.

When a depreciable asset is acquired, it goes onto the

balance sheet at a value equal to its acquisition cost, which may include various installation and setup costs. Every time we take a depreciation charge against that asset, its balance sheet value drops by the same amount – just as if you had spent cash. At any given time, the reported or "book" value will be the initial value minus all the depreciation charges to that point. At some point, that value will reach zero, and we say that the asset is fully depreciated, meaning having no value and no longer appearing on the balance sheet.

The actual, or market, value of the asset at any time may be more or less than the book value, sometimes dramatically so. This does not come into play unless the asset is scrapped or sold, in which case there will be an apparent gain or loss on the disposition, relative to the book value. This gain or loss does not reflect the actual cash flow effect of the transaction, but it does represent a taxable value, so we need to use it to calculate the tax effect, which is very much a cash flow item. So, when we dispose of a capital asset, there are two cash flows to consider. One is the actual cash received for the asset (or the cost paid to haul it away), and the other is a tax increase or rebate depending on whether the amount received was more or less than book value.

Supplement 10-2 – Using the Template; a Step-by-Step Guide

Throughout this guide, we will refer to the generic differential cost template shown in Figure 10.4. It is important to remember that this template is only a shell, and each of the categories will need to be expanded to capture any effects that are relevant to the decision at hand. It is also important to be clear about the decision alternatives under consideration. The cleanest way to do this is to designate case A as the proposed future state, and case B as the "base" case, which will normally be business as usual. If we do this, then any figures entered in the template will be in the form A − B. As discussed elsewhere, it is often much easier to identify the difference between cases than to come up with totals for A and B separately, however if you have the total values and wish to keep track of them, it would make sense to create two new pages for A and B in the workbook as backup. The difference A − B may be positive or negative, the former meaning that the value for A is larger than the value for B, regardless of whether it is a cost or a revenue item, and vice versa. If this convention is observed throughout, then the present value calculated at the bottom will be the present value of choosing alternative A over B, at the given discount rate. A positive value means that it is worth doing, and a negative value means it is not. Normally an IRR can also be calculated, which will give the return on assets from choosing alternative A. This rate of return can be compared to the company's hurdle rate for any investment required.

The first section of the template deals with changes in revenues attributable to whatever change we are considering. For most cost management activities, there will be no change here, but we do need to consider the possibility. As with all of the categories in this template, the value of the analysis is greatly enhanced if you get the responsible person, in this case a sales or product manager, to agree that there will be no change in revenue, or to give you a specific value if there will be a change. For our purposes, we really only need the total change in revenue, but it is sometimes useful to separate this change into volume and price effects, as discussed in Supplement 10-3. Price effects have no impact beyond revenue, but if there is a change in volumes, then all of the cost categories representing variable costs will also change, so we have to pay attention to that.

Changes in purchased goods and direct labor are fairly self-explanatory, the main caveat being that you should make sure that you are comparing the alternative to the real base case, not to the official standard cost values for both labor hours and purchase prices. The ancillary costs for both categories will normally show up under overheads, but if your company normally charges things like shipping, handling, scrap, etc. directly to purchased goods costs, you should itemize those here if relevant. Again, observe the sign convention: if alternative A has lower costs than base case B, the entry will be a negative number. If there is a volume effect in play, then the materials and labor categories will be changing for that reason alone. It is generally cleaner and more informative to not include that effect at the line-item level, but to add in a line further down for volume effect on variable cost.

The overhead categories are where most of the detailed itemization of cost items will take place and the level of complexity required depends entirely on the change being implemented. Depreciation for example, only comes into play if there is an acquisition or disposal of a capital asset, otherwise it can be assumed to be constant between alternatives. If an asset is acquired, then a yearly depreciation charge will appear from that point forward, and if an asset is disposed of, the depreciation associated with it will stop at that point. Both can be occurring at the same time. If there is such an event, the only reason we need the amount of depreciation involved is to calculate the tax impact of the decision, which means that the correct amount of depreciation to be used is whatever the tax code dictates. You can make an estimate if necessary, but it is far preferable to consult with your accounting department to obtain the values to be used.

The "Other" category covers all other indirect factory costs. If alternative A will use less electricity, calculate the difference and itemize it here. Likewise, if alternative A will require more supplier visits for quality assurance, calculate a cost and list it here. The list of items can be quite long, and must reflect a carefully thought-out schedule of all the things that will change from A to B. It will probably also be more detailed in some areas than your company's normal accounting records, so getting agreement from the affected areas as to the correct amounts to use is important. This is also the area where the tension between average and marginal costs will be most apparent. This will be a matter of judgment as discussed elsewhere.

The category also contains a line for volume effect. If there is no volume effect on the revenue stream (i.e.: no change in unit sales volume), then this line will be zero and can be omitted. However, if there is a change in unit sales, see Supplement 10-3. Fortunately, it is very rare that you will have to go to this level of detail.

The overhead category also contains a heading for corporate, or front office overhead, often represented as Sales, General, and Administrative (SG&A) expenses. These are generally assessed as a percentage of "factory" costs (basically, the sum of all the costs above this line). Notice the word 'assessed' as opposed to 'calculated', as the amount is not a natural consequence of the other activities, but rather, a matter of management policy. This leads to the obvious question; if you reduce other costs, does the SG&A assessment go down too? In the short-term, probably not – the budgets for the year are already set and don't usually get revised in that situation. However, over a few years, you would expect the budgets to converge to the new cost base. A reasonable representation might be to show no change in the first year, then an adjustment in subsequent years. Of course, there may be aspects of the decision that affect SG&A directly, and these effects should be captured. Some examples might be a product change requiring engineering validation, or the outsourcing of a support function. This question will be revisited in Chapter 16.

The next heading is changes in "other" income, specifically the gain or loss on disposition of assets – usually, but not necessarily, capital assets. A piece of capital equipment has a book value equal to its initial value minus all the depreciation accumulated to that point. Similarly, production material has a value (either its initial cost or its replacement cost, depending on your accounting system). When you sell or scrap either of these things, the tax authorities perceive that you made a profit or loss based on the selling price minus the accounting value. This is a fictitious number as far as we are concerned, but it does have a tax impact that is very real, so we need to include it.

This brings us to the gross income line, or effectively, the taxable income line. If alternative A shows a higher gross income than the base case, then there will be a corresponding increase in taxes too, and vice versa. To calculate the effect, you will need an effective tax rate, and most publicly-traded companies publish this number. As with any tax-related question, you are advised to get the input of your accounting department on the actual number to use.

Once we have taken taxes into account to arrive at the Net Income line, we can start to make the adjustments to turn this into a cash flow line. The line for depreciation was purely an accounting value, not a cash flow, so we can add that back. Similarly, the "income" from sale of assets was not a cash flow item, so we can subtract that to get to an adjusted net income line. From there, we have two more adjustments – basically we need to put in the real cash flow effects corresponding to the two imaginary lines we just took out. The first is capital equipment; when we buy equipment, the cash goes out all at once, so we can put these outlays in the capital equipment line. If we sell a piece of equipment, there is a cash inflow, so we can either put this on its own line, or just show it as a negative capital expenditure.

The final line is an important one, and often overlooked. For our purposes, working capital consists of inventory and the net of accounts receivable minus accounts payable. There are several ways that our decisions could change these values. Taking inventory first, any decision that increases the amount of inventory (raw materials, work in process, or finished goods) represents a one-time outflow of cash equal to the value change, and vice versa. So, a positive change in average inventory value is a negative value of cash flow. There are several ways in which inventory levels can change as a result of operating decisions, but this value can also be used as a hedge or as a proxy for other issues. For example, if you are considering switching to a supplier that is cheaper but is known for unreliable delivery, one way to quantify the latter is to decide on an incremental inventory buffer that would give you the same assurance of continued production as your base case and put that into the template as an increase in working capital.

The balance of receivables minus payables is really a matter of contract terms, but the effects can be quantified with this template. Most companies try to enforce standard payment terms for all of their suppliers, but if you were considering switching to a supplier that stubbornly insisted on faster payment, then this would be a one-time increase in working capital or cash outflow equal to the reduction in lead time times the average spend per period.

This raises the subject often referred to as Supply Chain Finance. This is worthy of a separate discussion, but here is the short version. Almost all companies are borrowing money from their suppliers by virtue of not paying cash on delivery. Many companies have discovered that they can borrow even more, usually interest-free, by extending their payment terms out to 90 days or even longer. This reduces working capital, which looks good on the strategic profit model and provides a one-time boost in cash flow with no apparent damage to the income statement. From an outsider's perspective, this is clearly a zero-sum game since the suppliers must increase their working capital by an equal amount to carry the receivables. Savvy suppliers will factor this into their pricing decisions to recover the cost, so in the longer-term, this is a net zero for all concerned. We can generally assume that a company trying to extend payment terms to extreme levels is exhibiting financial distress, either due to a shortage of cash flow or the need to dress up the balance sheet for re-financing or acquisition purposes.

That said, we need to show the effects of payment terms on our template. If we were to simply extend the payment terms for an existing supplier, the immediate effect would be a decrease in the working capital line equal to the change in payment time multiplied by the average spend per unit of time. This would occur once at the time of the change (Year 0), but this is not the whole story. It still represents a debt that has to be paid, so unless you expect the situation to continue for an infinite time, we need to account for it. We can do that by extending the template for as many years as we expect the terms to last and creating a residual term in the last year. This term will simply be the same amount (adjusted for inflation if that is a significant component of your model) added back to working capital, representing a negative cash flow. When this is brought back to a present value, we can see that the gain is just our cost of capital on the amount "borrowed." This assumes of course that there is no change in the price paid as a result of the action. Be careful about this: the change in price paid may look like zero, but there may have been a possible cost reduction that you didn't get, so it is easy to bury the true effect.

Finally, we arrive at a line showing the differences in actual cash flows between alternatives A and B. If we are given a discount rate, we can calculate the present value of these cash flows, and if we have observed the A – B convention throughout, this value will be the value of choosing A over B. A positive value tells us that the choice is worth making – at that discount rate. Since the choice of discount rate is sometimes a matter of debate, it may be useful to do a calculation of IRR as well. If that calculation is possible (it isn't always), this value shows you the discount rate at which you are indifferent to the choice between A and B. If this rate is higher than the appropriate discount rate, then A is preferred and if it is lower, then B is the better choice. This sometimes allows for a more informed discussion than looking only at present values.

A Note About Residuals

Conceptually we would choose the number of time periods to include in our analysis such that all foreseeable outcomes are covered and that anything beyond the cutoff point can be ignored. In practice it is not always that easy, and it may turn out that one alternative has some ramifications extending beyond the template, while the other does not, or has different issues. Rather than trying to forecast everything out to a distant future, we can treat the exceptions with residuals. A residual is just an entry in the last column of the table, capturing the discounted value (at that future date) of all impacts for that line item that extend beyond the template horizon.

Take for example, the simple lease versus buy comparison from Chapter 2. At the end of the five-year period, you have either an expired lease or a fully-depreciated piece of equipment. However, if you own the equipment, it might still have substantial value, so this wouldn't necessarily be a fair comparison. If you believe that the equipment will have residual value (hence the term), you could hypothesize that you would sell it at the end of the five years and the value received would show up as a negative capital amount in the last column. While this might not be what you plan to do, it would at least make the comparison more accurate. Other items that have impacts beyond the planning horizon can be treated in a similar fashion.

Supplement 10.3 – Dealing with Volume Change Effects

When prices, costs, and volumes are changing, common practice in managerial accounting is to separate the effects. The main reason is not to obscure the per unit effects of the changes we are proposing to price or cost by mixing them up with the volume changes. On the revenue side it is fairly simple; the total effect is:

$$Revenue\ Change = Price_{new} \times Volume_{new} - Price_{old} \times Volume_{old}$$

For our purposes, we could probably leave it at that, but in managerial accounting it is common to break this into Price Effect and Volume Effect:

$$Price\ Effect = Volume_{old} \times (Price_{new} - Price_{old})$$

$$Volume\ Effect = Price_{new} \times (Volume_{new} - Volume_{old})$$

And therefore (the algebra is left to the reader):

$$Revenue\ Change = Price\ Effect + Volume\ Effect$$

On the cost side, there is no price effect, but there is a corresponding cost effect that can be separated from the volume effect. The cost effect is what we are doing with our differential analysis – taking the unit cost differentials and multiplying them by the current production volume. This is similar to the price effect above, but itemized in greater detail.

The volume effect is where it starts to get a bit messy. If the volumes change, so will all of the variable costs associated with the product – not just the ones that we are focusing on to do our differential analysis. The analysis requires that you separate all current costs into fixed and variable categories. Anything designated as a fixed cost should, by definition, be independent of volume changes so there should be no volume effect associated with these. Variable costs on the other hand will vary proportionally with the volume change, and rather than trying to incorporate this in every line item, it is simpler and more informative to put in a line for a volume effect. This is one case where a total cost does matter: you will need the total of all variable costs in the proposed alternate (new) case in order to calculate the magnitude of the change. The issue of fixed and variable costs was discussed in detail in Chapter 7, and we know that the separation of the two is not always clear-cut. The cost file may break these costs down for you for the existing (base) case, and you may be able to use these values to estimate the new total. Fortunately, a reasonable estimate here is normally sufficient.

Volume Effect = Total Variable Cost$_{new}$ × (Volume$_{new}$ - Volume$_{old}$)

The way we would use this is illustrated in Figure 10-3.1. This is the generic TCO template used previously, with the addition of volume effects for both revenue and cost. All we have done on the cost side is to add a line for volume effect on variable costs, calculated as above. Since this is by definition a differential cost, we can add that number directly to our total differential cost line. This will give us the correct change to net income for tax purposes, and since it is a cash flow item, it will not be backed out for the adjusted net income line.

There is one additional item that we have to pay attention to, and it is very important. That is the change in working capital line. Here again we have broken this into cost and volume effects as we did with variable costs. The cost effect would be the change in working capital at the base case volume, that results directly from the proposed change, such as changes in inventories or payables. The volume effect recognizes that as a firm's volume of business changes, its total working capital (inventories plus receivables minus payables) changes in more or less direct proportion. To fill in this line, we need to know the company's total working capital position in the base case. Since this value is required for financial reporting purposes, it should be obtainable from accounting. The calculation would then be:

Volume Effect = Working Capital$_{old}$ × ((Volume$_{new}$/Volume$_{old}$) - 1)

Figure 10-3.1: TCO Template with Volume Effects

TCO Template With Volume Effects

	Year 0	Year 1	Year 2	Year 3	Year 4	Year 5
Change in Net Revenue:						
Price Effect						
Volume Effect						
Total						
Changes in Cost of Goods Sold						
Purchased Materials						
Shipping						
Other Items (duties, storage, etc.)						
Net Change in Purchased Goods						
Changes in Direct Labor (by category)						
Changes in Overhead						
Depreciation						
Other Overhead Categories (itemize)						
Volume Effect on Variable Overhead						
Sales and administrative expenses						
Total Overheads						
Volume Effect on Variable Costs						
Changes in Other Income						
Gain (Loss) on disposal of assets						
Changes in Gross Income						
Change in Taxes (at effective tax rate)						
Changes in Net Income						
Plus Depreciation						
Less Gain (loss) on disposal of assets						
Adjusted Net Income						
Less capital expenditures						
Less Increase in working capital (cost effect)						
Less Increase in working capital (volume effect)						
Changes to Net Cash Flow						

With the addition of volume effects, this shell template is as complete as we can make it and can be used for any kind of differential analysis that might accompany a business case.

Chapter 11 – Using the Template

Using a standardized format as presented in the previous chapter has numerous advantages. First, it is a form familiar to most business audiences, so explanation of the results should be straightforward. Second, it is broadly and transparently comprehensive, meaning that every possible financial impact of a decision has a place where it would show up. Now, in most cases it will be possible to skip many categories as being irrelevant to a differential analysis, but the template serves as handy checklist to be sure that certain effects are not overlooked. For example, it is tempting to say that a change of suppliers for a certain component will have no effect on labor (direct or indirect). But, are you sure? Will the packaging be the same, and will different handling be required? More importantly, does the Manufacturing Manager agree that there will be no impact? It is important to have concurrence from all areas on the effects of the change, including the areas where you project no change.

Finally, the template is flexible as a "what if?" tool. It is quite possible that not everyone will be convinced by the analysis, usually meaning that they disagree with the outcome. Having a comprehensive template allows you to redirect the attention away from the final number and toward the inputs. If someone wants to propose a different number for any of the detailed inputs, these can be updated and tested in real time.

As comprehensive as this template is, there are still some issues that are not readily captured, or need some sort of workaround. We can identify three main categories of such issues as residuals, uncertainty (risk) and intangibles.

Residuals

This issue comes up when there is a time dimension to the decision, and more specifically, when there are effects extending beyond the time horizon used for the template that differ between the alternatives. Another way to state this is that if, at the end of the analysis period, the alternatives are not in a strictly comparable state, some sort of adjustment is needed. One way to handle this is to extend the analysis period out as far as necessary to make the differences disappear, but this is not always feasible, or even worth the effort. Instead, we use residual terms in the analysis.

The commonest example is when one decision alternative (A) involves buying a piece of equipment and the other (B) does not. The equipment may still have useful life and value at the end of the analysis window, so if all else is equal, alternative A has a value that B does not. We capture this by imagining that we would sell the equipment at the end of the period, even if we have no intention of actually doing so, and showing the (hypothetical) cash realized as an inflow at the end of the last period. Similar logic applies to other assets. If we choose to buy a raw material in larger quantities to take advantage of a price break, one of the consequences will be an increase in average inventory held, which we show as a negative cash flow in period 0 as we build it up. However, at the end of any analysis period, this alternative will have residual value in inventory that the other alternative does not, so for a fair comparison, we should imagine that we liquidate that excess inventory and show a cash inflow as a residual in the last period. This holds true for liabilities as well as assets. If one alternative (only) requires signing a maintenance contract that will extend beyond the time window, then we need to add a residual item to the maintenance cost line in the last period to capture the value of the committed future payments. The way we would do this is to map out the expected payments and use the Present Value (=PV) function to calculate the future value of them at the end of the last analysis period and add that number to the maintenance cost for the last period. It would make sense to give it its own line and call it 'residual maintenance expense'.

In some situations, the residual effects of one alternative may extend indefinitely, or at least beyond any reasonable forecast horizon. In such cases a couple of useful formulas may be helpful in calculating residuals. One is for a perpetuity, in which a stream of revenue or cost is expected to continue indefinitely. The present value of a perpetuity is:

$$PV = A/r$$

Where A is the amount of the periodic cost or payment and r is our usual discount rate. It is also possible to have a perpetuity where the periodic amount is growing or shrinking at a constant rate (g) per period:

$$PV = A/(r\text{-}g)$$

Although neither of these formulations is likely to be truly representative of residual values, they may serve as reasonable approximations in some circumstances.

Dealing with Uncertainty

We all know that risk must be evaluated and weighed as part of a decision analysis, but that doesn't mean that there is any correct or widely accepted way of quantifying it. A common approach is to multiply the cost of a chance event (failure) by its frequency of occurrence to arrive at an expected value that can be used as comparative risk-severity index. There is nothing conceptually wrong with this approach but both risk and severity can be very hard to quantify, and you often wind up multiplying a large number by a small one, getting a very imprecise result. A broader discussion of risk is reserved for Chapter 18, but for our immediate purposes in performing a TCO analysis, a more useful approach is to consider the cost of mitigation rather than the cost of occurrence. We can think of this as insurance, either as a formal insurance policy or as operational choices that give us the same mitigation. Some risks can be priced in a market, as when formal insurance policies can be purchased for things like fire, earthquake, business interruption, crop loss, loan defaults, etc. If we are considering any decision that would cause a change to the cost of insurance for any such category, then we have a reasonable proxy for the cost difference between the alternatives attributable to their riskiness. This is true whether or not you would actually buy the insurance – that is a separate decision.

Futures are similar to insurance policies. If you buy commodity products with a global market (oil, coffee, copper, etc.) or if you buy product denominated in a foreign currency, you have a source of uncertainty that represents a risk. To some extent we can buy futures in commodities and currencies that will lock in our future costs. These normally sell at a premium to the spot market, that premium being the cost of the risk as determined by a market. A cost comparison that involves a change in exposure to currencies or commodities should, to be fair, price these changes at the values of their futures rather than current market values. Again, whether you actually buy the futures or not is a separate issue; this is used here as a way to quantify the difference between alternatives.

Some risks are too specific to a particular situation to be able to buy insurance or futures in an open market, and for those we can consider operational hedges as a form of insurance. Probably the commonest scenario is trying to compare suppliers. Price you know of course, but quality and delivery are probabilistic – how do you compare two suppliers with, say, 90% and 95% delivery ratings, respectively? If you were switching between these suppliers, either way, there are many things that you might do differently to compensate, or you could just live with it. However, for costing purposes, we need something more direct, and the most straightforward would be to estimate the change in safety stock of inventory that you would need to equalize the choices in terms of operating performance (as in product availability for production). This would show up on the template as an increase or decrease in working capital, and as any change in the costs of handling and storage. Again, that might not be what you would actually do, but it does provide an objective evaluation of the risk differential.

Assessing and quantifying overall business risks is very difficult, but the problem becomes much more manageable when it is confined to the risks attributable to the differences between decision alternatives. It is still not easy, but with the tools listed here it should be possible to construct an analysis that accounts for the main sources of risk. As a footnote to this, if the cost differential template is constructed in Excel, it is also possible to use it as the basis of Monte Carlo simulation, as available in various add-ins. What simulation does is allow you to express various elements of your template as a probability distribution instead of a single value. Simulation will not attach a price to this riskiness for you, but it will let you see a probability distribution of the outcomes. For example, a single-value analysis of an alternative might show you that a decision has a positive NPV of some amount. A simulation might show you that this is indeed the expected value, but that there is also a certain chance that the NPV of the decision could be negative. This is information that would be useful in making the ultimate decision. A more detailed discussion of this is found in Chapter 18.

Intangible Costs

In many cost analyses, there will be items that people will tell you that you cannot put a price on. These are what we call intangible costs – anything that you cannot express in currency units. These costs tend to have one thing in common: somewhere along the path from decision to outcome, there is a link that depends on a subjective, human evaluation and response, whether they be customers, suppliers or employees. This is quite obvious and hugely important in consumer marketing, but it shows up in even in the operating decisions that are the focus of this book. After all, decisions are ultimately made by people. Some of these evaluations can be priced in markets as we have seen in the discussion on risk, but in the end, we may have to deal with some factors that simply cannot be quantified with any credibility. We should be careful here though, often when we say that something is impossible to quantify, what we really mean is just that it is more difficult or unpalatable to quantify than we care to deal with. It is worth questioning that assumption to be sure that opportunities for quantification are not overlooked.

There are numerous examples of choices that defy quantification for comparison purposes, for different reasons. Among the more challenging ones are decisions that involve risk to human life. Operating decisions such as how many hospital beds to provide have these implications, and whether we like it or not, our decisions are implicitly attaching a cost to a life. Nobody wants to be quoted on such a value, but in most industries, there is a tacit understanding of the acceptable range.

Somewhat less consequential are decisions such as how much to pay for office furniture. More expensive furniture looks better, may convey a better image to customers, and may make employees happier. But, will any of these things translate into more revenue or less cost in the future? Some may argue that this will be the case, but for most situations this will be an unvalidated hypothesis. Similarly, we may prefer to place business with certain suppliers because we just prefer dealing with them or because we think they are more "responsive" to our issues. Again, if these are valid reasons, then the result should ultimately be lower costs over time, however this too defies quantification. Many decisions are made on the basis of such hypotheses, but unless there is supporting data, these will have to remain in the intangible category.

When we have exhausted all reasonable efforts at quantification, we may be left with a collection of intangible items that need to be reconciled. In most cases there will only be one or two key intangible items to deal with, but it still may not be possible to get broad agreement on what values to assign to them. In such cases, an alternate framing of the problem may help. Instead of asking what value to assign to the intangible items, we can ask whether they are worth a specific amount. Sometimes this is a much easier decision than the original one, and this is where use of our cost analysis template can be useful.

For many cost analyses, there is no real interest in the absolute amount of the difference, only a clear indication that A is better than B or vice versa. In such cases, some parts of the template are unnecessary, primarily the issues around taxation. Only in extreme cases, involving major time-value-of-money issues and changes in capital investment, would the tax impact change the decision one way or the other. However, including all the effects accomplishes two things. First, it makes the analysis complete and therefore pretty much bullet-proof when used for presentations to an executive audience. Second, it allows you to assign quite a precise price to the intangible items in the decision. If you have done a thorough job of quantifying everything that you can, then the difference in NPV between alternatives represents the price you have to pay (or avoid) for the intangible differences. If you are considering choices A and B, you may find that A is favored by a specific NPV amount, but you would prefer B for some intangible reasons, you are now in a position to ask whether those benefits are worth a specific currency amount. The decision may still be difficult, but if the analysis has been well done, the discussion can be very focused on the central issue.

Chapter 11 – Key Takeaways

1. Decision alternatives will sometimes have effects that extend beyond the time span of the template we choose, so for comparison purposes it is important to capture any differences in their residual values. In any affected category we can include a residual value in the final period to ensure that they are on an equivalent basis.

2. The TCO template does not explicitly address the risks associated with the decision alternatives, but these should not be ignored. One way to account for differences in riskiness is to include the costs of operational hedges or insurance policies that bring the alternatives to equivalent levels of risk. Inventory is one of the main operational hedges available.

3. The TCO template, by definition, cannot include truly intangible factors that may influence a decision. However, careful use of the template can quite precisely quantify the costs of gaining or avoiding those intangible features.

Part III Introduction

The first two sections dealt with defining and measuring cost respectively. Now that we have a set of tools to compare decision alternatives, we are ready to start a discussion of actively managing costs. Depending on one's position in the organization and the crisis of the moment, everyone will have a different list of priorities for the costs that need addressing. However, we will start with a whole-company perspective and start with the largest components of cost. Although it is not typically broken out cleanly on financial statements, if we add up all the costs that represent money paid to suppliers of goods and services, we will find on average that about two thirds of all revenue coming in is paid out in purchases. Direct materials are the most obvious category, but a significant portion of indirect costs may also represent purchases of one sort or another.

From this we can infer that the most powerful way to manage costs is to manage the purchasing process. We will look at this under three categories that we can summarize as: "Buying stuff right," "Buying the right stuff," and "Cutting the cost of what you buy." Excusing the grammar, this suggests that your first priority is to make sure that you are paying the "right" price for goods and services that you are already buying. For the most part, this is a matter of comparison shopping, analysis, and negotiating, so it is the quickest and simplest approach to cost management – but not quite as simple as it might sound! The details are covered in Chapters 12 & 13.

The second approach is more challenging because it requires careful examination of the designs and specifications for what you buy, or what you make for that matter. Many purchases are unnecessarily expensive because the specifications are overly restrictive or simply because the item being purchased is not the most appropriate one for the application. Making progress in this area will require advanced planning and also the cooperation and sometimes the education of downstream users of the product or service to make the necessary changes.

While it is possible to make these changes during ongoing operation, it is far easier to address them at the design or specification stage, so this approach is a critically important component of the new product design process. These topics are covered in Chapters 14 & 15.

The third approach is to reduce the actual cost of a product or service – not just the price, although that should follow. This means either changing an existing design or the process that creates it, and it doesn't make much difference if this process is at a supplier or if it is something you are doing internally. For that reason, the tools used in this category are applicable to cost reduction within your organization as well as in the supply base. Although this sort of cost reduction may be the first thing that comes to mind when one thinks about cost management, it probably offers the lowest return on the effort and cost to implement. Chapters 16 & 17 cover the tools and techniques of process improvement.

Chapter 12 – Pricing of Purchased Goods and Services

One of the most basic elements of cost management is ensuring that you are paying the right price for all of the things that you buy. This is one of the primary tasks of the purchasing function, but this is not intended to be a "how-to" book on purchasing and how to get to that price; there are several good texts on that subject. Instead, our interest is in determining what that price is, so that it can be a basis for action or negotiation. However, the purchasing function has traditionally suffered from two related problems that this book is intended to help address. One has been the common assumption by higher management that purchasing is simply a price reduction activity and therefore not particularly interesting strategically. A cause for this is the related problem that purchasing personnel have lacked the tools to argue for purchase decisions that are not made strictly on the basis of price. The templates and models presented in this text should help to properly quantify decisions and place them in the larger corporate financial context.

That said, price is still critically important. The importance stems from two factors; one is that these expenditures represent a very large percentage of the cash flow through a typical company, and the second is that pricing issues are usually more quickly and easily addressed than other contributors to overall costs. If we assume for the moment that *what* we are buying is not negotiable, we can turn our attention to what constitutes a "right" price to pay. The definition is somewhat subjective, and depends on who you ask! A broad definition is a price that is fair and reasonable to both buyer and seller. From a buying perspective, a "right" price is one that is no higher than it needs to be – after allowing for all of the adjustments that go into a cost comparison of alternatives. While it is easy to pay more than you need to, it is also possible, albeit difficult, to pay too little. Prices that are too low tend not to be sustainable over time and may lead to supply disruptions and other problems down the road.

Price Determination

Let's look more closely at how prices are determined. The basis of trade is that both parties are better off doing the transaction than not, so the fact that a trade takes place suggests that buyer and seller are both satisfied that they lack better alternatives. On either side, it is the alternatives that establish limits on a "right" price. As a buyer, there are three factors that determine the maximum that we are willing to pay for an item of trade:

1. Value created by the purchase: As a business, we buy things because they allow us to make money selling something to our own customers. If the price of a purchased item is high enough that we cannot do that, it would be folly to go ahead with the purchase. In other words, we will not pay more for something than the value it adds to our enterprise.

2. Prices offered by competitors: We may need to make adjustments for non-price factors as discussed in Part II, but once that is done, a price is not a "right" price if someone else is offering the same thing for less.

3. Prices of substitutes: Many products and services are substitutable in the sense that they are not the only way to do things. For example, you may have negotiated the best price in the industry for hard disk drives, but when the day came that solid state drives were cheaper, your price was no longer a "right" price. This threshold may not be as clear as the others as there may be switching costs involved and the need for validations or approvals.

Any of these three factors may be the one that sets the lowest bar, meaning the highest price you are willing to pay for an item. At the same time, the seller is facing a corresponding set of factors that will determine the lowest price it is willing to accept:

1. Profit created by the sale: As we have seen, profit is a somewhat slippery concept, and different suppliers may evaluate their situations differently, but it is safe to assume that, in the long run, a seller would not accept

a price that is lower than its average cost of production.

2. Prices offered by other customers: This is just the mirror-image of the buying situation: if other customers are willing to pay a given price, there is little reason for the seller to accept a lower figure. The exception to this rule is if the classes of customers can be kept strictly segregated from each other so that there is no dilution of existing sales. This is called price discrimination and is practiced in many industries, although in broad terms it may be illegal[1]. Where price discrimination may be present, a knowledgeable buyer will explore legal protections where appropriate.

3. Alternate uses of the assets: A price on a product may yield a large profit and still not be the best use of a company's resources. For example, a vineyard/winery may receive an offer for its grapes that is well above the cost of production, and above current market prices, yet if it feels that it can make more return by converting those grapes to its own label wine, then the offered price will be too low in spite of passing the first two criteria.

Bringing these all together, the buyer will consider the lowest of the three values as its upper limit and the seller will take the highest from its three criteria as a lower limit. Provided there is some gap between these, a deal is possible and there is some room for negotiation on the price. It should be pointed out that all of these categories apply to the longer-term and are subject to a certain amount of flexibility in the short term. For example, a spike in a commodity price may make your end product unprofitable, but you may choose to continue production in the belief that the situation will be temporary. Similarly, from the other side, a supplier may accept a price that is below its average cost of production (but likely not less than its variable cost) because of low capacity utilization and high fixed costs needing to be paid. The supplier would similarly be seeing this as a short-term situation, or as a form of price discrimination as described above. That would not be a long-term "right" price for the supplier, but might be

1   In the USA, this is the subject of the Robinson–Patman Act of 1936 (or Anti-Price Discrimination Act, Pub. L. No. 74-692, 49 Stat. 1526).

the best option available to it in the short-term. Whether it is a "right" price for the buyer depends on the time horizon. For a one-time buy or a short run, it might be OK, but as a basis for a long-term business plan, it is not a "right" price and may lead to bad decision-making on investment, pricing, etc., not to mention the potential for disruption of supply when the supplier finds more profitable uses for its capacity.

From the above, we can see that many elements of a "right" price draw on the existence of a market – a forum in which buyers and sellers compete to make the most favorable transactions. Economists like to envision a perfect market in which buyers and suppliers are freely interchangeable and price information is known to all. That surely does not describe the purchasing scenario we face as buyers, but we can still learn from the idealized situation. In a perfect market, with no structural capacity constraints, price will converge on the point at which suppliers' economic profit is zero – that is to say, cost plus enough margin to cover the cost of the assets employed, and no more. If there are cost differences between suppliers, the price will converge to the point where the second lowest cost supplier is making zero economic profit (the auction effect), so that the lowest-cost supplier will make some economic profit and the third, fourth, and so on lowest cost suppliers will be making increasing economic losses (although often showing an accounting profit). This mechanism forces competition on the basis of cost, with the result that costs will be continuously converging towards world-class low-cost performance. So, in a perfect market, the "right" price for a commodity will be the lowest feasible cost of production plus enough margin for economic break-even. This value can be calculated, or at least estimated even in the absence of a market. We can think of this as a "should cost" figure and should serve as a target for the prices we pay. Since there is really no such thing as a perfect market, we will never achieve this, sometimes not even close, but we should know what that figure is as a benchmark.

The task in cost management is to determine whether a price is acceptable or not, and acceptable in this context means that it is the best you can do under the circumstances. While an estimate of the "should cost" figure as described above will help identify areas of opportunity when there are large gaps, the price you will pay ultimately depends on the limit of suppliers' willingness to sell to you. To find where that limit is, there are two basic tools at your disposal. These are price analysis and cost analysis.

Price Analysis

Price analysis is what we as individuals do every day in our buying. Most things we buy are traded in some sort of market with multiple suppliers, so we can compare prices to see what is fair. We can select the lowest offer, or we can ask a preferred supplier to price match using our price information as bargaining power. There is little value to us in asking about our supplier's costs or profit, because even if those are better than all its competitors, they will not lower the price it is willing to offer.

We do much the same thing in business. Some commodities are traded in a market where prices are known to everyone. Buying in such markets may involve difficult decisions about how and when to buy (spot market vs. futures, etc.), but for a spot buy, the right price can often be found in a daily newspaper. Again, it is not particularly useful to know an individual producer's cost of production as it is unlikely to have an impact on the price. Where a commodity market does not exist, we try to simulate one. The traditional method is to solicit bids from a number of suppliers and compare these numbers to identify a right price. This is, in effect, a sealed-bid auction where the bids are not visible to competitors. An alternative approach that has been enabled by communications technology has gained some popularity in recent years, and that is the reverse auction. This is conducted in real time and competitors can see each other's bids, although not their identities. Provided the necessary conditions are met, either of these approaches can generate enough information for a buyer to evaluate a price to decide if it is "right" or not – at least, in the sense of whether it is the best you can do. It is important to remember that prices may not be directly comparable from supplier to supplier, even for the identical item. In Chapter 10 we gave some examples of adjustments that might have to be made to compare the TCO values for different suppliers.

For the use of competitive bidding to establish a "right" price, a number of conditions have to be met, some obvious, some perhaps less so.

- The pool of competing bidders must be sufficiently large. Your best bid will only be as good as the best bidder in the pool, so you must cast a wide enough net to find that one. Sometimes you know pretty closely in advance which one that will be, other times you may have no idea, so the requisite size of the pool will vary according to your knowledge. The pool must also be large enough that the bidders know that there will be significant competition – and not just from the competitors they know.

- There must not be collusion among the bidders. Although direct collusion is generally illegal, there is potential for tacit collusion among industry players to respect a certain price structure. This is one reason to increase the size of the bidding pool, potentially including a bidder that would not normally be considered, as a way to detect collusion among a smaller subset.

- All requirements must be explicitly stated. This sounds obvious enough, but it is not unusual for businesses to have unwritten expectations for what a product or service will do, or how it will be delivered, or how a particular test is to be performed. If there are incumbent suppliers, they will usually know about these expectations but new suppliers may not, and may not include them in their bids. This creates an unfair dilemma for the incumbent suppliers who must choose between bidding on what you asked for, or on what they know you want. Either way, chances are good you will not get what you want and you may damage your relationship with existing suppliers.

- The bids must be "honest," meaning backed by an honest commitment to supplying the good or service at that price. This will only happen when the bidder believes that it has a fair chance of winning the bid and being awarded the business. If a supplier believes that you are only fishing for information, or are trying to pressure another supplier, or are not serious about giving it the business for any other reason, it has little incentive to quote you an accurate number. Whether the resulting bid is too high or too low may depend on many factors, but either way, you do not have a good data point. A bid may be less than "honest" in another way. In a competitive environment, suppliers often find that, if they take their projected costs and add a reasonable margin, they will not win the business. In such cases they may adopt a "bid and chase" scenario, where they quote an initially unprofitable price, with the intention of reducing costs sufficiently over the product life so that the overall business is profitable. There is nothing particularly wrong with this from the buyer's point of view unless you have expectations of future price reductions on that product – which you often do. There is a darker side to bid and chase strategies, where the supplier never really intends to supply product at that price. It is unusual for a product to go from bid to production without some sort of change to the design or specifications. Some suppliers have a conscious strategy of using these changes to recover the profit margin they gave away with the initial bid – once switching costs have become significant. Contractual terms on price adjustments may help with this, but the best defense is better discipline in the design process.

- Switching costs must not be a significant factor. Bids will not reflect a true market price if the buyer is constrained in its ability to accept them. In particular, an incumbent supplier may feel free to quote an above-market price if it perceives that it will be costly for the buyer to switch. Anticipating this, competing suppliers are apt to modify their bids as well.

- All bidders must be equally informed. Although the formal request for bids will almost certainly be equal for all, some suppliers may have back-channel communications with the buying company that might selectively leak certain information that would be helpful in preparing a bid. Companies should treat this as a serious ethics violation and should perhaps consider extending training in procurement ethics beyond the purchasing function.

For purposes of evaluating pricing, the value of a commodities market or a competitive bidding process goes beyond establishing the "right" price for a specific product. We have seen that costs contain a mix of things that are readily quantified and those that are not and have to be priced in a market. Suppliers are faced with certain intangibles (mostly the perceived riskiness of the business) when placing bids and may include a risk premium that is difficult to evaluate from a buyer's perspective. When prices are established through a robust bidding process, this pricing of intangible elements has been factored in. As a result, we can use such prices as a basis for evaluating prices on similar products for which no bidding information is available.

This is done by building a "bridge" from a known right price to a new situation. This bridging process requires first of all that you have a solid base to build on. Not only must you have confidence that the price of the reference product is a true market price, it must be similar enough to your target product that the inherent business risk can be assumed to be equivalent. If this is the case, then a differential analysis as described in Chapter 10 can be used, although the format does not need to be as comprehensive. Differences such as direct labor, materials, and certain aspects of overhead are readily estimated to provide an approximation of the "right" price for the target product. Cost modeling (Chapter 7) can also be used if there are volume differences between the base and the target. If there are differences in the technologies or assets used, then bridging may not be feasible. It is also unwise to bridge across different industries on the demand side. For example, injection-molded plastic parts are used in many different downstream industries and the parts and technologies may look very similar. You will find however, that these industries have very different characteristics that show up in overheads (e.g.: requirements for documentation and certification) or in cost of capital (market assessment of riskiness of demand) that make cost comparisons problematic.

When used judiciously, price analysis provides a tool for evaluating the acceptability of a quoted price without the necessity of an in-depth cost analysis. In many cases, price analysis will make it clear what price level is achievable and if you are at or near that level, there is little reason to invest additional effort – better to move on to the next cost reduction target.

Cost Analysis

Price analysis in the form of competitive bidding is the base of traditional purchasing. Solicit a sufficient number of bids, select the best one and issue the purchase order. While that model is still useful for many items, that is simply not how purchasing operates today for the larger and more strategically important elements of the portfolio. Many of the conditions listed above for effective competitive bidding are not met, requiring a different approach. The pool of potential bidders may be small, there may be significant switching costs, and in a new product development situation, the ultimate specification may not be known – but rather will be developed interactively with the selected supplier.

In these situations, the actual price will be negotiated between buyer and seller, and from a buyer's perspective, the objective is to pay a price that is as close as possible to what it would be if the item were actually priced in a competitive market. To approximate that, we take advantage of the observation above that in such a market, price would be lowest achievable cost, plus enough margin for the supplier to make a positive, but small, economic profit. Putting aside the margin question for the moment, the first task is to identify what it should cost to produce the item in question. For obvious reasons, this is often called a "should cost" figure.

This is essentially the same task as coming up with the standard cost figures used in our own company, but now we need to do it from an outsider's perspective. In that respect, the calculation suffers from all of the same difficulties enumerated in Chapter 6, compounded by the reduced transparency. There are several ways to go about this, the most straightforward being a zero-based, ground-up calculation by your own personnel. Although quite costly and time-consuming, most large companies employ dedicated cost analysis staff to estimate costs for both purchases and in-house manufacturing. This of course, requires fairly intimate knowledge of what goes into the product and how it should be made. When this knowledge is not present, some reverse engineering may be required, or it may be appropriate to hire an independent expert to perform the evaluation. In most cases, direct costs (labor and materials) are fairly easy to evaluate, but overheads are much more difficult. Companies doing cost estimation on purchased products may use their own overhead rates if the operations are similar, or may turn to industry averages. In the U.S., the Bureau of Labor Statistics publishes a large amount of data on this, and in the field of defense contracting, the Department of Defense also publishes much information on the calculation of overheads.

An alternate approach to estimating the "should cost" figure is to ask (or require) the supplier to provide its own cost data for evaluation. This is often requested in a specific format that may or may not match up with how the supplier approaches the calculation. There are obvious difficulties with this approach, the main one being the willingness of the supplier to comply. This can vary greatly from company to company and from industry to industry. It is worth considering why a supplier would be reluctant to provide this information, because some of those reasons can be addressed:

- The supplier may feel that its costs are a trade secret, just as much as their processes, and may not trust the buyer's ability to keep this information confidential. An unscrupulous buyer, or anyone with access to the information, could leak it to a competitor to the detriment of the selling company. Non-disclosure agreements (NDAs) can help with this, but are rarely able to correct the damage if there is a leak. Developing a solid reputation for integrity may be the best way of overcoming this objection.

- Disclosing cost information means that the negotiations will be about profit, which tends to be an uncomfortable subject, particularly when not all of the negotiators really understand the concept of economic profit. Many suppliers will feel that disclosing cost information is an unnecessary weakening of their bargaining position. It is of course, so it should be met with a similar concession on the buyer's part – such as a commitment to protect the supplier's economic profit.

- Cost information reveals more than just the break-even point, it also shows the price at which contribution margin is zero – in other words, just how far the supplier could be pushed in extreme situations. An opportunistic buyer could take advantage of this, at least in the short-term.

- Cost information could contain assumptions that are at odds with the buyer's request for quote (RFQ). Usually this will involve volume forecasts, where the supplier may regard the buyer's estimates as unreliable and in need of discounting. There may also be disagreement on the trajectories of future costs that would serve to make the negotiations more contentious.

- Cost information could also show that the price being offered may be too low, potentially alerting the buyer to the supplier's intention of recovering margin through aggressive pricing on any changes that may be required.

All of these, except possibly the last one, are valid concerns, suggesting that trust will play a role in a buyer's ability to obtain reliable cost information from suppliers. Trust can be established in several ways, but establishing a reputation for integrity in purchasing relationships is an important first step. The ability to obtain this information will depend somewhat on industry norms, and on the relative bargaining power of buyer and seller. If a seller firmly declines to provide this information, but is still the preferred source, you have a difficult decision to make – yield on your demand, or find an alternative.

One tactic that is useful in extracting cost information is to develop your own cost model. With this in hand, you can tell the supplier that, "we think your cost for this product should be xxx." Most suppliers will tell you that your model is wrong and that their costs are higher. You can then ask them to show you exactly where it is wrong, and as long as your model is credible you will normally get some data. If you judge it to be valid you can use it to revise your model and reach a better estimate of cost.

When a supplier does provide you with a cost breakdown, for each line item there are two questions you need to ask. The first is whether the numbers the supplier is giving you are really true, and the second is whether the numbers are what they should be in a competitive market. Answering the first one is really an auditing process, much as you might do in your own company as described in Chapter 6. Answering the second one requires more creativity, and certainly leaves some room for negotiation. Mirroring Chapter 6, we can look at a supplier's cost data in more detail.

Purchased Materials

These are normally quite transparent; there will be a bill of materials with part numbers and prices for all direct purchases. For each item, the questions to ask are whether the price shown is actually what the supplier is paying, and whether it could be purchased more cheaply elsewhere. To answer the first question, you may ask to see actual supplier invoices, but the answer to the second one is more important. You might ask the supplier about its own supplier selection process to decide whether it is rigorous enough, or you may try to establish market pricing of the components by other means. Usually this will be some sort of price analysis, but in important situations it may be worth doing a cost analysis on your supplier's suppliers.

In the purchased parts category, it is also important to pay attention to allowances for freight, handling, scrap, etc. The main thing is to be sure that the figures that are presented to you are consistent with the supplier's own internal accounting so that there is no double-counting when you get to the overhead component. You can also make an assessment of whether the numbers are reasonable in their own right.

Direct Labor

As with purchased parts, the first question is whether the reported numbers match reality. For a new product, it is helpful to have your own estimate of the labor content, but for an existing product you should be able to visit the supplier's facility and observe the operations. A few minutes of discreet observation should give you the basis of a reasonable estimate. Whether or not the labor content could be reduced is a rather different analysis that we will defer to Chapter 16. The actual cost of labor (cost/hr.) is usually fairly well-known and is not normally negotiable. When you choose a supplier, you are effectively agreeing to pay its going rate for labor. However, if the rate is abnormally high, that should be a hint that it might be worth reconsidering the supplier selection, or entering into discussions about alternate manufacturing strategies. In the U.S., the BLS (Bureau of Labor Statistics) publishes extensive data on wage rates throughout the country, allowing you to compare numbers, but keep in mind that direct labor is usually a very small percentage of the total and is probably not the deciding factor.

Overheads

This is an opaque area in cost analysis. We have already discussed the difficulties in calculating a "true" overhead in your own operation, and now you have to do the same thing in one where you are missing many of the details. Large contracting agencies, such as most government departments, rely heavily on published tables of industry averages, and may enforce these in price negotiations. Much of this data is publicly available and provides a baseline. You may also ask your supplier for a detailed breakdown in an Activity-Based Costing format, although it may not always be to your advantage to do so. When you are presented with figures by your supplier, you need to satisfy yourself on two points: is it real (does it truthfully and accurately capture the supplier's costs?) and is it right (is it a competitive number in a marketplace?).

Published industry data will help you answer the second question, and an ABC model of cost allocation may help answer the first. However, most companies don't have very detailed ABC models for the reasons given in Chapter 6. Principally, if the company's products are relatively homogeneous, a detailed model won't reveal very much and you are probably best off to rely on industry average data to evaluate the amount.

However, industry averages do not generally reflect the amortization of special equipment, fixtures, and tooling that are specific to a particular product. To the extent that any of this is classified as capital equipment, there will typically be a separate line item in the cost file for the depreciation charge associated with it. This charge will be based on assumptions about sales volumes and product lifespan, where the buyer and supplier may have different opinions. Since capital investment involves assumption of risk (mostly risk of premature obsolescence), the supplier's assumptions will necessarily be conservative. There are several reasons why it makes sense for the buying company to pay for and take ownership of special tools and fixtures, but a major one is that it cleans up the cost estimation and takes a major source of uncertainty out of the supplier's calculations. From the buyer's perspective, it is a way to make sure that you only pay for these once!

When the supplier's products are not homogeneous, your principal concern is whether the product you are buying is over or under-allocated. For example, if your supplier runs mostly high-volume, automated production, but is producing something for you that is more labor-intensive, and if the supplier allocates overhead on the basis of direct labor, then your product will be charged with a disproportionately high portion of the total overhead costs. You would be fully justified in asking the supplier to revise its cost model. On the other hand, if the situation were reversed, you would be under-allocated and getting a free ride. If you let this go, you are taking advantage of a supplier's mistake, and whether or not you want to do this depends on the sort of relationship you have, or want to have with that supplier.

When we say that products are homogeneous, we mean in terms of the indirect costs associated with them. Normally, products that require similar process technologies will be homogeneous in this respect, but not always. Different customers may place very different demands on the supplier for design and engineering support, testing, documentation, warranty, batch sizing, packaging, and a host of other details. Often, these costs are just dumped into a common overhead bucket and allocated on a simplistic basis, meaning that all customers share in the costs. If your supplier sells similar products to your competitors (common), and if one competitor is demanding and getting enhanced services in these areas, chances are good that you are paying a share of your competitor's costs, but not getting the benefits. Of course, as a buyer, you can turn this into a conscious strategy. If you are the one making the demand for indirect services, you can be the one getting the subsidy. The key lesson from all of this is that you must understand your supplier's basis for allocation of indirect costs in order to properly evaluate its cost data.

Sales, General and Administrative Expenses (SG&A)

The so-called "front-office" or non-factory costs are difficult to evaluate because, while some of them are clearly costs of running the business, others are a sort of tax that is not necessary for the current product, but may be essential to the long-term viability of the company. In most cases, industry averages will be the best benchmark, but it is also possible to form an opinion about the reasonableness of these charges by visiting the supplier and getting a good understanding of its business practices and strategies.

The nature of the problem is illustrated by the charges for engineering and R&D expenses. Cost for the development of new products is clearly not a cost of producing the current product, but on the other hand, the costs that were incurred to develop the current product are typically not reflected anywhere in the cost file, so it somewhat evens out.

An arguably better approach is used in the calculation of Economic Value-Added where these development costs are treated as a capital investment with a depreciable life. This is actually a truer representation of what is going on; the main reason that this is not done in conventional accounting is that the investment is not something that can be pledged as collateral or recovered in liquidation. Very few companies do this however, so the only option is to evaluate the level of expenditure against what is normal for that industry. Other expenses such as advertising also fit this profile and are ultimately a matter of management policy rather than a cost in the usual sense.

If R&D expenses are viewed as an investment, the same thinking applies to these as it does to tooling and fixtures. It is generally to the buyer's advantage to pay for these in a separate, upfront charge (and to claim ownership of the resulting intellectual property). This again simplifies the cost analysis, although it begs the question of how the supplier gets paid for exploratory R&D that isn't ultimately commercialized. Depending on the industry, a percentage of total costs may be allowable for this. Paying separately for R&D cleans up the cost analysis and is standard practice in much government procurement, but in many instances, suppliers will strongly resist this. The argument would be that they are not in the business of doing contract engineering; they are in the business of selling well-engineered products and that R&D expenses are an integral part of that. Where you wind up on this will be a matter of negotiation, but from a cost management perspective, it is much easier to manage costs if you take ownership of them.

Profit

This the final element of cost analysis as a means to arrive at a "right" selling price. Unfortunately, profit is something of a dirty word that no one wants to talk about. This is a mistake as a mature discussion of the subject would greatly facilitate price negotiations. From the buyer's side, it would be helpful to acknowledge from the outset that we expect and want our suppliers to make a profit. If their costs are competitive, we expect that they will make a positive economic profit, meaning that their margins must not only be positive, they must be sufficient to cover the costs of the assets employed – at the cost of capital applicable to the supplier's industry. From a cost analysis point of view, this gives us a target: if we can establish a "right" value for the supplier's costs, we then need to calculate the costs of the assets deployed as a margin value that will bring us up to a "right" price that yields the supplier a modest economic profit. Unfortunately, this is much easier said than done, so alternate methods come into play.

The simplest method of calculating a profit margin is to add up the costs and add X%. Although this sounds very simplistic, it actually works quite well, with the proviso that the costs used as a baseline are "should" costs, not necessarily the supplier's actual costs. The reason it works is that companies in the same industry tend to converge to similar levels of assets deployed so that the accounting margin correlates fairly well with the economic profit. If we know what is normal or average in a particular industry[1], we have a base to start with. The average is just that, an average, so a best-in-class supplier should be making somewhat more than that. Again, it is important to emphasize that the best-in-class margin should be added to best-in-class costs. Or, we can say that an average margin should be added to average costs. Either way, if our supplier's costs are below average, it should make an above-average margin and vice versa.

Government contracting is often faced with the problem that prices must be negotiated for products or services for which there are no other buyers and very few suppliers. As a result, there is no market average for profit margins and an acceptable figure must be built from the ground up. The overall intent is the same – to identify the point of economic break-even.

---

1   Several factors contribute to large differences between industries. These include: level of competition, degree of capital intensity required by the process, and inventory turns. This last item is often underappreciated: grocery stores look like a very low margin business, but they turn over their inventory much more frequently than some other businesses, which reduces the amount of capital (fixed and working) required relative to a business that must hold inventory for a longer period.

A method called *weighted guidelines* is described by Burt et. al.[1] and shows the basic structure of this approach. The idea is to identify a number of categories in which contracts may differ and assign percentage points of profit margin based on whether the job in question rates high or low in each category. Whether building up from zero or attempting to develop a variance from an industry average, the same factors will apply, but some of them will be embedded in the average already. The baseline will be a percentage of the total cost amount that is nothing more than payment for the cost of the working capital involved. Additional percentage points are awarded for the amount of fixed capital employed (over and above depreciation). Further adjustments can be made for risk, particularly any cost risk on materials that the supplier is assuming and for risk associated with any uncertainty of volume demand forecasts. What we can see from these categories is that most of what we call profit is not profit at all from an economic perspective, but is actually a cost. In broad terms, a supplier's profit is the cost of the risks that you are asking it to assume. If you find this to be excessive, it is an indicator that perhaps you should be making the product or delivering the service yourself.

Pricing Summary

For establishing pricing on a product that already exists, or is similar to existing product, it is likely that the only question you will have to address is getting the "right" price for a well-defined product. The simplest way to do this is to let a market sort it out through competition. If there is a market price for what you are buying, then you can be comfortable that you know what the "right" price is. Likewise, if you can use market prices as a reference and convince yourself by comparison that a particular price is in line, you can also be reasonably sure that you have a "right" price. When this is the case, there is little point in going any further – you know, and the seller knows, that the price is "right," and there is little more that you can learn that will change anything.

1   See: Burt, D. N., W. E. Norquist and J. Anklesaria (1990). <u>Zero Base Pricing</u>. Del Mar, CA, Byline Publishing. According to the authors, the method they describe is no longer accurate for D.O.D procurement, but it serves as a general guide for how to approach the problem.

When a useful price analysis is not possible, cost analysis is the only tool left to establish what we would consider to be a "right" price. Of course, suppliers won't necessarily agree, and in a transactional[1] relationship, the actual price will depend more on negotiating skill and strength. Cost analysis is more useful when used in a collaborative environment and particularly in cases where work has to start before the final configuration is known. The ability to establish a price after the fact is a key to such relationships, and cost analysis is the basis of that ability.

Cost analysis doesn't have to be complete to be useful. Chapters 7, 8, & 9 discuss cost modeling and the way costs change with various factors. Even if you don't do a full breakdown, it is still useful to know things like: the split between fixed and variable costs, the amount of cost addressable for productivity improvement, the amount of cost represented by certain volatile commodities, and potentially other partial breakdowns of cost. This is important because, even if you have accepted a price as reasonable, things will change. Sometimes the supplier will ask for an increase because of these changes, and sometimes you should be asking for a decrease. Good cost modeling will allow these discussions to take place in an objective manner.

---

1   The word 'adversarial' would apply here, but not with the suggestion that there is any animosity involved – just a zero-sum game, arguing over who gets what share of the profits.

Chapter 12 – Key Takeaways

1. A major component of cost management is paying the "right" price for goods and services.

2. If prices are set in, or can be referenced to a competitive marketplace, those prices can be accepted as "right." This determination can be called price analysis.

3. If a market does not exist, cost analysis can be used to approximate the same result. This is an increasingly important part of price determination.

4. Analysis of cost also requires analysis of profit. This is a contentious topic, but there are guidelines to help. It is also important to understand the concept of economic profit.

Chapter 13 – Contracts and Contracting:

In many cases, a price is not the whole story, even if carefully evaluated on a TCO basis – it is just a number at a point in time. If there is any time dimension to the transaction, things will change and the transaction price may or may not change with them. Many changes are driven by the business environment: commodity prices change, sales volumes may be more or less than expected, and so on. Frequently, changes will be initiated by the buyer and there will be expectations about how the price should or should not change as a result. What happens in response to all of these changes depends on the type of contract that exists between buyer and seller. Contracts are important for the obvious reason that they represent an agreement between the parties on how prices will be managed, but they are also important because they create incentives for certain behavior by either party. Some of these are what we call *perverse incentives* because they motivate one party or the other to behave in ways that help itself, but are detrimental to the overall relationship, so these need to be minimized. Finally, no contract can anticipate all eventualities, so it is important to have agreement on how unforeseen events will be managed.

Types of Contracts

The essential difference between types of contracts is how risk is apportioned between the parties. Risk in a transaction derives from two main sources: uncertainty over the actual nature of the item of exchange, and changes in the economic environment over time. The simplest case is one where no risk is involved – it is a one-time purchase and the item being purchased is a known entity. In this case we agree on a price and the deal is consummated with no ongoing commitments or expectations on either side. This is the simplest case of what we call a fixed-price contract, sometimes called a firm fixed-price contract (FFP).

Now, let's introduce some uncertainty – suppose you take

your car to a mechanic for a brake job. Nothing is going to change much in the time between you are quoted a price and time the work is completed, so there is no uncertainty in the business environment. There is however, some uncertainty in the job itself – parts may be corroded, studs may break, etc., so there is unforeseeable variability in the time it will take. Hypothetically at least, there are two ways you could pay for the job: you could agree in advance on a firm price, or you can agree to pay for actual time and materials expended on the job at an agreed rate. In the first instance, we have a firm fixed-price contract, and any risk of unexpected difficulty is borne by the mechanic. In the second case, what we call a time-and-materials (T&M) contract, that risk is borne by you, the buyer. These represent the opposite ends of the contracting spectrum, and there are many intermediate versions that have been developed.

The same dynamic plays out when there is a time dimension to the contract. If we issue a purchase order for our office supply company to deliver us printer paper every week, it is normally for a fixed price, and may specify a time period over which that price will remain firm. If there are variations in the price of paper, or the cost of delivery over that time, it will be absorbed by the supplier. Or, that risk could be passed back to you by way of a market price adjustment or a fuel cost surcharge.

Whenever there is risk involved, what we have learned about economic profit tells us that whoever absorbs it needs to get paid for doing so – riskiness is a major driver of the cost of capital. Notice the very deliberate use of the word 'absorb' – it's not so much that one party *takes* a risk so much as they soak up the uncertainty and protect the other from it (and, of course, expect to get paid for doing so). Accordingly, we should expect that a firm fixed-price contract will be at a higher price than the *average* time-and-materials contract. This will not always be the case because of some difficulties with the incentives and the monitoring costs associated with T&M contracts, but it is true in principle. This raises the question of which type is better, and who should be absorbing the risks of uncertainty. FFP contracts have some distinct advantages in the areas of incentives and monitoring as just noted (and discussed in more detail later), and they are generally advocated as the best form of contract to use – if possible. Purely from a risk allocation perspective, this will not always be true. If we re-frame the question, it is whether you should absorb a risk yourself or pay someone else to do so (should you buy insurance, or self-insure?). The key factors in a decision on contract type are: who understands the risks the best (and is therefore best able to manage and price them), and who is able to diversify[1] the risks. On both counts, the nod usually goes to the supplier. Suppliers normally understand the risks associated with their businesses better than you do and so are better positioned to put a price on it. Our mechanic above knows far more about the likelihood of trouble on a brake job than you do, so is comfortable quoting a fair price with an allowance for that included. Suppliers are also often able diversify their risks across multiple customers and industries, and so are less exposed to fluctuations. Again, our mechanic does lots of brake jobs, so even a bad experience on one will not matter much in the long run.

However, there are situations where it makes more sense for the buyer to take on the uncertainties, and in some cases, the seller will insist on it. These are the cases where you, the buyer, are the source of uncertainty. Typically, these uncertainties are demand volume and specification changes. The supplier gets its demand forecast from you, the buyer, and while you may feel that you don't have much control over actual demand, you certainly have more knowledge and control than the supplier does. Plus, there is a degree of moral hazard[2] involved in relaying that forecast, particularly when the supplier has no way to triangulate the information from other sources. If you force the supplier to quote a firm price, it will necessarily include a significant risk premium. Specification changes are also a source of uncertainty, particularly in jobs with long development phases, such as

1   Diversification of risk is discussed in detail in Chapter 18.
2   Moral hazard, in this sense, means that it would be to your advantage to give the supplier an overly optimistic forecast of demand in order to secure a better price. The supplier knows this of course and will discount your forecast by an amount that may depend on your reputation for integrity.

building tooling. Some buyers are in the habit of changing their minds frequently about what they want, and the supplier will, a) want to get paid for what it does, even if it has to be re-done later, and, b) will not want to go through preparing a full quote for every design modification that comes along. In such cases, the supplier is likely to insist on a T&M contract. This makes sense for both parties, but it does create an incentive problem. There is a need to monitor the supplier to ensure that the work it bills for was actually done and that it was what the buyer specified at the time. This monitoring can be an expensive undertaking, but the cost can be greatly reduced if buyer and supplier have respect for each other's integrity.

There is a third form of contract that does not lie neatly along the spectrum from FFP to T&M, and this is often called a level-of-effort contract. This is usually used for the procurement of professional services such as legal services, advertising, or R&D. These contracts will specify an amount, and the deliverable is "the best you can do for that amount." In such cases, the amount to be spent is pre-determined as a matter of management policy, so it doesn't really fall within the cost management arena. However, there is still the concern about getting the most value from the money spent. Such contracts are usually placed with recognized professions with standards of qualifications and codes of ethics that give us some assurance of value.

Role of Incentives

As noted above, and in Supplement 13-1, "Setting Taxi Fares," contracts provide incentives for the parties to behave in certain ways; some desirable, some not. Many of the intermediate forms of contract along the spectrum from FFP to T&M were devised as ways to minimize the undesirable incentives.

Let's start with the FFP contract. The supplier knows how much it will get, so its main incentive is to reduce costs as much as possible to maximize its own profit. In general, this is a good thing, but the buyer is not going to benefit from it, at least not right away – maybe when the contract gets renegotiated. However, cutting costs can also mean cutting corners. That is why the basis of an FFP contract must be a comprehensive specification of what is to be delivered. Comprehensive in this case means every detail – not just a physical description, but also requirements for testing (and interpretation of testing), packaging, delivery, and any other possible requirement of the transaction. This is another one of those things that is much easier said than done, and often we rely on the supplier to take care of this. If I order an Acme Electronics part #123, I am relying on Acme to give me what I am expecting on the basis of its brand and reputation. Other times, we have to write the specification and own[1] it ourselves. The reason a comprehensive specification is so important is that things change. If material prices increase but the price doesn't, our supplier is going to start feeling pinched for profit. One of the first things it is going to do is follow the cost management procedures we will cover in Chapter 16, and one of those is to get out your specification and a magnifying glass to look for any opportunities to reduce cost. Anything unspecified or ambiguous is a potential source of cost reduction for the supplier and unfulfilled expectations for the buyer.

There are also incentives on the buyer's side. Again, the price is fixed, so there is incentive to try to get more for the money. We may place demands on the supplier for extra services, specification adjustments and other such things, arguing that they are within the scope of the original contract. At the same time, the buyer has no incentive to help the supplier reduce costs, especially if it involves any effort or expense on the buyer's part. As a result, cost reduction opportunities will go unexplored.

When we go to the other extreme, the T&M contract, the incentives are different. Here the supplier has no motivation to reduce costs at all; in fact, it has every incentive to increase them, as it will likely make a profit on every extra unit of cost. To counter this, the buyer must be prepared to monitor and audit the supplier's performance, which is not only costly,

1   The word 'own' is used here because a specification embeds significant product and application knowledge and can be an important piece of intellectual property.

but requires knowledge of the supplier's business that the buyer might not have or wish to acquire. These are the main reasons that T&M contracts are widely disfavored in commercial trade, although as we have seen, they have their place.

The majority of intermediate contract types that have been developed are intended to align the legitimate goals of both parties and counter the perverse incentives inherent in either of the main types. The most promising, from a cost management perspective, is a cost-sharing type of contract. In broad terms, the way it works is this: the parties must first agree to an initial price for the defined product or service. This price may be determined by a competitive bidding process, or by a bottom-up cost analysis. From that point on, the price will be adjusted to reflect changes in cost, with the change being shared between the parties at an agreed proportion. There are several requirements for this type of contract to work well. The price of the product or service must be based on analysis and negotiation, not set by a competitive market. For the effort to make sense, there must also be a time dimension to the contract. This could be open-ended in the form of an "evergreen" contract that renews continually year over year, or it could be as short as the period from initial design to actual product launch. The most important factor though, is the need for transparency on costs. The supplier must be willing to reveal its cost information and to make it auditable. Otherwise, the incentive for the supplier is to exaggerate cost increases and hide cost decreases. If the necessary conditions are met, this type of contract provides incentives for both parties to contribute to cost reduction efforts that will improve the profitability for both.

Variations on this theme are possible. If a large part of the supplier's cost is a commodity with a volatile market price (e.g.: copper), it doesn't make sense to require the supplier to absorb that risk and include it in its pricing. A feasible alternative is to agree on a baseline cost for the commodity and establish a separate account for variances. Periodically, a payment will be made one way or the other for the accumulated surplus or deficit on the cost. This takes the commodity risk out of the pricing and transfers it to the buyer, which can hedge this exposure or not, as it chooses.

T&M contracts can also be modified: one version that is appropriate for development projects is the cost-plus-fixed-fee agreement. This requires identifying a fixed amount that is effectively the supplier's profit for the job. This does not change, but actual costs are reimbursed. The cost risk remains with the buyer, but the incentive for the supplier to inflate costs is removed. On a profit margin basis, there is some incentive for the supplier to reduce costs. As with all contracts other than FFP, the buyer must have the ability to monitor and audit supplier costs. Not only must the reimbursed costs be actual values (and free of rebates or kickbacks) but they must be reasonable as well.

It is appropriate to inject a note of caution here: it is easy to devise all sorts of complicated contracts that balance risks and incentives, but there is the issue of follow-up. Such contracts require continuous monitoring and occasional interventions. Except in certain highly-regulated sectors such as defense procurement or public utilities, very few companies have dedicated contract management staff and it is very easy to lose track of these agreements.

Conclusions

The type of contract used for the procurement of goods and services is an important part of cost management. The contract may address this directly, in the form of a schedule of how the price is to evolve over time. An example would be awarding a contract on the basis that the supplier is expected to generate productivity improvements resulting in a specified price reduction, year over year. In other cases, the role of the contract is to create the right incentives for the supplier to engage in cost management activities, and to involve the buyer in that process. These cost management activities are a mirror of what takes place in your own company. The first priority is to be sure that the supplier is paying a "right" price for its own procurements. Normally the supplier will have incentive enough to be doing this, but may need a push in that direction. The next priority will be cost reduction activities in the supplier's own operations using the methods we will discuss in Chapters 14 – 17. The role of the contract is to align the incentives to encourage these activities for mutual benefit.

A key element of any contract other than FFP is the sharing of actual cost information. Historically this has been a major sticking point, but it seems to be increasingly accepted as a basis of doing business. When this information is shared, there is the opportunity for win-win efforts on cost reduction. However, achieving this requires a level of maturity and integrity on both sides as there will always be some incentive to mis-state or misuse the shared information.

This notion of integrity, or trust if you prefer, is a recurring theme in supplier relationship management and is an important component of cost management. The role is most visible where trust is absent. If you don't trust a supplier to perform in certain ways, you will at least mentally add some intangible cost to its price for comparison purposes. If a supplier doesn't trust you to provide honest volume forecasts, it will discount your forecasts and add a cost to compensate. If a supplier doesn't trust you to handle its cost information properly, it will decline to provide that information, or will distort it. Contracts are designed to minimize the need for trust as much as possible, but are not able to do so completely. Clearly, the presence of trust, or something like it, can reduce the cost of doing business to the net benefit of both parties.

Chapter 13 – Key Takeaways

1. The purchase of goods or services is based on some sort of contract, and the type of contract chosen has a major impact on how costs will change over time.

2. The key parameter for contract type is the manner in which risks are assumed by each party.

3. Most contracts lie along a spectrum from FFP, where all risks are borne by the seller to T&M, where all risks are borne by the buyer.

4. All contracts give the parties certain incentives to behave in certain ways, and sometimes to conceal or mis-state information.

5. Any contract that passes risk to the buyer creates the need for monitoring to ensure that the costs being passed through are both real and right.

6. A key enabling factor for most contracts is transparency of costs between buyer and seller. This is often strongly resisted by sellers.

Supplement 13-1 – Setting Taxi Fares

Getting into a taxi is a classic time and materials contract: you don't know what the final cost will be, but will pay for the time and distance covered by the trip. The perverse incentive of the T&M contract applies here: it is to the driver's advantage to prolong the trip as much as possible to generate the maximum revenue and profit. To protect the unknowing customer, most municipalities have historically regulated taxi operation, the first requirement usually being the installation of an approved taximeter to ensure that time and distance are accurately recorded. This fulfils the monitoring requirement for a T&M contract, but doesn't help with the perverse incentive. To combat that, several approaches are used, one being a flat rate for certain trips such as from the airport to the hotel zone (an FFP contract, where the cost of any delays is borne by the driver). Another tool is the rate structure. Usually there is a significant charge for the first increment of distance with a declining rate for longer distances. The idea is that the marginal value to the driver of prolonging the trip is low and that it would be better to get the trip done quickly and take on a new fare. This of course, only works if there is a good chance of getting a new fare, so the authorities have to step in again, and what they do is to limit the number of taxi licenses available. This improves the driver's chances of getting additional work, but is clearly not an economically efficient solution, as supply is restricted relative to what the market would take. The unintended consequences are that it is harder to get a taxi than it should be, and that taxi licenses become a valuable commodity.

The key enabler of the ride-share model (Uber, Lyft, and other similar services) is the availability of mapping and traffic information to anyone with an internet connection, including the ride-share services. This can be processed into a "should cost" figure for any specified trip so that every ride can be an FFP contract with no risk to the buyer and only minimal risk for the driver. So long as regulation doesn't intervene, prices can float so that any given moment, supply will mostly match demand. There is still a perverse incentive in FFP contracts, and that is the temptation supply sub-standard goods. We generally use specifications to limit this, and for ride-sharing, these specifications are provided by the ride-share company in terms of vehicle type and condition, and using monitoring of compliance via the rider's feedback when paying.

Viewed from a contracting perspective, we can see that the ride-share model is based on a better type of contract for the purpose. When choosing a contract type, allocating risk is the primary concern, but attention must be paid to the role of incentives and the costs of monitoring.

Chapter 14 – Cost Prevention/ Avoidance

With this chapter we address cost avoidance as a fundamental element of cost management. We hinted at this in the chapter on differential analysis when we noted that the baseline, typically the "do nothing" case, was not always a constant. If a long-term purchase contract avoids what would have been an inevitable future cost increase, then you have done a good thing, even if the agreed price is above the current going rate. Such actions are vitally important for cost management, but they tend to be difficult to quantify. The tricky part is establishing a credible baseline – what would have happened in the absence of a particular action. In the above case, a forecast of market pricing would be the baseline, but it has to be credible and generally accepted within the organization.

Things like market price fluctuations can be difficult enough, but it is mostly a matter of quantification, using the tools that we presented in Chapters 7 through 11. The big rewards, however, are in new product development (NPD), where the challenge is to keep cost out by making sure that you are designing or specifying the right or best thing in the first place. If, during the development process, a designer has a bright idea to revise the design to use lower-cost materials, this is also a valuable cost avoidance. But, quantification here is even more difficult than in the first example above. You could compare the design to the previous revision level, if formal documentation actually exists, to estimate a cost change – but is that previous revision level representative? It could be argued that a better designer would never have done it that way in the first place! For this reason, engineers and designers tend to object to being measured on cost avoidance activities as they feel it requires excessive documentation and penalizes them for doing the job right the first time. So, while cost avoidance is highly important, and there are formal tools available, there are also significant implementation issues that are as much a part of cost management as the actions themselves.

Specifications

Specifications are a suitable starting point for this discussion because they uniquely define what it is you will make or buy. We use the term 'specifications' here as a broad term for a set of drawings and documents that define all of the important details of a product or service, including the criteria for acceptance or rejection. We will simply call this entire package the *specification*. These elements usually describe physical products, but services are subject to the same thinking although the terminology is a bit different. Closed-end service activities such as a consulting report or a software implementation are usually governed by a *statement of work* (SOW), while ongoing services such as a call center operation or running the cafeteria are specified by a *service level agreement* (SLA).

As we saw in Chapter 13, the specification is the basis of a contract, and given the incentives involved, if you neglect to specify something you need, you probably won't get it[1]. Conversely, if you specify more than you need (very common) you probably will get it, but will surely pay for it.

If you send a specification to a supplier, whether internal or external, the supplier's first step will be to decide exactly *how* it intends produce the deliverable. This is called *process choice*, and involves both equipment and processing steps. Whatever process is chosen has an inherent capability to deliver product within certain acceptability limits. This is called *process capability*. That process choice also defines the supplier's cost to a large extent, and therefore the price that you will be charged. Ideally, the supplier will select the lowest-cost process that can reliably deliver what you have specified, and use that as a basis for estimating a cost and quoting a price. The role of the specification is clear here: the more demanding it is, the higher your costs will

---

1   There are exceptions to this: a supplier may know that the specifications you issue are not sufficient to guarantee that you get what you expect, but regards this knowledge as a trade secret. It is happy to give you what you really need, even though you didn't specify it, because it knows that if you tried to give your specification to a competitor, it would fail to deliver a working product if it was not privy to the "secret" specification.

be. Processes, once chosen, are not readily changed, so this effect will be with you for the life of the product. You need to be a bit careful here. It is not unusual for suppliers (including internal ones) to be a bit too optimistic about their process capability in order to be able to offer a lower price and win the contract. If you fall into this trap, you will not be paying a "right" price and the hidden cost you will pay is quality problems for the life of the product.

Avoiding over-specification is an important element of cost management, but that is not to suggest that it is productive to start challenging all specifications. For one thing, it is not usually all that helpful to relax specifications in mid-production once a process choice is made. It is more useful at the initial design stage. To address over-specification at the design stage, it helps to understand why it happens and work on the causes. Fundamentally, the reasons for over-specification boil down to either ignorance, meaning the designer's lack of some key information, or favoritism in the sense that specifications are written to favor a particular supplier. The two can overlap to some extent. Before digging into the roots of these causes, it is helpful to discuss the two opposing philosophical approaches to writing specifications, so see Supplement 14-1: "Black Box vs. White Box."

There are two types of ignorance that can result in less-than-optimal specifications. One is that designers may not be fully aware of the cost impact of their designs and specifications, and the other is that they may not have full knowledge of the actual requirements.

Cost Awareness

Actually, it is often quite difficult for designers to get cost information as it is not accessible to them, or worse, if purchasing staff regard it as secret. Actually, purchasing staff actually do often act this way, and not just out of narrow-mindedness. As we saw in Chapter 6, the numbers in a cost file often have stories attached to them, and may not represent the current state. As a result, cost impacts are hidden and there is not much motivation for designers to seek out more economical alternatives. There are some solutions to this, one being to outsource design by using a functional (black box) specification. That way, competitive pressures will (hopefully) force suppliers to seek out the best solution. However, this doesn't work when the supplier is an internal operation, or when requirements are constantly shifting such that a T&M contract is required. In these cases, the best approach is constant interaction between product and process designers so that alternatives can be quickly and easily evaluated for cost impact. This comes under the broad heading of *concurrent engineering*, (see Supplement 14-2) and is now considered to be standard practice when the manufacturing operation is internal to the organization. Physical co-location of these functions is a very effective way to achieve this although it can also be made to work remotely.

Concurrent engineering should be straightforward enough for internal operations, although there are sometimes cultural barriers to overcome, but it gets more complicated when the manufacturer will be an outside supplier. There is a chicken-or-egg problem here: concurrent engineering implies that the discussions are taking place before the specification is finalized, yet it is typical practice to not select the supplier until the specification is finalized and competing bids can be compared. This presents a dilemma for cost management. While many suppliers will provide a certain amount of free consulting, true concurrent engineering will require some commitments. The topics of early supplier involvement (ESI) and early supplier selection will be covered in Chapter 15.

In the absence of a designated manufacturing partner, designers must use a more "open-loop" approach, meaning that they must observe certain design rules that they know will result in lower-cost designs, more or less independent of the choice of supplier. There are many variants on these themes, so we will just try to summarize the main streams below. All of these are backed up by dedicated textbooks and other resources, so we will only provide an overview and some commentary here.

Value Analysis/Value Engineering (VA/VE)

These two terms are usually mentioned in the same breath

although, strictly speaking, they apply at different phases of the design process. Value Engineering describes a process used at the initial design phase, while Value Analysis is the same sort of analysis applied to existing products. As such, VA really belongs in Chapter 16, but we'll address it here. Value Engineering tends to be more system-oriented, focusing on the needs of the final customer, while Value Analysis is more component-oriented, looking at the functions performed in the context of the complete product.

The central idea in both methods is that we design things to create value for some user. Value is conceptually defined as benefit divided by cost. In consumer products this is a balancing act as we try to find the "sweet spot." In B2B commerce, we usually find that the benefit required is strictly specified, meaning that exceeding it does not increase value, even if it is free. Anything that does not increase value is waste. That leaves us with trying to find the lowest cost approach to meeting requirements.

Applying this process during the design phase can be awkward. Ideally, we would expect designers to be thinking that way constantly and to only produce designs that had already been subjected to that sort of analysis, even if only in the designer's head. There are often benefits to additional sets of eyes on the problem, so it would seem to make sense to have some sort of peer-review process before the design is too far along. Since this consumes both design lead-time and costly engineering resources, it is not all that popular, particularly since the benefits are hard to quantify and subject to manipulation. What can be very valuable is the exercise of formally articulating the design requirements, and this can be done quite early in the process. Being very precise about what is required helps strip away preconceptions about things that might seem to be required, but really aren't. (See Supplement 14-3 on rocket motors.)

Design for Manufacturing/Design for Assembly (DfM/DfA)

As is often the case, these terms reflect concepts that originated in different places, but have converged until there is substantial overlap, and the two are often combined as DfMA. The idea of designing for specific conditions has spawned multiple such designations, to the point that we often talk about DfX meaning design for X, where X can be any particular requirement that you want to observe, so that we can have design for service, design for recycling, design for disassembly, design for packaging, etc. However, in their original form, DfM and DfA were intended to achieve much the same result as concurrent engineering, but without necessarily involving a supplier.

At its heart, DfMA is a set of design rules that reflect typical process capability in various industries. There are different sets for different processes such as machining, manual assembly, circuit board assembly and so on. Since these vary so greatly, there is little point in trying to list them here. There are several software providers[1] that have analysis tools to apply these design rules, and there is a useful spinoff from these analyses in the form of a cost estimating function. Although these cost estimates may not always be up to date on their absolute values, they will show clearly the effects of changes in the design – further echoing the emphasis in this book on the value of differential analysis.

As with VA/VE, implementation is the main challenge. The preferred way to implement the use of these tools would be to commit to a software package and make the output of that software part of the design review process. Of course, if you design enough parts of a certain type to justify the purchase of the software, chances are good that your designers already know the rules pretty well, so the gain may not be great. Trying to implement DfMA on a case-by-case or ad hoc basis doesn't usually work very well, but it may be useful to invest in a library of design handbooks that designers can consult when they feel they are getting out of their depth.

Implementation Issues

It has been demonstrated that all of the above techniques can work to reduce (avoid) costs and it often seems that they

---

1   The oldest and best-known of these is Boothroyd-Dewhurst (https://www. dfma.com/).

are not as widely-used as they should be. In the author's experience, attempts to apply any or all of them in a formal way have not proved to be sustainable. There are several reasons for this.

One is that the design process often takes place under severe time pressure, and any sort of review process cuts into available time. This is a valid concern, and if time-to-market is valuable, then time spent to get the design perfect is not a good investment. However, if you take the fast route, it is important to realize that to remain competitive it will be necessary to continually review and improve the design over time. This requires allocation of significant resources to the review and improvement effort, something that relatively few companies are prepared to do. It also requires a continual improvement mindset in the initial product and process design to not lock in too much of the cost. Specifically, this means avoiding fixed costs such as special purpose equipment. Remember the old saying: "there's never time to do it right, but there is always time to do it over."

A second reason these programs fail is that product designers don't much like participating in review processes. Some of this is quite legitimate; some of these protocols require documentation of multiple iterations of a design to show the improvements made. To many designers, this is just wasted effort – they have already gone through multiple iterations in their heads and see no reason to document the intermediate steps. There is also a natural human resistance to being second-guessed on our design choices. Most people don't like having their design choices and assumptions exposed and questioned. Add to this the fact that the personnel assigned to the review roles are rarely the firm's top design talent, so there is the sense of being questioned by persons less qualified to do so. Although most designers will go along with an edict to subject their designs to this kind of review, resistance can be expressed in many ways, including continual questioning of the true value of the process.

Another main reason that such programs tend to disappear over time is cost. Adopting any of these protocols requires commitment of resources: personnel, software, or both.

Conceptually, these investments should pay for themselves, but actually demonstrating that is very difficult. The differential analysis template in Chapter 10 provides a tool to generate a present value of any design change, but the difficulty lies in establishing the baseline – what would have been the case without the change. For a product in current production this is feasible, but for a new design it is more hypothetical. It is also subject to manipulation if one is trying to demonstrate a certain level of cost savings. Ultimately, it is uncertainty about the value of such programs that causes them to be abandoned. The tools in this book will not remove all uncertainty, but do provide a rigorous platform for the analysis.

Design Requirements

The second form of ignorance that leads to potential over-specification, is lack of knowledge of the true design requirements. In practical terms, this means that a designer must sign off on a product or service that will be launched into an uncertain world where it is not possible to know all of the conditions or issues that might arise. For some of these products or services, failure is unacceptable – as in those cases where human life or large investments are at stake. Faced with this dilemma, there is a natural tendency to specify the best of everything, just to be safe. Designers don't generally like to discuss the factors of safety (also known as factors of ignorance) that are built into their designs, so it may take some digging to discover the extent. The problem, of course, is that these factors of ignorance run up the cost, maybe unnecessarily, but also maybe not.

There is no easy answer to this, as it is one of those cost vs. risk tradeoffs that has no correct answer. Obviously, it is helpful if the designers have full awareness of the cost impacts of their decisions, via the means just described, so that the more obvious tradeoffs can be dealt with. Going beyond this requires creating a culture where uncertainty can be admitted without penalty, and the cost vs. risk tradeoff can be discussed objectively in a cross-functional setting. That, unfortunately, is beyond the scope of this book.

Favoritism

After ignorance of various factors, the second main reason for specifications being more costly than necessary is favoritism; by which we mean that they are written to favor (or exclude) certain suppliers. This is not necessarily as insidious as it sounds! If it has been decided for good business reasons that a particular supplier will be used, and that contract terms are in place to work out the pricing, then it makes perfect sense that the specification should be written to conform closely to that supplier's processes and capabilities. This would occur fairly naturally through a concurrent engineering or APQP (see Supplement 14-2) approach. The downside is that such a specification may not be portable if there were ever a need to change suppliers. Suppliers naturally like this as it creates switching costs for the buyer and gives the incumbent supplier an advantage in any price negotiations that take place. Even though the initial price might be "right," there is potential for it to drift over time as design changes are implemented.

Less desirable favoritism can occur in several ways. One is the factor of ignorance as discussed above. If a designer is concerned about some factor, say corrosion resistance, it is tempting to look at suppliers' data, and then write a specification at the best level available. In other words, the designer has chosen the supplier without actually mentioning it by name. In some industries, designers may be even more explicit about it and declare a sole-source supplier. The result is the same, but the latter is more visible.

Just as incumbent suppliers like specifications that are written in ways that favor them, so do potential suppliers. Writing specifications is difficult and tedious, and potential suppliers are often eager to help with the process by providing their own versions for adoption. The hope being that when the package is sent out for quotes, they will be best-positioned to bid on the requirements. This is not all bad. There is no need to re-invent wheels, and suppliers often have detailed product knowledge that they can embed in specifications – to your benefit. The downsides are fairly obvious. The specification may contain elements that are unique to one supplier and hard for others to meet. Also, the specification will likely be provided by a supplier with a high level of technical and design support (overhead), one that is probably not the low-cost supplier. Since the use of supplier-generated specifications is a mixed bag, the key is awareness: understanding where the specifications came from and why. A good designer will take suppliers' inputs and take advantage of them, but remove any content that is supplier-specific.

Writing specifications to favor or disfavor a particular supplier can be done with good intentions, or it can be done for reasons of convenience (a polite term for laziness), but it can also cross an ethical line. Suppliers may attempt various means to persuade specification writers to write them a certain way, and this can range from dubious practices such as lunches and golf outings to outright bribery. The writing of specifications is a weak point in many companies' financial control mechanisms, and in cost management efforts, it deserves more attention than it often gets.

Design for Supply Chain

Previously we described DfX, as in design for X, X being any particular concern. What we have seen in the above discussions is that the issuing of a specification is a critical point in cost management and is actually a very strategic decision. The choices of black box versus white box specifications and the tolerances required have a major impact on which supplier will be used and what the cost will be. We often hear estimates that something like 80% of a product's cost is determined when the design is released, as there is very little to work with after that point. We have already discussed DfMA as a way to control costs, but now we want to introduce the idea of DfSC – Design for Supply Chain.

When we think of supply chains, logistics often come to mind, and we could think of Design for Logistics as a subset of DfSC. The logistics part would include considerations of how components and final products are to be packaged, shipped, and stored – issues that are not normally top-of-mind for product designers. Some examples of how logistics can shape product design are given in Supplement 14-4.

However, this is only a small piece of the overall puzzle. The success of a company depends on its ability to obtain competitively-priced product, reliably, over an extended period of time. This is what we call supply management as opposed to the more clerical function called purchasing. As we have seen, the design details and the manner in which they are specified have a major impact on what suppliers can be used and who owns what parts of the intellectual property associated with the product. This, in turn, drives how the contracts will be written and how pricing is likely to evolve over time. All of these are strategically important issues and suggest that product design has to be undertaken with a keen understanding of the commercial aspects of the supply chain as well as the technical details.

Modularity

Just as the commercial structure of the supply chain is an important element, so is the physical structure. By physical structure, we mean the manner in which the component parts move and come together to create the final product, i.e.: who does what, where. We can discuss this under the heading of product *modularity.* One of the concerns is just the movement of goods as discussed above, but it also has important effects on inventory management, product life-cycle issues and supplier interchangeability. We are talking here about physical modularity – the degree to which the final product is sub-divided into separate, stand-alone modules that can be "bolted" together to create a final product. A module in this sense is something that can be sourced and delivered by itself and is interchangeable as long as interface requirements are met. The classic desktop PC is an excellent example of a very modular product. Virtually all of the components have industry-standard interfaces so that they can be plugged or screwed together in almost any combination. It should be noted that service operations are also amenable to modularization, such as separating immunizations from standard doctor visits, or breaking out background checks as a separate exercise so that they can be used for multiple purposes.

Modularity comes at a cost. In a PC, the electrical connectors are more expensive than hard-wired connections, the size of the cases must be large enough to handle all potential hardware and its necessary cooling, and so on. The excess cost of modularization has to be offset by other savings, and in the case of the PC, it is. The main advantage is the ability to offer a wide variety of final products without having to hold inventory of every possible variant. This is called *postponement* and is a well-known supply chain strategy, but can only be used if enabled by the design.

Modularization has other, somewhat less-obvious advantages for inventory and cost management. Imagine a product with two components, A and B. Part A is only available from a few suppliers, has long lead times and uncertain deliveries. Part B is readily available from a variety of sources on short notice. You would probably want to hold a fairly high level of inventory of Part A, but there would be no sense in doing so for Part B. But if they were designed as an integrated whole (non-modular), that is what you would have to do. Modularization may cost more initially (for example, adding a pair of electrical connectors), but allows for reduced inventory on Part B, and also allows for more competitive sourcing. Further advantages emerge when the components in question have different life cycles. Extreme examples of this can be found in the aerospace industry where airframes may have a production life of twenty years or more, but the electronic control systems may depend on semiconductor chips that will be obsolete and unavailable in less than two years. When the chips become unavailable, the product will have to be re-designed around what is available at that time. If the high clockspeed items are confined to small modules, this will be less costly than if they are more broadly integrated.

Trying to pull all of these pieces together to create effective DfSC is a circular, iterative process, not the neat linear model often used in the new product development literature. A designer must create a product that satisfies the design requirements in a cost-effective way, and to do so must be aware of the supply chain implications, including which supplier(s) can be used, and how the product structure must reflect the distribution of work. In many cases, the answer to the question of which supplier will be used may be something like: "any competent plastic molder," in which case the process becomes more linear and the tools discussed above can give a reasonable result. However, it is often the case that there are only a few suppliers who are proficient in a technology and are equipped to deal with the particular requirements of your industry (usually documentation and certification issues). Some of these suppliers may have close ties to your competitors or other characteristics that would make them unsuitable as partners. In extreme cases, it may not even be commercially feasible to use certain technologies, even though they make sense from an engineering perspective (see Supplement 14-5 on the sourcing matrix).

The key message here is that for effective cost management/ containment/avoidance, new product design and supply chain management need to be joined at the hip. This reflects the major role that suppliers (and sometimes distributors) play in determining your cost and ultimately your profit. It should be apparent that, for non-commodity items, suppliers have an active role to play in the design. This means that suppliers must be involved, and must sometimes be selected, before the design is anywhere near complete. This is a complicated issue and deserves its own chapter (Chapter 15).

Chapter 14 – Key Takeaways

1. Cost avoidance, particularly at the product design stage is the most productive form of cost management.

2. However, cost avoidance is very hard to quantify.

3. There are several design protocols that are designed to ensure low-cost designs, but they suffer from the quantification problem and are difficult to sustain.

4. There are many aspects of a design that create cost, not just manufacturing cost. Design for Supply Chain (DfSC) takes an integrated approach to ensure that products can be supplied not only at a low cost, but with high reliability for extended time periods.

Supplement 14-1 – Black Box vs. White Box

When creating a specification, there are two ways to tell a supplier what you want. One way is a *descriptive* specification in which you supply detailed drawings or other descriptions of the characteristics of the item in question. For example, if you wish to buy automobile wheels, you might send the supplier a detailed drawing of the shape, dictate the material to be used, including its processing, heat treating, etc., plus the particular type and color of paint to be applied, and so on. The supplier doesn't need to know anything about wheels, as long as it knows about casting, painting, etc. This is sometimes referred to as a *make-to-print* situation.

The opposite approach is a *functional* specification, in which you define the result you are trying to achieve and leave it to the supplier to figure out the best way of achieving that. This is sometimes referred to as a *black-box* specification, a term originating in electronics where there are many situations where the user specifies the outputs expected from defined inputs, but doesn't care about the actual method of achieving it. For example, if I want a battery charger, I want it to deliver certain voltages and currents in response to different battery states, but I don't know or care anything about the internal electronics that manage this. Because of the widespread use of the term black-box to describe this type of specification, it has become common to use the opposite term and describe make-to-print situations as *white-box* specifications. Hybrids of both methods are also possible of course, so you may encounter the term *gray-box* in these situations.

The decision on which specification type or mix of types to use is strategically important for several reasons. You can get a sense of this when you realize that if you had both types of specification package available to send out for quotes, you would almost certainly be sending them to non-overlapping lists of potential suppliers. Right away, your choice dictates the type of supplier you will be able to use and this will have a cost impact. Often, product designers are not well-equipped to make this choice from a strategic viewpoint. From a cost management perspective, it is vitally important to have purchasing involvement at the earliest stages of design.

Either type of specification can be better in various circumstances, so let's look at the pros and cons.

If you use a descriptive or white-box approach:

- You must do the detailed design work yourself. Not only does this incur a cost, but you must also be confident that your design work is first-class and that you have up-to-date knowledge of the technology involved *and* of potential competing technologies.

- You will most likely be using a low-cost supplier that will not be able to provide much design support. Suppliers that do have design capabilities probably won't want to talk to you because they don't want their knowledge translated into a specification that you will send elsewhere.

- You will get the lowest possible purchase price for the item that you have specified, but it is up to you to be sure that your design has not overlooked better approaches.

- You will assume sole responsibility for whether or not the component works in your application. This means that you must have full understanding of the requirements of that application and what it takes to meet them.

- Your specification package will tell the supplier relatively little about the end use requirements. This can be an advantage or disadvantage.

If you use a functional or black-box approach:

- Suppliers will do the detailed design work for you. They will charge for this one way or another, but it opens the door for innovative suppliers to develop solutions that are better (cheaper) than what you might have done on your own.

- You do not have to have detailed knowledge of the technology involved, which may be totally outside your area of expertise.

- You can rely on market mechanisms to be sure that the chosen supplier is up to date in its field and providing you with best-in-class designs.

- You must communicate the actual performance requirements to suppliers. In many fields, this is valuable, proprietary information, and possession of it may allow your supplier to become a competitor, or to sell to your competitors.

- Since design responsibility falls to suppliers, you can ask them to provide a warranty of performance.

So, which is better? Both approaches have their advantages, but in general, the functional approach tends to be preferred for the simple reason that it allows a competitive market to bring forth the lowest cost solutions. The two main reasons to not use a functional approach would be, a) you have best-in-class design capability in the specific field and want to take advantage of it, or, b) you regard the functional requirements of the application to be proprietary knowledge that you do not choose to share with suppliers.

Supplement 14-2 – Concurrent Engineering and APQP

Concurrent engineering is not a new concept by any means, but it really started to attract attention in terms of formalizing its key elements c. 1980. As changes in technology started to accelerate and product complexity continued to increase, it was no longer feasible to rely on tribal knowledge to ensure that designs could be put into production with satisfactory performance. The primary driver was quality, and the recognition that a production process had a certain inherent capability to produce outputs within specified limits. Lack of full understanding of the statistical capability of chosen processes often resulted in product that failed to consistently meet expectations – in other words, poor quality. This discovery was what motivated the development of the Six-Sigma methodology at Motorola, now better known as Lean-Six-Sigma.

Process capability can be measured in several ways, the best-known probably being C_{pk}[1]. This measurement assumes that a process results in a measurable output, subject to statistical variance. This variability of output is conventionally assumed to follow a normal distribution. It is also assumed that there are known upper and lower acceptance limits. The capability of the process is defined as the range that spans the mean, plus or minus three standard deviations ($\mu \pm 3\sigma$). As long as these values are within the acceptance limits, the process is said to be *capable*. If one of the ends of the capability range coincides with one of the acceptance limits, the process is only just capable, with a C_{pk} = 1.0. Higher is better, as C_{pk} is the ratio of acceptability range to capability range. There are rules of thumb about this, and values less than 1.5 are usually viewed with suspicion.

This capability problem is the same one that we have when sending a specification to a supplier, just viewed in the opposite direction. Our concern here is cost, but we are assuming quality capability to be a given. When we send a specification to any supplier, we are hoping that it will

1   For a comprehensive definition, see: https://www.itl.nist.gov/div898/handbook/pmc/section1/pmc16.htm

choose the lowest-cost process that will achieve that. If the specifications we send are more restrictive than they need to be or are not well-matched to the supplier's capabilities, our costs will be higher than necessary. We also have to assure ourselves that the supplier truly is capable to the levels we need, so it is common to insist on some sort of validation testing before accepting production deliveries. Clearly, the best way to address these concerns is during the design and specification process, not afterwards, and this is where concurrent engineering comes in.

The best-known formalization of concurrent engineering is the APQP (Advanced Product Quality Planning) model. The formal model was developed by AIAG[1] based on a study of quality practices across multiple industries, but drawing heavily on aerospace practices. This model has diffused widely and is now found embedded in many software platforms for new product development (NPD). The basic model looks like this:

Figure 14-2.1: The APQP Model

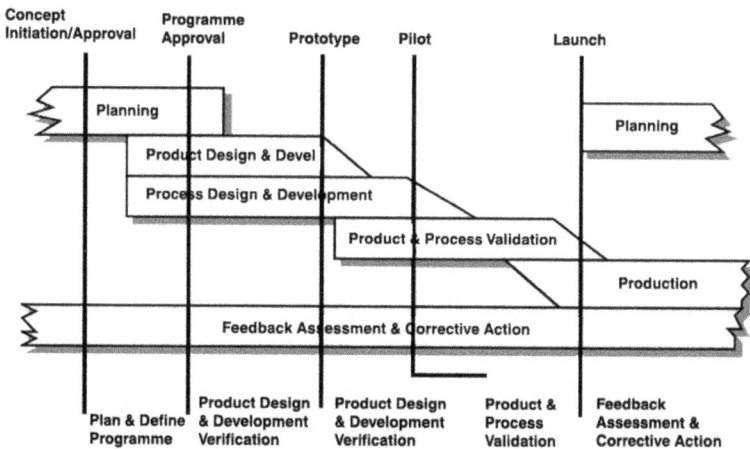

The key feature to note is the overlap between the product and process stages of development. What the full APQP process does is create formal sign-offs as the various stages are completed to ensure that when production begins, both

1   Automotive Industry Action Group – a consortium of the North American auto manufacturers set up to reduce costs across the industry through the commonization of processes. (https://www.aiag.org/)

the product and the process perform as intended and are *capable* with respect to their acceptance ranges.

From a cost management perspective, the critical feature is that process design must begin before the product design is completed – in fact they should start more or less simultaneously as shown in Figure 14-2.1. This is manageable when the supplier is either internal or has been pre-selected, but cannot be applied when the supplier remains unknown. The original model makes no distinction as to where the various functions are performed – in-house or at a supplier. To get the full benefit of concurrent engineering, we need to select our suppliers early, on the basis of their capabilities. This has its own pitfalls, as discussed elsewhere, but the main issue is that we will have to arrive at a mutually agreeable price after the development work has been done. That is where cost, and cost analysis become critically important.

Supplement 14-3 – Wally and the Rocket Motor

Wally, a colleague of the author, had, in a prior life, been employed by an aerospace components company that supplied products for spacecraft. One of these products was a valve that controlled the flows of propellant and oxidizer into the combustion chamber of a rocket motor. The requirements for these valves were extremely demanding, particularly for the oxidizer (liquid oxygen). The valve of course had to operate with complete reliability, and the allowed leakage specifications were extremely low. On one side of the valve was Florida sunshine, heat, humidity and salt air. On the other side was liquid oxygen, one of the most corrosive substances known to man, at cryogenic temperatures (-300°F). Not surprisingly, the product was a costly one, involving lots of precision machining and exotic materials.

NASA was a cost-conscious purchaser, and one day announced that it was replacing Wally's company with a competitor as a supplier for these valves. The competitor's product cost a small fraction of the original, was demonstrably more reliable, and had exactly zero leakage. How did they do it?

The answer is that the competitor studied the requirements more carefully. Wally's company had designed a beautifully-made product that would open reliably under field conditions, *and could close again.* There was no such requirement in the specifications – rocket motors are one-shot machines, and once that valve has opened, there is no need to be able to close it again. So, instead of being designed like a faucet, the competitor's product was designed like the familiar tear strip on a soft drink can. It is easy to see how: a) this design would be superior in all ways, and, b) how being very careful about articulating the design requirements can lead down a better path.

Supplement 14-4 – Design for Logistics: Case Examples

The handling, shipping, and storing of product represent a major portion of cost. "Logistics" costs average about 10% of GDP, and offer significant opportunities for cost reduction. Logistics requirements also impose constraints on design that might not be apparent when looking only at the end use. Some examples will illustrate.

Regular buyers of Costco cashews may remember that they used to come in cylindrical PETE jars. The round cross section has many advantages; it uses the minimum material for the volume, it is easy to blow-mold because of its radial symmetry, and labels are easily applied without the need for indexing. So why are these jars now square in cross section? The square section is more costly for all of the above reasons. The answer is shipping and storage costs. Since cashews are fairly light, they can fill up a truck without fear of going over weight, so the shipping cost per jar is the cost of a truckload divided by the number of jars that can be squeezed in. The square sections pack more closely, with a theoretical reduction in shipping cost of about 11%. The same holds true for storage: normally there is a fixed charge per pallet location, so the same reduction in unit cost is possible. Retail shelf space also carries a fixed charge, so the ability to squeeze product into smaller volume reduces cost too.

Similar thinking applied when Chevrolet introduced the now long-forgotten Vega. This vehicle had several innovative features, with mixed results. One was the design for shipping. The car was short enough (unusual at the time) that it could be stood on end in a railcar, and this would allow more vehicles to be loaded on a train. This required several design changes, the most visible being that the battery had to be redesigned to have its fill ports along the rear edge instead of in the center as is normally done. This idea doesn't seem to have caught on.

In another rail shipping story, Cadillac dealers noticed that a significant portion of a certain model were being delivered with transverse dents across the trunk lid. It was discovered that the trunk lids were coming open while being transported on rail cars, and when they did, they struck the cross beam above them. The reason was something called inertial unlatching – when you vibrate a latch at the right frequency and in the right direction it can "float" and come unlatched. The railcars vibrated in a way that was never experienced on the road, but a new requirement had to be added to the specification (probably unnecessarily increasing the cost of many subsequent designs!).

Supplement 14-5 – The Sourcing Matrix

The way you design products that will be purchased has a large influence on how that purchasing relationship is going to work. As a way of categorizing things and making sense of this factor, it is useful to introduce the strategic sourcing matrix. This matrix is an adaptation of one originally created by Peter Kraljic[1] and is therefore often referred to as the "Kraljic" matrix. Many versions exist, but most take this form:

Figure 14-5.1: The Sourcing Matrix

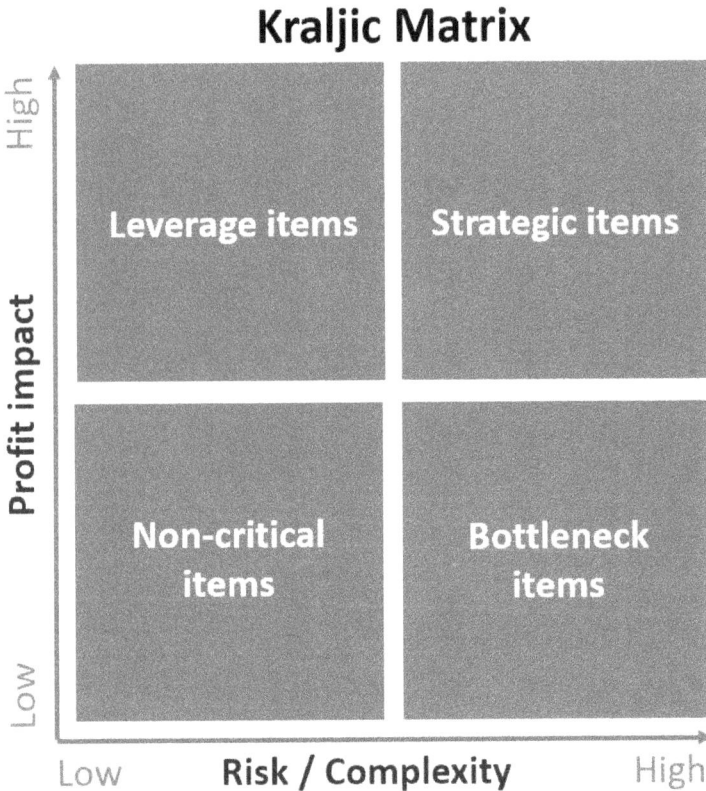

Products to be purchased will fall into one of these quadrants. For the axes, "Profit Impact" really just means whether or not this product represents a lot of money to your company. "Risk/Complexity" refers to the suppliers in the marketplace and is roughly the same thing as the inverse of the number of

1   Kraljic, P., "Purchasing Must Become Supply Management," Harvard Business Review, Sept. – Oct. 1983

potential suppliers. Low means that there are lots of suppliers, and high means that there are only a few. The idea is that you take a different approach to purchasing depending on what quadrant your product falls into. There is a major limitation to this analysis and that is that it fails to account for how your purchases look to the potential suppliers. If something is a large spend to you, but peanuts to most suppliers in the market, that would change the dynamics a bit. We can put that concern aside for the time being.

The guidelines are these: if a product falls into the lower-left quadrant, your main interest is in purchasing it as efficiently as possible. You aren't all that concerned about getting the absolute best price, you just want to execute the purchase orders as simply as possible. This often means picking a supplier and just ordering from a catalog at a standard trade discount. However, if you land in the upper-left quadrant, it is important that you get the best price possible because the product itself doesn't differentiate you from your competitors – it only affects your costs. The large number of suppliers allows you to use a number of purchasing tools to drive pricing down. The upper-right quadrant is more interesting strategically. These are often the products that allow you to differentiate yourself and the small supply base suggests that it is more important to cultivate a strong working relationship with key suppliers than it is to get the lowest possible price. Price is never unimportant, but it will have to be negotiated rather than set in a marketplace. Finally, we come to the lower-right quadrant. This is a sort of no-man's-land; there are only a few suppliers, and you aren't buying enough to be an interesting customer. As a result, you will pay too much, and get poor service in return. The best strategic actions for products in this quadrant are those that get you out of it.

Product design will determine to some extent which quadrant your purchases will occupy. It is perfectly OK to have products in all quadrants except the last one, in fact, it is best to have a portfolio balanced across the other three. Unfortunately, it is very easy to design one's way into the lower-right quadrant, especially if designing without adequate knowledge of the commercial market. It is often easier to design a custom part than to look up the details and incorporate an existing one, or to use an industry standard. It is also easy to be tempted by higher performance options than to work with more common technologies. Defense contracting has been prone to this for many years, hence the strong push to use COTS (commercial, off-the-shelf) technology wherever possible. The message is clear: for effective cost management, do not design yourself into the "Bottleneck" quadrant.

Chapter 15 – Early Supplier Involvement

We have seen in the above chapters that one of the most productive approaches to cost management is to keep it out in the first place, by designing products that are cost-effective to produce and deliver. Key to this is coordination between those who define the specifications and those who must produce the product. The implication of course, is that this coordination must take place before the specification is considered final. When it is known in advance that production will be internal to the firm, most companies practice some sort of concurrent engineering to ensure that this takes place. However, when the supplier will be external, this becomes more complicated.

The title of this chapter is Early Supplier Involvement (ESI), but the term is quite broad and needs better definition. "Early" in this instance means prior to the release of a specification for production, but that can be as short as a few days, or as long as several years. There is another milestone along the way, and that is when a commitment is made to purchase from a particular supplier. If this occurs prior to the release of the specification for production it is called Early Supplier Selection (ESS), meaning a somewhat binding commitment to a particular supplier.

The timing points and the level of involvement are somewhat fuzzy and hard to pin down precisely. In particular, the commitment to a supplier is rarely total. When a company works closely with a particular supplier on the development of a product, it is usually understood that the ensuing purchase order is the supplier's to lose, but this is rarely committed to in writing. If a more formal statement is required, it is normally in the form of a letter of intent (LOI) that has multiple escape clauses conditional on the supplier's performance and pricing. There are a few situations (best avoided) when the supplier is unequivocally designated from the outset. It may be the case that engineering is adamant that only product from a certain supplier may be used, or it may be that your own customer makes that requirement. This is obviously bad in terms of your ability to negotiate pricing (although the tools in this book will help!), but at least there will be clarity on who you need to work with to reduce costs. Whether the supplier is motivated to participate in cost reduction efforts is another matter and may depend on contract terms.

Types of ESI

Since ESI is such a broad term, we will try to break it down into some typical scenarios:

Free Consulting

This is probably the commonest form of ESI. It is very normal for designers to contact potential suppliers (and vice versa) to discuss potential approaches to their problems. It is equally normal for these suppliers to provide this technical support at no charge, regarding it as part of their sales expenses. In fact, some of their best technical people are often assigned to this role since it is such an important sales tool. All of this can be very beneficial to a buyer, but the pitfalls are fairly obvious. Since the potential supplier's goal is to win new business, it will steer the technical discussion in directions favorable to itself, and may neglect to mention better alternatives. There is a danger that a particular supplier may give such excellent technical assistance (including help with writing the specifications as discussed in Chapter 14) that the designer feels no need to explore other alternatives. In effect, a supplier selection is being made, raising the critical question of whether the designer chose to work with a supplier that is also a viable commercial partner. This is very difficult to manage, as these relationships evolve relatively slowly and there is no key decision gate along the way.

One way of managing this that has been observed to work is to assign a purchasing person to handle supplier relationships in the NPD phase. This person would not necessarily be the regular production buyer. The person designated needs to be both technically and commercially knowledgeable and the goal is to help the designers, not to be a gatekeeper. The first priority is to make sure that discussions don't progress too far if a potential supplier is not a suitable commercial partner. A second priority is to manage the sharing and ownership of intellectual property. Designers tend to be a bit lax about this, so it is helpful to have some oversight. Critical documents in this regard are *non-disclosure agreements* (NDAs) where the supplier agrees not to share or use any of your trade secrets, and *waivers of confidential disclosure*. The latter is the reverse of an NDA, where the supplier agrees that anything it tells you is considered to be public knowledge unless it is specifically designated as proprietary. This is to prevent suppliers from sharing ideas with you and then suing you if you use them – it happens! There is a bit of a catch to both of these documents. If you agree not to disclose or misuse confidential information, then the onus is on the owner of the confidential information to clearly designate what is and is not confidential. This requires a certain amount of discipline.

Preferred Supplier Designations

This state is hard to pin down exactly as it lies on the continuum from casual free consulting to formal supplier selection. Essentially, it means some sort of acknowledgement by the buyer that a certain supplier has an inside track on winning the business and is at least guaranteed a fair shot at it. It can be something as simple as a verbal statement to the effect that: "you are the only guys we're working with on this, and as long as we can agree on price, the business is yours." This general idea can also be expressed in letter form, and while it has almost no legal significance, it is often an inducement to the supplier's management to allocate pre-production development funds to your product.

Most companies have (should have) an approved supplier list (ASL), containing only suppliers that have passed certain tests of performance and are approved for use without further qualification. A subset of this list is often given a *preferred supplier* designation. This list is of suppliers that have demonstrated superior performance on the golden triad of price, cost, and delivery. A supplier on this list can assume that if it participates in development of a new product, that it will have at least a tie-breaker when it comes to awarding a purchase order.

However a supplier preference is communicated, the goal is the same: to encourage the supplier to commit more effort to development and to share more information.

Sole Supplier Designations

We will use this heading to cover situations where a supplier has been formally designated in advance of development work. The designation may be for either technical or commercial reasons. The problem with this situation is that it largely removes incentives for the supplier to be cost-conscious. As discussed in Chapters 12 & 13, price will usually have to be established on some form of cost-plus calculation, so reducing its own costs is not good for the supplier, and they aren't all that motivated to help you reduce your costs either! That is why companies avoid this sort of commitment wherever possible. The most they will typically give is an LOI saying that they intend to award this business to the supplier, provided that…. followed by a long list of conditions and escape clauses.

In principle, working with a pre-selected supplier should be similar to working with in-house manufacturing. The difference is that your own manufacturing operates as a cost center, while the supplier is operating as a profit center. As a result, the incentives are flipped and will need to be addressed through contract terms (Chapter 13). Companies that must buy from sister divisions or affiliated companies know this phenomenon only too well – your in-family suppliers will always be your worst ones in all respects: price, quality, and delivery. The use of internal suppliers also raises the issue of transfer pricing. This is similar in many ways to establishing pricing after the fact, and is a sufficiently thorny and contentious issue that it deserves its own discussion (Chapter 18).

Cooperative Research & Development Agreements (CRADAs)

These agreements are popular in government procurement, and are sometimes seen in private industry. These typically are used without a specific product in mind, but in recognition that developing complementary technologies would be mutually beneficial. The parties to a CRADA agree that when they do research and development in a particular area, they will share their findings with their partners. The idea is that this exchange will help all parties advance faster toward some commercially valuable goal. The key feature of a CRADA is that no money changes hands, so the parties can effectively extend their R&D capabilities at no cost – an obvious aid to cost management. Any agreement beyond the simple sharing of information, such as an agreement to commercialize the results starts to fall under the heading of a joint venture, which is beyond the current discussion.

Does ESI Work?

The whole point of ESI is to create cheaper and better product through concurrent engineering. While this seems fairly believable, it is a hypothesis that needs validation. Empirical studies in this area, although often focusing on attributes other than cost, have yielded equivocal results. Basically, the conclusion is that sometimes ESI helps, sometimes it doesn't. When faced with this sort of conundrum, it is appropriate to identify the factors that separate the apparently opposite conclusions. We can try to summarize research in this field[1] as follows.

The essential difference is the manner in which development progresses. One characterization is that development is either *linear* or *iterative*. Linear means that you basically know where you are going, you just need to go through the process to work out the details. An iterative process on the

---

1   Specifically, see: Eisenhardt, K. M. and B. N. Tabrizi (1995). "Accelerating adaptive processes: product innovation in the global computer industry." Administrative Sciences Quarterly 40(1): 84-110. and: Terweisch, C., et al. (2002). "Exchanging Preliminary Information in Concurrent Engineering: Alternative Coordination Strategies." Organization Science 13(4): 402-419.

other hand is one where many paths have to be tried and there is often need to loop back and try alternates. Another way to characterize development is whether the specification is evolving in *precision* or in *certainty*. Imprecise information would be a situation such as: "we will use an electric heater; we just don't know what wattage yet." Conversely, uncertain information would be illustrated by the statement, "we know what our heating requirements are, but we haven't decided whether to use electricity or gas."

These two characterizations are very similar, and similar results were found. Where the development is linear and the information is lacking only in precision, early supplier involvement was helpful in getting to the end result faster and better. In other situations where the technology is uncertain, early supplier involvement didn't help and could actually hurt as it tends to restrict the range of options that are explored. A bad outcome really means that you chose to involve a supplier that was ultimately not the right one. So, putting all of this in plain language; the time to involve a supplier is when you have reached a state of certainty about the technologies and capabilities that are required. At that point, you can evaluate potential suppliers to see if they are appropriate and move forward from there. Involving a supplier too deeply prior to that is likely to limit your options and risks leading you into poor choices.

Chapter 15 – Key Takeaways

1. Early supplier involvement (ESI) means engaging with potential suppliers before the specification for a product is finalized – and using that engagement to develop the specification.

2. The goal of ESI is essentially the same as that of concurrent engineering: to produce better products faster and more cheaply.

3. ESI adds another dimension, and that is the commercial relationship that is being developed at the same time. Consequently, there should be at least a preliminary evaluation of a supplier as a business partner before allowing significant involvement.

4. Managing the ownership of intellectual property during ESI requires an increased level of attention and discipline.

5. Although ESI is generally beneficial, it can be detrimental if the supplier(s) involved do not have a wide enough range of technical capabilities to evaluate all of the alternatives.

Chapter 16 – Cost Reduction on Existing Product

Given all of the normal reasons to want to reduce costs, it is natural to want to reduce the cost of products or services that are in current production. We have already addressed the need to ensure that you are paying the "right" price for everything on the supply side, but once that is taken care of, all that you have left is to either change the design, or change the process by which the products are created. At this point, it makes very little difference whether these changes take place within your own organization or at a supplier. A process improvement at a supplier's facility should result in a price reduction to you by one mechanism or another, depending on your contract terms. As a result, the techniques discussed in this chapter are applicable wherever the activity takes place.

Changing product or process design on the fly is hard (read: costly) for several reasons. For one, the design activities have been done already, and depending on how well they were done, the available gains may not be all that large. This necessitates an assessment activity to identify the most promising candidates for cost reduction. Secondly, it requires an investment of resources that is not absolutely required, and must therefore be justified. This investment will include the time of technical personnel and may involve capital investments as well. Time and capital are both scarce resources, so there is likely to be resistance for allocating either to cost reduction rather than to new product. The good news is that the justification for changes to current product is easier to make because the baseline is well established. Companies know what it is currently costing them to make a product (or think they do; after reading Chapter 6 you may be skeptical), so if the analysis is well-done, it will be an easier sell than say, cost avoidance on products that are still in development. The template provided in Chapters 10 & 11 is an important tool for this. That said, the implementation issues are still similar to those that impede cost avoidance in new product design.

Finally, one of the largest obstacles to making changes to an existing product is the sunk cost problem. Normally, some fixed costs are created in the initial process design, and these may be very large, as in tooling or automation. These are normally "recaptured" with a depreciation term that will show up in the overhead part of the cost file. Changes that obsolete some of that investment will seem to be a cost savings as they will reduce the depreciation charge – but this is not cash flow, since that money has already been spent. You can't reduce the cost of money you have already spent unless there is some recovery of value from these assets. When looked at on a differential basis, comparing the existing state to a proposed one, the existing equipment may be effectively free to use, making it difficult to come up with an alternative that is cheaper than free. This is not totally true, as there are tax implications associated with disposal or write-downs of capital, so the analysis has to be done carefully. See the chapter supplement to see how this might work.

Implementing a cost reduction on an existing product is an exercise in creativity – there is no linear set of steps that will address all of the possibilities. That said, we can identify some different approaches that have been formalized and that will help to identify the opportunities. These approaches overlap since they are trying to accomplish the same thing, and may be used in combination although they reflect different points of approach. We don't claim that this list is exhaustive, rather it is a starting point for developing your own strategy.

Value Analysis

This was discussed in Chapter 14 in the same breath as Value Engineering, so only a brief summary is needed here. Value analysis tends to be detail and component-focused, primarily because it is too late for major system changes. It also tends to be product-focused rather than process-focused. Although the same thinking can be applied to both, process re-design is usually approached differently. Value Analysis can be performed formally or informally, but in contrast to new product development, current product often doesn't have a clear "owner" who is responsible for continuous improvement of the design. As a result, VA is more often an ad hoc exercise, targeting particular products. The approach is straightforward: each feature and component of the design is specified in terms of the function it is intended to fulfill. This statement of function needs to be stripped down to its most basic level, and often requires several iterations to strip away the things that are not really necessary. At that point, creativity comes into play as the participants search for more cost-effective ways to accomplish the necessary functions.

Process Optimization

There are many situations where the basic structure of a process is set by design, but there are detail decisions that have to be made on a continual basis in order to get the best results. Some examples:

- What route should a package delivery driver take each day to minimize distance traveled?
- How much inventory of milk should a grocery store carry?
- How many checkout lanes should the grocery store have open at different hours?
- In project management, what start times should be given to each task to delay expenditures as long as possible while completing the project in the minimum possible time?
- How frequently should preventive maintenance be performed on a machine?
- How should an airline price its seats?
- How many distribution centers should you have in North America?
- How many patients should a doctor schedule in a day?

Once you become sensitized to such issues, you will see countless examples around you every day. Some of these decisions have been made and will remain set until altered, while others have to be made anew every time. It is usually the former that represent the best opportunities for improvement, as the conditions are apt to have changed over time, to the point where better options are available.

These types of decisions fall into two categories: those where the operating conditions are stable and it is possible to calculate a single best solution (deterministic), and those where decisions have to be made in the face of uncertainty, where you try to get the best result on an expected value basis (stochastic). Both types of decision can be automated, and often are – making them more or less invisible to the user. The danger is that the automation algorithm may be based on out-of-date data, or the algorithm itself may no longer be appropriate for the situation. For example, an ERP system will generate and execute replenishment orders for your inventory every day, but do you know what order logic was specified, and what data the system uses to generate the orders?

There are several techniques that can be used to make optimal decisions in these situations, but all require that you develop a mathematical model of the process you are trying to optimize. The development of these models and their analysis are subjects for their own textbooks, but we can give a quick summary here. Bear in mind too, that many larger companies have staff specialists in this area who can be called upon for assistance.

If the relationship between the decisions in question and the results desired is linear, then a well-established technique is linear programming. The math behind the technique is fairly complex, but what you need to know as a user is that the linearity condition allows even very large-scale problems to be solved efficiently, and more importantly, the solution is guaranteed to be optimal. The requirement for linearity may seem to be a restrictive condition, but in practice, a huge variety of problems can be formulated this way. Non-linear problems can be optimized too, but the algorithms are much less efficient and come without the optimality guarantee. As a result, the usefulness of non-linear models tends to be limited to small-scale problems[1].

For many decisions, uncertainty in the environment is a critical factor. In these cases, the term optimization doesn't

---

1   "Small-scale" here means something like two or three decision variables, while "large-scale" can mean thousands.

properly apply, as it is unlikely that any one solution will be the best in all possible cases. What we have to do instead is find a solution that gives us the best *expected value* of the outcome. This means that we must know something about the probability distributions of the uncertain parts of our model. A prime example is consumer demand, where we can't know what it will be tomorrow, but based on past data we might believe that it has a certain probability distribution, perhaps log-normal, with an observed mean and standard deviation. For simple models we may be able to use this assumption to calculate a probability distribution for the possible results of any decision and hence choose a decision that delivers the best expected value, either analytically or by trial and error. For more complex models, such a calculation becomes infeasible, and the preferred tool is Monte Carlo simulation. This still requires you to know or assume the statistical properties of the uncertain parts of your model, but gives a numerical solution for the result rather than an analytical one. Some examples of the use of simulation are given in Chapter 18.

The formulation of models and the use of optimization techniques may be beyond an operating manager's sphere of expertise, in which case getting expert help may be worthwhile. Larger companies may have internal staff with these skills, or it may be possible to find consulting firms with what you need. It is worthwhile though, to acquire at least a basic understanding of the approaches, and some useful textbooks are listed in the References section. It is important to be able to understand and interpret the results of optimization and simulation. If the operating conditions are stable, and an optimal result has been obtained by using linear programming, then that result can be used with confidence that it is actually optimal. If non-linear programming was used, you do not have the same guarantee, so you would need to be sure that there was a thorough evaluation of alternate solutions. Finally, if the operating conditions are uncertain, and simulation was used to arrive at a best expected value, you need more information before committing to a decision. A solution that gives the best expected value may not be the best one. The output will have an expected value (mean), but it also has a variance, and two solutions with similar expected values can differ greatly in their variance. If you are more or less risk-neutral, and can play the averages over a large number of repetitions, then this doesn't matter much. On the other hand, if this is a one-shot deal that can make or break the company, you will give a lot more weight to solutions with less downside variance. We will have more to say about risk in Chapter 18.

Process/Value-Stream Mapping, Lean Production

We'll start this section with a brief description of Lean Production, since it provides the philosophy for process mapping approaches. Lean is widely misunderstood as operating without inventory and without unused capacity. It may look like this when you are done, but it may not. To explain Lean, it helps to define its philosophical opposite, which we will call Mass Production. In Mass Production, the problem statement is to maximize output from a given set of resources. This thinking makes sense when demand, for practical purposes, is unlimited – as was the case in most of the Western world in the second half of the 20th Century. Lean assumes that demand (including both its mean and its variance) is a given, and re-frames the problem as minimizing the resources deployed to satisfy that demand. From this we can see that if demand is stable, then a Lean process will match the stereotype: minimal inventory and little unused capacity. However, if demand is variable, then it will have to be satisfied with buffers of either inventory or excess capacity[1]. As a side note, firms quickly discovered that if you cut the buffers down to just what is necessary to cover variance in demand, your own processes must be error-free or you will have to add an additional buffer to compensate for that. This buffer is of no value to the customer, so in a competitive marketplace, you will not get paid for it. For this reason, Lean is frequently coupled with quality improvement initiatives, and a widely-used term is Lean-Six Sigma.

When you start to focus on customer demand or value as

1   In service applications, the equivalent of inventory is a customer waiting line, or order backlog.

the motivator, it becomes natural to think about all the cost-generating activities and whether or not they add value for the customer. If we can map out these activities, we can put them in one of three categories: value-adding, non-value-adding but necessary, and waste. This, then, is the basis of value-stream mapping, for which there are many guides (and consultants willing to help). This mapping must not be done as an armchair exercise – you must go out into the shop and actually follow product and information through the system to see exactly what *is* being done, not what you *think* is being done. Inevitably there will be some surprises.

The standard cost file will usually have quite detailed information about all the labor and machine steps that are required, and this will be reflected in the direct costs and some of the overhead. The blind spot is that these are just the value-adding steps. There is no accounting for the non-value-adding steps – these just disappear into general overhead. For example, a cost file may tell you that a particular part gets a machining process, followed by a paint process. Those are costed quite accurately, but there is no mention that in between these processes, the part was packaged up, shipped across town to a warehouse, received, stored, then packaged up again, shipped back for painting, received and delivered to the paint line. Once you see this on a process map, you are likely to have some ideas about reducing costs!

To be useful, a process map must not only list the activities, and the time they take, but also the time between the activities and the inventory build-up between them. Reducing throughput time is a central focus of Lean because it is the easiest and most direct way to reduce the assets deployed. If you do the mapping correctly, you will find that for most products, the actual value-adding time is around 1% of the total throughput time. The other 99% of the time, the product is sitting waiting (no value to the customer there!) or being moved from one place to another (again, no value to the customer). After doing the exercise and fixing the obvious wastes, you might get the non-value-adding time down to 98%, which doesn't sound like much of an improvement, but it is a 50% reduction in throughput time – and a 50%

reduction in WIP, plus other benefits. None of these benefits show up in the cost file, so you will need the differential analysis template in this book to demonstrate the value!

Cost Driver Modeling

We discussed cost modeling in Chapters 7, 8, & 9 as a way to predict how costs will change with various factors. If we can do that, we can use the same approach to identify the things we can change that will reduce costs. Chapter 8 in particular shows how costs can be associated with "drivers" – activities or choices that actually create elements of cost. Process mapping gets us part of the way there, although we still need to add costs to all of the parts of the process that are not in the cost file. In effect, this is a very detailed activity-based costing model. We must remember though, that the process that <u>creates</u> the product is not the only one creating costs that <u>relate</u> to the product. There are processes for advertising, customer service, warranty claims, etc., all of which can be modeled as the outcome of measurable cost drivers.

Clearly it doesn't make sense to drill down to the ultimate level of detail on every aspect of every product, so this approach is best taken in a more focused manner after a period of exploration to discover the areas of greatest criticality or opportunity. The Anklesaria Group (www.anklesaria.com) has developed this project-based approach, and more to the point, has published a book on the subject[1] that is worth reading if you intend to pursue this kind of formalized approach to cost reduction of current product.

The use of cost drivers integrates well with Value Analysis and Value Stream Mapping. Once identified, drivers can be used in two ways. One is to look for drivers that are responsible for large amounts of cost, or to look for drivers with high coefficients. In either case, small changes to the driver can have large effects on cost. These situations often show the most productive ways to tackle cost.

---

1   Anklesaria, J. (2008). Supply Chain Cost Management: The AIM & DRIVE® Process for Achieving Extraordinary Results. New York, NY, AMACOM.

Chapter 16 – Key Takeaways

1. To change the true cost of a current product or service (as opposed to changing its price), it is necessary to change either the design of the product or the process that produces it.

2. Cost reduction opportunities are not evenly distributed and require search and assessment activities that can be costly in their own right.

3. Several techniques have been developed to discover these opportunities and predict the effects of changes. These include: Value Analysis, Value Stream Mapping, and Cost Driver Modeling.

4. To the extent that cost reduction activities require investment of funds, they must be justified. The TCO template can be used for this purpose.

Supplement 16-1 – Costing a Process Change

Let's take a hypothetical case example. You, (or your supplier), are manufacturing a particular product, with a cost file that looks like Figure 16-1.1 (this is the top-line summary version – in practice it would be broken down more finely, but we don't need that at the moment).

Figure 16-1.1: Product Cost File

Product Cost File	
Direct Costs:	
Net Purchases	$2.00
Direct Labor ($20x5/125)	$0.80
Total Direct Cost	$2.80
Overhead:	
Specific Depreciation	$0.40
General Overhead (@250% of DL)	$2.00
Total Overhead	$2.40
Total Factory Cost:	$5.20
Sales and administrative expenses (10% of Factory Cost)	$0.52
Total Cost:	$5.72
Target profit (10% of total cost)	$0.57
Target Selling Price:	$6.29

There is some important information that is not shown in the cost summary (but should be in the package of records associated with the cost file). For the sake of this example we will assume these key points:

- The product is now entering the third year of a planned six-year lifespan, at which point it is assumed that it will be discontinued and replaced with something completely new.
- Estimated sales are 500,000 units per year and are assumed to be constant for the remaining life. Running two shifts, this is about 125 pieces per hour.

- In the initial process design, $2M was spent on an automated assembly carousel and recorded as a capital investment. Since this investment was unique to the product, it will have no salvage value worth mentioning should it become unnecessary.
- Assume further that this machinery will be depreciated over 10 years on a straight-line basis. As a result, there will be book value at the end of the product life, but no actual value.
- Based on these assumptions, the depreciation charge will be $0.40 per unit produced. As a side note, the pricing decision on this product should have recognized that this depreciation charge is insufficient to recover the full investment, unless the forecast information was different at that time.
- In addition to the automated portion of the assembly (run by one operator), the remaining process steps (final assembly, test, packaging, etc.) are handled by a four-person linear "assembly" line.
- We will assume a cost of capital of 12%, a labor cost of $20/hr. (fully loaded), and an effective tax rate of 35%.

Now, let's consider some cost reduction proposals:

Case 1: Your industrial engineers decide that the four-person, linear assembly line is inefficient and that the work loads are not well balanced. By rebuilding and rearranging the work stations, one person can be eliminated, reducing direct labor by 20%. The rearrangement will cost $100,000 and will be treated as an expense (not capital).

There is a pay-back issue here, albeit a pretty simple one, but we will do a multi-year comparison just to be sure. A couple of questions need to be addressed. First, is the labor reduction real? The surplus person may or may not be laid off, but as long as the person is no longer associated with this product, the answer for our purposes is "yes." Second, is the cost of the rearrangement real? If the cost is for maintenance personnel who are going to be paid regardless and who aren't doing anything else, the answer could be "no." However, unless this is very clear, it is best to assume that by using these personnel for this job, we are forgoing their potential use for other such projects, so we will assume the answer is "yes."

It is quite evident that this is actually a cost reduction, and will pay for itself, but the questions are: how much of an improvement is it, and more importantly (especially if you are the buyer of this product), what should happen to the price? After the change, the cost file would look like Figure 16-1.2, using the standard formulas shown.

Figure 16-1.2: Revised Product Cost File

Revised Product Cost File	
Direct Costs:	
Net Purchases	$2.00
Direct Labor ($20x4/125)	$0.64
Total Direct Cost	$2.64
Overhead:	
Specific Depreciation	$0.40
General Overhead (@250% of DL)	$1.60
Total Overhead	$2.00
Total Factory Cost:	$4.64
Sales and administrative expenses (10% of Factory Cost)	$0.46
Total Cost:	$5.10
Target profit (10% of total cost)	$0.51
Target Selling Price:	$5.61

The buyer in this case would be hoping to see a price reduction to $5.61, conveniently ignoring the cost to implement! Let's dig a little deeper. Because general overhead in this company is calculated on the basis of direct labor, the standard cost will show a 20% reduction from the previous case. Is this real? The answer is, probably not. Nothing about the overall operation is going to change as a result of this modification, not the floor space or utility usage, nor the material handling, nor anything else really.

What should really happen is that accounting should re-calculate the overhead allocation percentage based on the total costs (that didn't change) divided by a reduced number for total labor hours. Then all of the standard costs for all products should be re-calculated. We know this isn't going to happen, so that is why we get what we see here. If it were done the "right" way, there would still be a reduction, but a much smaller one, and the exact amount would require more information than we have here. Alternatively, if the overhead had been calculated using a detailed, activity-based costing methodology, we would probably see that the overhead allocation would hardly change at all, as very little of the firm's overhead is directly caused by labor hours. So, an argument can be made for a variety of numbers for the reduction in overhead cost, ranging from zero up to the amount shown here, and the result is the potential for lively debate between buyer and seller! For this analysis, we will take the conservative view and say that actual overheads will not change.

Similar logic applies to the SG&A line although the situation is a bit different. Most of the front-office expenses are not so much caused by the production activity as they are mandated by management to facilitate the activity. The % allocation is just a way to divide the total cost up among products, even though there may be no direct connection. R&D is a good example – by definition it comes before production, so there is no reason to charge it to a current product, except to make sure that it is recovered when pricing is being established. The actual decision is usually to spend a certain amount on these front-office activities and the allocation percentage follows from that. So, in this case, what should happen is that when the cost base changes, the allocation percentage should be recalculated and a new cost calculated for all products. Again, that's not going to happen, at least not this year. So again, an argument can be made for a cost reduction of any amount from zero up to the amount shown here. From the manufacturer's perspective, the conservative view is that the total amount is not going to change as a result of this action, and that the cost change should be zero.

Then we come to the ever-contentious issue of profit. Should the manufacturer receive a lower absolute amount of profit as a result of making a cost reduction? From the buyer's view, the profit should be reduced by $0.06. Using the seller's point of view, and the standard formula, a reduction of $0.01 is calculated. These may seem like small numbers, but percentage-wise they are quite significant. Since what we call profit is mostly the cost of using the company's assets to perform some economic activity, we can argue that the amount of "activity" has declined a little bit and a small reduction of profit may be in order – probably close to the $0.01 value.

Figure 16-1.3: Re-Revised Cost File

Re-Revised Product Cost File	
Direct Costs:	
Net Purchases	$2.00
Direct Labor ($20x4/125)	$0.64
Total Direct Cost	$2.64
Overhead:	
Specific Depreciation	$0.40
General Overhead (Unchanged)	$2.00
Total Overhead	$2.40
Total Factory Cost:	$5.04
Sales and administrative expenses (unchanged)	$0.52
Total Cost:	$5.56
Target profit (10% of total cost)	$0.56
Target Selling Price:	$6.12

The total effect of these assumptions on the manufacturer's side is shown in Figure 16-1.3, but this does not have any accounting for the cost of the reorganization. For pricing purposes, the manufacturer would want to add in the $100,000 cost divided by the projected remaining product volume of 2,000,000 units, or $0.05/unit. So, the buyer expects a new price of $5.61, and the seller sees $6.17 as the price where it breaks even. What is the right number?

To do a definitive analysis, we will use the differential template as described in Chapter 10. We will define B as the base case (no change) and A as the alternative. All numbers are expressed as A - B, so that a positive NPV will mean that A is better than B by that amount. From Figure 16-1.4 we can see that making this change would represent a positive NPV of $92,942, if the selling price does not change.

Figure 16-1.4: Case #1 Differential Analysis

Case #1 Differential Analysis	Now	Year 1	Year 2	Year 3	Year 4
Change in Net Revenue					
Price Effect	-	-	-	-	-
Volume Effect	-	-	-	-	-
Other Revenue (e.g.: scrap recovery)	-	-	-	-	-
Total	-	-	-	-	-
Changes in Cost of Goods Sold					
Purchased Materials	-	-	-	-	-
Shipping	-	-	-	-	-
Other Items (duties, storage, etc.)	-	-	-	-	-
Net Change in Purchased Goods	-	-	-	-	-
Changes in Direct Labor		(80,000)	(80,000)	(80,000)	(80,000)
Changes in Overhead					
Depreciation	-	-	-	-	-
Other Overhead (rearrangement)	100,000	-	-	-	-
Volume Effect on Variable Overhead	-	-	-	-	-
Sales and administrative expenses	-	-	-	-	-
Total Overheads	100,000	-	-	-	-
Changes in Other Income					
Gain (Loss) on disposal of assets	-	-	-	-	-
Changes in Gross Income	(100,000)	80,000	80,000	80,000	80,000
Change in Taxes (at 35%)	(35,000)	28,000	28,000	28,000	28,000
Changes in Net Income	(65,000)	52,000	52,000	52,000	52,000
Plus Depreciation	-	-	-	-	-
Less Gain (loss) on disposal of assets	-	-	-	-	-
Adjusted Net Income	(65,000)	52,000	52,000	52,000	52,000
Less capital expenditures	-	-	-	-	-
Less Increase in working capital	-	-	-	-	-
Changes to Net Cash Flow	(65,000)	52,000	52,000	52,000	52,000
NPV @12%	$92,942				
IRR	71%				

What we can do with this spreadsheet is use the Excel Goal Seek function to find a revenue reduction that would bring the NPV to zero. This is the point of indifference: if the manufacturer cannot get at least this much revenue, the change is not worth making. The result in Figure 16-1.5 shows that a revenue reduction of $49,354 per year would do this, corresponding to a unit price reduction of $0.10 or a price of $6.19 – $0.02 higher than even the seller might have suggested based on a more simplistic analysis!

Figure 16-1.5: Case #1 Break-Even Analysis

Case #1 Differential Analysis - Breakeven

	Now	Year 1	Year 2	Year 3	Year 4
Change in Net Revenue					
Price Effect	-	(49,354)	(49,354)	(49,354)	(49,354)
Volume Effect	-	-	-	-	-
Other Revenue (e.g.: scrap recovery)	-	-	-	-	-
Total	-	(49,354)	(49,354)	(49,354)	(49,354)
Changes in Cost of Goods Sold					
Purchased Materials	-	-	-	-	-
Shipping	-	-	-	-	-
Other Items (duties, storage, etc.)	-	-	-	-	-
Net Change in Purchased Goods	-	-	-	-	-
Changes in Direct Labor	-	(80,000)	(80,000)	(80,000)	(80,000)
Changes in Overhead					
Depreciation	-	-	-	-	-
Other Overhead (rearrangement)	100,000	-	-	-	-
Volume Effect on Variable Overhead	-	-	-	-	-
Sales and administrative expenses	-	-	-	-	-
Total Overheads	100,000	-	-	-	-
Changes in Other Income					
Gain (Loss) on disposal of assets	-	-	-	-	-
Changes in Gross Income	(100,000)	30,646	30,646	30,646	30,646
Change in Taxes (at 35%)	(35,000)	10,726	10,726	10,726	10,726
Changes in Net Income	(65,000)	19,920	19,920	19,920	19,920
Plus Depreciation	-	-	-	-	-
Less Gain (loss) on disposal of assets	-	-	-	-	-
Adjusted Net Income	(65,000)	19,920	19,920	19,920	19,920
Less capital expenditures	-	-	-	-	-
Less Increase in working capital	(12,339)	-	-	-	12,339
Changes to Net Cash Flow	(52,661)	19,920	19,920	19,920	7,581
NPV @12%	-				
IRR	12%				

Notice that with either price or volume changes, the value of working capital comes into play. We assume that a total revenue reduction of a certain amount means a one-time reduction in accounts receivable of that amount times the payment terms. We also have to add that back in as a residual in the final year when we do differential analysis. Here we assumed payment terms of 90 days (1/4 year). As is often the case, the impact is minimal, but it is an area often overlooked, and may be significant.

Case 2: By some small re-designs, and by buying some of the components pre-assembled, the automated assembly equipment can be retired, and the operator can be eliminated. Some of the processing steps that were previously automated can be added to the four-person line, making it more balanced and not requiring additional labor. As a result, there will be an increase in purchased parts cost of $0.25 per unit and 20% reduction in direct labor.

Figure 16-1.6: Case #2 Revised Product Cost File

Case #2: Revised Product Cost File	
Direct Costs:	
Net Purchases	$2.25
Direct Labor ($20x4/125)	$0.64
Total Direct Cost	$2.89
Overhead:	
Specific Depreciation	$0.00
General Overhead (@250% of DL)	$1.60
Total Overhead	$1.60
Total Factory Cost:	$4.49
Sales and administrative expenses (10% of Factory Cost)	$0.45
Total Cost:	$4.94
Target profit (10% of total cost)	$0.49
Target Selling Price:	$5.43

The revised cost file is shown in Figure 16-1.6. In this case, some of the reduction in general overhead may be real, but probably not as much as calculated by the standard formula. We can make the same arguments about SG&A and Profit that we discussed in Case 1. Using the standard rates, if this change were implemented, the buyer would expect a price of $5.43 – a significant reduction.

As you might expect by now, a thorough differential analysis shows another picture. Figure 16-1.7 shows that this change has a positive NPV of about $247,000, provided that the price does not change. Notice that because of the price increase on purchased parts, there is an increase in accounts payable, and in value of inventory, both representing an increase in working capital. To do an accurate calculation, we would need to know not only the payment terms, but also the inventory turns on components and on finished goods. Since the impact is likely to be minimal in this sort of business, we will just use the same assumption (90 days of cash flow) as we did in Case #1. Note also that this is one of those cases where the distribution of cash flows over time makes the IRR calculation meaningless. Using the same technique as in Case #1, Figure 16-1.8 shows that a price decrease of $0.26 ($131,244/500,000) to $6.03 would make this change neutral to the seller. This analysis may not be what the buyer wants to see, but it is invaluable to the seller for negotiating prices, and also for internal purposes in trying to justify a cost-reduction exercise.

Figure 16-1.7: Case #2 Differential Analysis

Case #2 Differential Analysis

	Now	Year 1	Year 2	Year 3	Year 4
Change in Net Revenue					
Price Effect	-	-	-	-	-
Volume Effect	-	-	-	-	-
Other Revenue (e.g.: scrap recovery)	-	-	-	-	-
Total	-	-	-	-	-
Changes in Cost of Goods Sold					
Purchased Materials	-	125,000	125,000	125,000	125,000
Shipping	-	-	-	-	-
Other Items (duties, storage, etc.)	-	-	-	-	-
Net Change in Purchased Goods	-	125,000	125,000	125,000	125,000
Changes in Direct Labor		(80,000)	(80,000)	(80,000)	(80,000)
Changes in Overhead					
Depreciation	-	(200,000)	(200,000)	(200,000)	(200,000)
Other Overhead (rearrangement)	-	-	-	-	-
Volume Effect on Variable Overhead	-	-	-	-	-
Sales and administrative expenses	-	-	-	-	-
Total Overheads	-	(200,000)	(200,000)	(200,000)	(200,000)
Changes in Other Income					
Gain (Loss) on disposal of assets	(1,600,000)	-	-	-	-
Changes in Gross Income	(1,600,000)	155,000	155,000	155,000	155,000
Change in Taxes (at 35%)	(560,000)	54,250	54,250	54,250	54,250
Changes in Net Income	(1,040,000)	100,750	100,750	100,750	100,750
Plus Depreciation	-	(200,000)	(200,000)	(200,000)	(200,000)
Less Gain (loss) on disposal of assets	(1,600,000)	-	-	-	-
Adjusted Net Income	560,000	(99,250)	(99,250)	(99,250)	(99,250)
Less capital expenditures	-	-	-	-	-
Less Increase in working capital	31,250	-	-	-	(31,250)
Changes to Net Cash Flow	528,750	(99,250)	(99,250)	(99,250)	(68,000)
NPV @12%	$247,153				
IRR	-13.9%				

Figure 16-1.8: Case #2 Break-Even Analysis

Case #2 Differential Analysis - Breakeven

	Now	Year 1	Year 2	Year 3	Year 4
Change in Net Revenue					
Price Effect		(131,244)	(131,244)	(131,244)	(131,244)
Volume Effect		-	-	-	-
Other Revenue (e.g.: scrap recovery)		-	-	-	-
Total		(131,244)	(131,244)	(131,244)	(131,244)
Changes in Cost of Goods Sold					
Purchased Materials		125,000	125,000	125,000	125,000
Shipping					
Other Items (duties, storage, etc.)					
Net Change in Purchased Goods		125,000	125,000	125,000	125,000
Changes in Direct Labor		(80,000)	(80,000)	(80,000)	(80,000)
Changes in Overhead					
Depreciation		(200,000)	(200,000)	(200,000)	(200,000)
Other Overhead (rearrangement)		-	-	-	-
Volume Effect on Variable Overhead		-	-	-	-
Sales and administrative expenses		-	-	-	-
Total Overheads		(200,000)	(200,000)	(200,000)	(200,000)
Changes in Other Income					
Gain (Loss) on disposal of assets	(1,600,000)	-	-	-	-
Changes in Gross Income	(1,600,000)	23,756	23,756	23,756	23,756
Change in Taxes (at 35%)	(560,000)	8,315	8,315	8,315	8,315
Changes in Net Income	(1,040,000)	15,441	15,441	15,441	15,441
Plus Depreciation	-	(200,000)	(200,000)	(200,000)	(200,000)
Less Gain (loss) on disposal of assets	(1,600,000)	-	-	-	-
Adjusted Net Income	560,000	(184,559)	(184,559)	(184,559)	(184,559)
Less capital expenditures	-	-	-	-	-
Less Increase in working capital	(1,561)	-	-	-	1,561
Changes to Net Cash Flow	561,561	(184,559)	(184,559)	(184,559)	(186,120)
NPV @12%	$0.00				
IRR	12.0%				

Chapter 17 – Supplier Relationship Management

If we were to extend our process mapping exercise all the way back to raw materials, we would discover that the majority of the cost-creating activities occur at our suppliers or their sub-suppliers. To be clear, these costs are not just the costs of value-adding activities, they include the non-value-adding activities and waste too. Even if the prices at which goods transfer from one company to another are market-tested, that doesn't mean that there isn't room for improvement; primarily through the reduction of waste. Our level of interest may vary depending on our contract terms, but it is always true that we have a vested interest in reducing costs anywhere in our supply chain. Even if we are buying on a fixed-price contract, it is better for us to have a profitable supplier than an unprofitable one, plus we might be able to negotiate a better deal in the future.

We can exert pressure on these upstream costs through the typical purchasing tools of competitive bidding and aggressive negotiation based on cost modeling, as these will create pressure on our suppliers to actively pursue cost reductions. Not only is this process more confrontational than it needs to be, it tends to exclude cost reduction opportunities that span the buyer-supplier interface. Something as simple as changing some of our ordering practices might result in useful cost savings at the supplier, but this is unlikely to come up unless there is a joint willingness to explore them and to make the appropriate price adjustments. This suggests two key points, a) there are aspects of the relationship between the parties that can be managed for mutual benefit, and b) the ability to have mature, honest and well-informed discussions about costs and prices is an important enabler of this. The majority of this book has been devoted to being well-informed about costs and their impacts, but in this chapter, we want to discuss the more relational aspects of this discussion.

Strategic Supplier Relationship Management

The term Supplier Relationship Management (SRM) would seem to cover this nicely, but just like many other terms, it means different things to different people. If we look at textbook treatment of the term, we find two trends. One is that SRM is primarily an information systems issue: the ability to access all information related to transactions with all suppliers and the ability of those suppliers to access the information they need to perform. This is clearly valuable if you are trying to manage a relationship, but it doesn't address your reasons for doing so. A second theme that we find revolves around the relationship with a specific supplier, and describes how firms might go about creating deeper and stronger relationships – with the implication that this is how business should evolve. We will take a more pragmatic view and look at the types of relationships that we want to have in different situations and how to manage them.

We have already introduced the Strategic Sourcing, or Kraljic Matrix (supplement to Chapter 14, and reproduced here as Figure 17.1) where we used it as a guideline for designing products that can be sourced effectively. Now we will look in other direction, and say, "given that we have a product in this quadrant, what sort of relationships do we want to cultivate with suppliers?" In Chapter 14, we pointed out the major limitation of this matrix, which is that it is a one-sided view that doesn't take into account how suppliers see us. We could draw the corresponding matrix from the suppliers' viewpoint, where the axes would be the number of available customers (high to low) and the profit impact of the product in question. What we find when we do this is that for anything beyond a purely transactional relationship to exist, there needs to be a symmetry of interests between the parties.

Figure 17.1: Strategic Sourcing Matrix

Kraljic Matrix

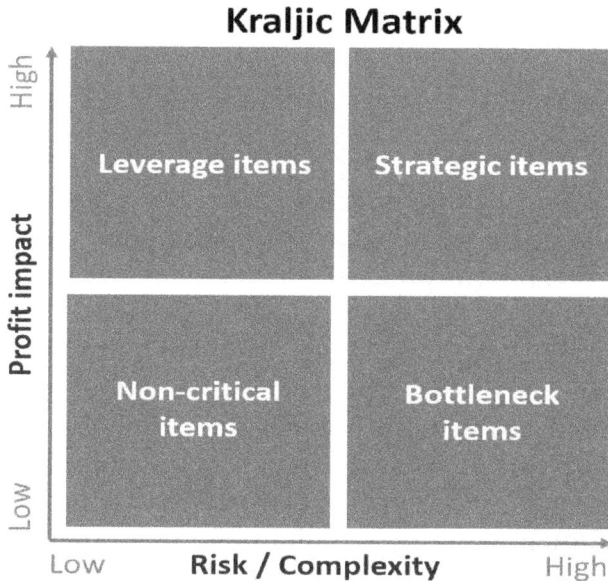

Taking the matrix quadrant by quadrant, let's start with the top left where we have many potential suppliers to choose from. This implies a commodity-type product, and it is in our best interests to let market forces set the price. Since these products also represent a large share of our spend, we need to be quite ruthless about pricing – as soon as another supplier offers a lower price, we switch. In these circumstances, we have no interest in cultivating a relationship with any particular supplier because we wouldn't get any benefit from it. If we are but one of many customers, the suppliers will feel the same way about us – as soon as another customer offers a better price, they are gone. However, if we are one of only a few potential customers, the suppliers will see us differently, and many of them will be clamoring to establish some kind of "relationship" with us. Since there is no symmetry of interest, we are unlikely to respond to that.

Moving to the lower-left quadrant, we are still dealing with commodity-type products, but ones that don't represent a great deal of cost to us, so we can't afford to be constantly shopping around for a better deal. In this case it might benefit us to establish some sort of relationship with a supplier, mostly for convenience in purchasing, as long as there is a mechanism to ensure that pricing remains more or less competitive. Again, unless we are one of only a few potential customers (unlikely), the supplier will have little interest in any kind of special relationship. We may call it a relationship, but mostly it will just consist of a negotiated trade discount.

We have already suggested that the lower-right quadrant is one to avoid during the design process if possible. The pitfalls are obvious, a unique product with few potential suppliers and not enough money involved to get their interest. Here, some sort of established relationship with one of those suppliers could be an asset to us, if only for assurance of stable supply. Whether this can work or not will depend on the perspective of those suppliers. Most likely, if the spend is small by our standards, it will be by theirs too, and they will regard us as more of a nuisance than a profitable source of business. No kind of collaborative relationship is likely to emerge in that situation. The exception may be if some of the suppliers are small enough that the amounts involved are significant to them. In that case, one of them *may* be interested in some sort of collaborative effort. The emphasis is on 'may' here, because these are usually evolving situations where it is not clear which customer is going to emerge as the leader, and suppliers would be unwise to commit themselves to any particular one too soon. So, while we would like to cultivate collaborative relationships with suppliers of products in this quadrant, we are unlikely to be successful.

Finally, we arrive at the top-right quadrant where opportunities for relationships are more likely to be found. Products purchased in this quadrant are important for two reasons. The first, obviously, is that they represent a significant share of your spend, but the second and more important reason is that these are the products that will differentiate your final product from your competitors. In all the other quadrants, the battle is to maintain parity, but here there is the opportunity to be unique. As always, there must be symmetry of interests; if the field of potential buyers is similarly small, then it is likely that buyers and suppliers will be jockeying to form strategic pairings, for which collaborative relationships are a requirement. This is not a given, though, so you must understand the competitive landscape – it may be that certain suppliers take the position that the buyers are all competing for the same market and whoever wins will have to come to them eventually, so there is no need to give away anything upfront.

Where collaborative relationships are possible, there are two things we want from a cost management perspective. One is concurrent engineering on new product development as discussed in Chapter 15, and the other is a joint commitment to pursuing ongoing cost-reduction activities for mutual benefit. The mutual benefit aspect is vital, but also very difficult to sustain; once a product is in series production, it is too easy to revert to a zero-sum mentality where each party tries to capture as much benefit for itself as possible. Executive level commitment is a necessary ingredient for this to work, and so is the sharing of much information that most companies consider to be sensitive or proprietary. To do the sort of cost analysis illustrated in Chapter 16, and to use it as a basis for a price adjustment, both parties must be confident that they are working with the same, true numbers. This state is referred to as open-books accounting, and is not a normal state of affairs in B2B transactions.

While open-books accounting opens up many opportunities for win-win initiatives, several hurdles must be overcome. One is confidentiality; both parties must have confidence that any shared data will not be leaked to third parties. There is also the potential for opportunism – once information is shared, it cannot be taken back, so if one party takes advantage of new information to renege on a prior agreement, recourse is limited. Finally, there is moral hazard – the partners do not possess the same information and while the sharing of information is supposed to overcome this, there is always the temptation to omit or misstate certain data points. Much scholarly work in business and economics has been done to discover how these hurdles can be overcome, and much of this work relies on something called trust. While we have a good sense of what trust means between individuals, it is not so clear what it means in a corporate context. For our purposes it is more useful to talk about trustworthiness.

Trustworthiness covers the data that is transmitted, and the actions taken on the basis of data received. We have emphasized earlier that the cost of capital – the cost of committing assets – is dependent on the level of risk involved. When a supplier acts – meaning: commits assets – on the basis of data received from you, there is normal business risk involved that the data may not be accurate or that forecasts may be wrong, and that is ultimately factored into pricing. If there is suspicion that you are being less than fully honest[1] about the data provided, this increases the risk level, so your un-trustworthiness effectively adds to the supplier's cost, and ultimately to your own cost. In practice, suppliers don't recalculate their cost of capital in these situations, they just discount your projections or add margin for error, but the result is the same: you will pay more. The same logic applies to the supplier's perception of how you will act on the basis of new information. If you have an agreement with the supplier that you will jointly seek cost reductions and that the benefits will be shared[2] (usually 50/50), the results will depend on the extent to which the other party trusts you to hold up your end of the deal. Absent that trust, the supplier may conceal cost-reduction opportunities in an attempt to keep all of the value for itself. You may see some cost reductions, but you will still be paying more than you should.

The lesson in all this is that, in the situations where it is beneficial to you to have a collaborative relationship with a supplier, it is in your long-term best interest to be seen as trustworthy. This can be difficult to maintain, as there is always the temptation of short-term, opportunistic gains, and because the benefits of trustworthiness are largely invisible

1   This is the *moral hazard* issue, the state where you possess information that your trading partner does not, and where it may be in your best interests not to disclose the truth. An over-optimistic sales forecast is one of the more obvious examples.

2   If you do have such an agreement, it is critical that you define benefits and sharing. As shown in the supplement to Chapter 16, these can be calculated in multiple ways. Our recommendation is that you base it on a full business case using the differential template. You can then specify that the price adjustment should be half-way between the current price and the price at which the supplier sees an NPV of zero.

to our accounting systems. Assuming that you want to be seen as trustworthy, there are some things you can do that will enhance that. If you can show your supplier that the data you are sharing is actually the same data that you are using internally, it can remove the moral hazard premium, to your benefit. With modern information systems, it is feasible to give suppliers access to the relevant internal data so that they not only trust it, but are kept updated in real time. Showing trustworthiness in your actions is more difficult, but can be accomplished by what are called *weak commitments*[1]. This means that you take certain actions that create penalties for yourself should you deviate from collaborative behavior. There are many ways to do this; for example, you could terminate a relationship with a competing supplier, thereby making it more expensive for yourself should you need to go back to them. The commitments need to be weak as opposed to total so that if your supplier behaves inappropriately, you have a realistic option to disengage. Cost management through relationship management is something that can't really be undertaken at ground level; it is a high-level strategic initiative and has to be approached and treated that way.

Supplier Development

In our context, the term *Supplier Development* means taking actions and committing resources to help our suppliers get better at what they do. This may involve their production processes as we have been describing in some detail, but it may include other things such as helping them to upgrade their information systems to be better able to work with us. Ideally, such efforts would take place in the presence of a formal agreement about what will happen with the results and what will change in pricing, if relevant. However, it can also be beneficial without such agreements – effectively gifting the supplier with resources. This goes against the grain for many companies as it seems like spending money to improve supplier profits, but many companies can be seen offering free consulting to their suppliers, and free access

1　This approach to establishing trustworthiness is explored in more detail in: Hanson, J. D. and J. Henkel (2020). "Collaborative Innovation: Weak Commitments and Unenforceable Contracts." International Journal of Procurement Management 13(1): 63-82.

to internal training resources as well. This works best in larger corporations that have central training and process improvement staff – effectively, internal consultants who can just as easily be deployed to assist suppliers as operating divisions.

It takes a leap of faith and commitment from higher levels to implement supplier development on a large scale like this, but it can also be done with a more informal, grass-roots approach. Usually, the trigger is a quality issue, and most companies have Supplier Quality Assurance (SQA) personnel who will go out to look at the problem and assist with solutions. If a process redesign is required, process experts from the buyer's side may be deputized to a special project to help with this. If a there is a cost reduction as a result, there may be no formal contract about what that means, but the buyer will know about it, and it will likely come up during the next round of pricing discussions. Funding and justifying such projects can be difficult, particularly since you don't know in advance how much cost reduction, if any, you are likely to achieve. The best way to think about it is the same way that we treat R&D: recognize it as a worthwhile, even necessary, activity and establish a budget for it. Normally this budget item would be under the Purchasing function which would be responsible for targeting it at the most promising opportunities.

Reverse Marketing

It is sometimes the case that the available supply base is too small for you to find a cooperative supplier or to establish competitive pricing. In extreme cases, it may be that no one is willing to supply what you need. This was a fairly common occurrence in Eastern-Bloc countries with planned economies, so manufacturers became adept at *reverse marketing* – persuading somebody to sell to you as opposed to persuading somebody to buy from you. To do reverse marketing you need to identify the *capabilities* that are required to deliver what you want. Depending on your strategy with respect to specifications (Chapter 14), those capabilities may involve manufacturing processes or design abilities, or both. You probably won't find any companies that have all of them, otherwise you would have a supplier.

The first place you should look for new suppliers is in your own existing supply base, as you know that many of the requirements are already met. Typically, the target suppliers will be those who don't currently make or do what you want, but could if they were given some encouragement such as the promise of a long-term contract. Another approach is to identify which set of capabilities you are best equipped to assist with in a supplier development mode. If you can then identify target companies that are lacking only those, you can propose new business opportunities to them. A common example of this would be a company that makes something very close to what you want, but for a different industry. It may be unwilling to deal with you because it doesn't understand the particular requirements of your market. Since you do, that is something you could offer to help with.

An alternative to persuading existing companies to sell to you is to start or enable the startup of a new company. You can actually start a new company yourself, with the option of divesting it when it becomes viable or keeping it. You may find entrepreneurial employees in your own organization who would seize the opportunity to run their own business. Many cities and universities have start-up incubators where you may find someone with the right sort of capabilities, needing only a viable commercial contract to get started. This is also an excellent opportunity to develop an SWMB (small, minority or women-owned business) supplier. If your company has contract requirements for such sources, this can provide an important competitive advantage, and corporate funding is often available to support the development.

These discussions are leading us away from our principal focus on cost management and into the broader field of supply management, so we need to bring it back into scope. The main point is this: in non-commodity situations, there is value to be gained by establishing and using collaborative relationships with suppliers. That value comes from improving the entire process as it spans company boundaries. These improvements may show up as price reductions, or they may not. Sometimes they will appear as price increases, albeit offset by cost reductions elsewhere. A thorough business case analysis as outlined in Chapter 10 may be needed to demonstrate the benefit – and to establish the basis for any re-negotiations of price.

Chapter 17 – Key Takeaways

1. Most of your costs are incurred by your suppliers, either through their activities or by their assumption of risks that you pass on.

2. Anything you can do to help suppliers reduce those costs will be beneficial to you, directly or indirectly. This is primarily true in non-commodity items where there is no market price.

3. Helping suppliers identify and implement cost reductions requires access to much confidential information that is not typically shared. In these situations, it is in the buyer's long-term best interests to be seen as a trustworthy partner, and there are mechanisms that can reinforce this.

4. For best results, cost reduction must be a system-level analysis, not specific to a single company. The negotiation on the sharing of benefits is a separate discussion, and can be facilitated by the type of analysis presented in Chapter 10.

Part IV Introduction

To this point in our discussion of cost management, we have treated cost as an objective, deterministic measure of what we give up in exchange for whatever it is we want to do. Granted, there are differences of opinion about the assumptions that need to be made, but these are at least quantifiable. We have also acknowledged that there is uncertainty, especially about costs in the future, and we have made the point throughout that uncertainty creates cost. The mechanism for this is through the effective cost of capital, implying that uncertainty can be priced in a market.

For our purposes, this is not always feasible – in fact, rarely so – so we need to be able to evaluate the costs of different scenarios in a probabilistic manner. This does three important things; a) it introduces subjectivity into the discussion in the form of utility and risk aversion, b) it allows us to consider the use of options, specifically real options, to maximize our position in an uncertain world, and, c) it forces us to rethink our concept of profit and how it should be evaluated. These are covered in the final chapters as we explore the subjective side of cost management.

Chapter 18 – Dealing With Uncertainty

It is a fact of life that when you operate a business, you put assets at risk. The returns that you make on those assets are not perfectly predictable, and the more unpredictable they are, the higher average returns investors are going to want as compensation. These risk premiums are priced in a market (the stock market), resulting in an effective cost of capital for any particular firm. The market may decide, for example, that a firm operating in a consumer-packaged goods market needs to generate a return some percentage above the current risk-free rate, and may make additional adjustments based on the specific firm's quality of management, or other attributes. For these reasons, we have used a cost of capital figure as a discount rate throughout when dealing with any cost situation that has a time component to it. Exactly what figure to use can be a matter for debate, and we have made the point that the true cost of capital depends not on where it came from, but how it is going to be used. For routine cost reduction exercises that are consistent with the company's overall business profile, there would seem to be little reason to use anything other than the company's market cost of capital, that can be inferred from stock price activity[1].

Unfortunately, this is not usually how it works. In most companies, capital is treated as a scarce resource, meaning that it should be allocated to its most productive use. Some of the projects competing for capital will be new product or business ventures that are inherently riskier than business-as-usual, and therefore must promise rates of return substantially higher than the base rate. As a result, companies tend to have a "hurdle rate" that all capital projects must exceed to be funded. This hurdle rate will obviously be higher than the market cost of capital. This is not really the right way to think about it – different projects should have different hurdle rates based on their nature, and the money should go to those that yield the highest premium over those

---

1   If the company is not publicly traded, a reasonable proxy would be to identify a company or companies with similar business profiles that are publicly traded, and use that value.

rates. Feel free to make that argument if it supports your case, but be prepared to use the going rate!

Many of our cost reduction efforts will not involve capital (per the accounting definition of the term), so any changes in expenditures, up or down, will show up in different budgets and will not be subject to the same constraints as capital. That doesn't mean that there won't be budgetary constraints, but the evaluation will be a bit different. Here, the argument for using the baseline cost of capital is even stronger, but may still be countered by any sense of risk in the initiative. You are still subject to general business risk, but one of the great advantages of differential analysis is that most of these cancel out. The commonest place where it won't cancel out is when you make changes to the split of fixed versus variable costs. You may add fixed costs (such as automation) to reduce per unit costs, but at the cost of increased sensitivity to future fluctuations in demand. Clearly, this increases the riskiness of the business and deserves a higher discount rate – but how much? Again, the commonest approach is to simply insert an arbitrary hurdle rate that feels comfortably above the baseline. This sort of works, but there are better ways to think about it.

Risk Sensitivity

Up to this point, we have presented the result of a cost comparison analysis as a single figure, typically the NPV. If there is no uncertainty in any of the differential data, this is just fine. However, if there is any uncertainty in the relevant costs (the ones that change), then this figure will only be the expected value of a probability distribution. To be interpreted meaningfully, it must be accompanied by additional information, typically its standard deviation. Similar information can also be conveyed by giving upper and lower bounds of the 95% confidence interval. Suppose, for example, we did a thorough differential analysis of a proposed process change and determined that the NPV of the change was $1M at whatever discount rate you were required to use. If the change does not introduce any uncertainty, then this number is the whole story and the company will be $1M better off by doing it. Now suppose there is some uncertainty – it may not be guaranteed that the process change will work as well as planned, or there may be an increase in exposure to fixed costs as mentioned above. Through analysis (simulation is the preferred tool for this kind of analysis), you determine that the NPV value has a standard deviation of $0.75M. The expected value is still $1M, but now there is approximately a 9% chance ($z = -1.33$) that the change will actually be worse than the present state. Do you still want to do it?

There is no correct answer to this question; the decision depends entirely on the level of risk aversion of the company and the actual decision-maker. Most companies are at least a little bit risk averse, so the answer is not automatic. Notice also the role of individual decision-makers. Some may be very risk-averse, feeling that they will be the ones to shoulder the blame if things turn out badly, while others may seek out risky options with large upside potential in the hopes that they will advance their careers with a big win. Ideally a company perspective will override any individual biases, but there is still no single, right answer. If this project is a one-of-a-kind deal, and if a negative outcome could be very damaging, then the company should be quite risk-averse, and the 9% figure may be enough to stop the deal. However, if the company makes hundreds of such decisions every year and no one bad outcome would be too serious, then the company should be more risk-neutral and accept projects right up to the 50-50 win/lose point.

Risk Pooling

The latter case illustrates the concept of risk-pooling – one of the key strategic-level cost management tools. Figure 18.1 shows the basic principle. Suppose you have fluctuating demand from one customer. To maintain an agreed service level, you have to have surplus capacity or inventory, and the more volatile the demand, the more you will need. This obviously has a cost. Now suppose you have three customers, all with equal volatility of demand, but uncorrelated with each other[1]. If we add the three streams of demand together, we can see that even with only three customers, the overall volatility is noticeably reduced. This means that we need a smaller percentage of surplus capacity or inventory than we would for one customer – so the average cost is reduced. The effect is greater as more customers are added to the mix, with the standard deviation decreasing as 1 over the square root of n, where n is the number of customers.

Figure 18.1: Risk Pooling

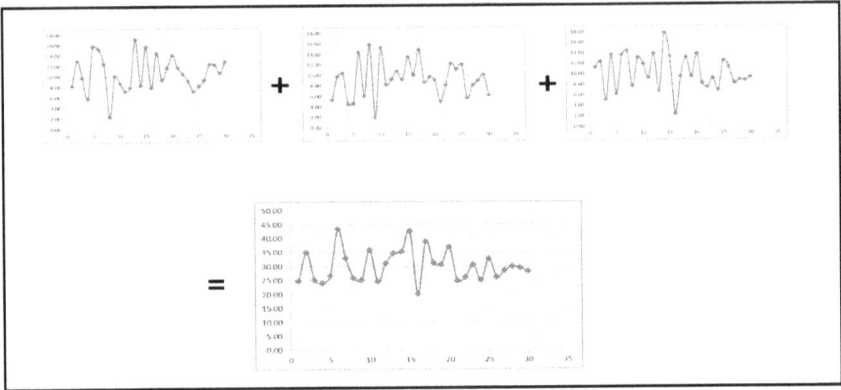

Risk pooling is an important cost management tool and can be deployed in several ways. Many applications of risk pooling are not strictly product-specific, so they tend to get overlooked and require a more strategic overview. One simple way to take advantage of risk pooling is centralization of inventory. There are costs associated with doing this, so you have to run the numbers, but the fewer places you store inventory, the less total safety stock you have to carry to maintain a given service level. A similar effect is achieved by modularization and standardization of parts. The more common content you have across your product line, the less capacity or inventory you will need. Careful analysis is required as the benefits may not show up on a single product analysis. As with all strategies to reduce the cost of risk, the benefits are greatest when the uncertainty is large.

1   This uncorrelated requirement is very important. In the example from the previous paragraph, if the company were making hundreds of small cost reduction decisions, but all of them dealt with exposure to the same fluctuating customer demand, then the variances would be highly correlated and there would be no reduction in risk through pooling.

Another less obvious way to pool risks is through outsourcing. If you make a part for your own use, your demand looks like one of the customers in Figure 18.1. If you outsource the part to a generalist supplier that serves multiple customers and industries, that supplier's demand profile looks like the combined curve, or even better if there are more customers. As a result, even if everything else is equal, the supplier's costs will be lower than yours, and you should be able to pay a lower price than what it would *really* cost you to do it yourself, although that real cost may not be immediately obvious from the accounting figures.

Make vs. Buy

The outsourcing scenario gives us an opportunity to address some issues that are often raised in the course of a make-versus-buy decision, and ultimately, to re-think what it is that we call profit. In the all-else-being-equal case, you have probably heard the argument: "we should make it ourselves – that way we only have to bear the actual costs and we won't have to pay the supplier's profit."

Let's examine that argument, particularly the part about profit. If you have been with us since the beginning, you will know that the majority of what the accountants call profit is actually the cost (market price) of dedicating and putting assets at risk to achieve some purpose. When we pay a supplier a price that includes a profit, we are paying it to commit those assets and to shield us from the risks associated with that business. The supplier's profit is our cost to have that risk taken off our hands.

Now consider what happens when we make it ourselves. First, it increases our asset base – and by assets, we mean not just capitalized assets, but all the resources we have tied up in inventory, wages, etc. Also, because our demand is not pooled at all, we will have to invest in more capacity or inventory than the supplier would. All of that drives our real (economic) profit down. Granted, our net accounting costs (incremental internal costs minus the purchase price) may go down too, but unless our cost of capital is less than the supplier's (doubtful), or we are a more proficient manufacturer than the supplier (even more doubtful), and assuming that we were buying at a competitive price in the first place, we will still see a net loss of economic profit. The accounting records may show a different picture, but a detailed differential analysis will tell the truth.

Transfer Pricing

Similar logic comes into play when we discuss transfer pricing, which is why it is covered in this chapter. When a company receives products or services from another closely-affiliated company, most parent organizations have policies that determine how the two companies record costs and revenues – what we call transfer pricing. In some corporations, this is an arm's-length policy: the selling company is free to charge whatever it wants, and the buying company is free to buy elsewhere if it can find a better deal. This means that if the transfer takes place, it will be at something close to a market price. The managerial accounting literature tells us that this gives us the best blend of performance incentives and operational efficiency. This is a perfectly acceptable way to operate, but may not work in many situations.

The most obvious exception is where it is decided, for reasons of either strategy or expedience, that the in-house supplier will be the supplier, period. This pretty much eliminates the ability to use market forces to set a price, and also messes up the incentives for the respective managers if they were to attempt to negotiate a price, so some sort of formula must be used. In Chapter 12 we showed how to generate a "right" price in the absence of a direct market test, and the same approach applies here. Ultimately it comes down to some sort of cost-plus calculation. As with any supplier, the costs should be scrutinized, not only to be sure that they are real, but also that they are close to where they should be. The "plus" part is typically determined by industry averages (the seller's industry) and the degree of capital intensity involved. Needless to say, both parts can be contentious. Buying managers often have difficulty understanding why there should be any "plus" at all, but once we understand that most of the apparent profit is just the cost of using assets, this should be easier to explain. However, the buying manager might reasonably argue that because the business is guaranteed, it is less risky than the supplier's other accounts, and a lower markup would be appropriate.

There is a situation in which formula-based transfer pricing can be detrimental to the company as a whole, and that is where the selling division has some competitive advantage and is able to produce the item at significantly less cost than any potential competitor. This is not as common as selling divisions like to think, but it can happen! In this case, using a cost-plus formula would have two undesirable consequences. It would fail to reward the selling division for good performance, and it would distort the buying division's calculation of cost. As a result of the latter, the buying division would likely underprice its products in the market, and would feel less pressure to reduce its own costs.

Another situation where a transfer price calculation can be tricky is when the company that is doing the buying is, itself, selling product in a situation where the price is being determined by cost analysis. From a corporate perspective, there is an obvious temptation to set a high transfer price in an attempt to persuade to ultimate customer to pay a higher price. The final customer will naturally suspect this and will want to scrutinize the transfer price closely; particularly the "plus" part. This may lead to some negotiation, so it is helpful to document clearly why you are using the formula you do.

Transfer prices can also be used to minimize taxes, at least when the companies involved operate in different tax jurisdictions. The more that costs can be transferred to the higher-tax location, and that profit is transferred to the lower-tax location, the lower the total tax bill will be. Companies have been known to set up dummy corporations to reap the profit in low-tax regions to take advantage of this. Ethical issues aside, governments are well aware of this dodge, and will in many cases have rules about what is allowable for transfer pricing. The interplay between these interests may result in a transfer pricing policy that does not conform to the ideal described above. In such cases, the tax amounts paid are real costs, but the actual transfer price may not be, and it is important to recognize this for decision-making purposes.

Hedging

Companies, like people, don't like uncertainty. Under the heading Risk Sensitivity, we explained how a company, faced with decision alternatives with equal expected values, would normally prefer the one with the lowest variance. In fact, most companies would pay some premium to reduce variance. In other words, a firm might prefer an alternative that has a lower expected value, but also a lower variance. If you are faced with a business situation that is attractive in general, but subject to more risk than you would like, one way to manage this is through hedging.

Hedging works in much the same way as an insurance policy. As an example, when I own a house, I am taking on certain risks, including the small, but not zero, risk that it might burn down. I can self-insure, but if I don't care to assume that risk, I can pay someone else to assume it for me by buying an insurance policy at a set price. In effect I am switching risk distributions to one that has a higher expected value of cost, but a much lower variance. The risk-pooling effect discussed above allows the insurance company to assume my risk at a comparatively lower cost than mine.

We can do similar things in business, and we can do it through financial instruments or through operational choices. Financial hedging is somewhat out of scope for this book, but operational hedges are very much in scope. There is interplay between the two, so we will begin with a brief overview of the financial approaches. The commonest form of financial hedging is the buying and selling of futures. A future is a contract between a buyer and a seller that they will transact a certain exchange, at an agreed price, at some point in the future. If I buy a future in, say copper, I am agreeing with a seller that I will take delivery of a certain quantity at a specified price at a given future date[1]. The advantage to both parties is that we know with certainty what our future costs and revenues will be. Future contracts of this type are commonly traded in a market, so there are transaction costs involved, and the long-run expected value to both parties is somewhat lower than it would be for market price transactions, but the reduction in uncertainty may make it the more attractive option.

The transactions for which there is a futures market are primarily in known commodities; oil and coffee being two of the most actively traded ones. Another important class of futures contracts is national currencies. This can be important if you are transacting in a foreign currency, for which future exchange rates are uncertain. Whether you are buying or selling, this introduces uncertainty into your costs or revenues, and you may be willing to pay a premium to reduce or eliminate it. Either way, it is possible to buy or sell futures in the currency of interest, accepting the transaction cost penalty to reduce uncertainty. On the buying side, the commonest way to "hedge" currency risk is to insist that the seller quote you a firm price in your own currency. This is an invisible hedge that transfers the uncertainty to the supplier and has no visible transaction cost. However, this increases the supplier's costs, and these must ultimately be recovered in the price it charges you. So, one way or another, the cost of the risk winds up in your lap. Whether this is an intelligent way to handle exchange rate risk or not depends on the situation. If the seller is a multi-national corporation or trading company that processes transactions in all the world's currencies on a daily basis, then the risk-pooling effect will make it the low-cost choice. On the other hand, if the seller is none of the above and doesn't often deal with foreign currencies, the exchange rate risk would come at a high cost. In such a case, the risk is better borne by the buyer, and can be hedged on the futures market, if necessary.

---

1   Many individuals and firms will buy futures with no intention of ever receiving the goods; their intent is to resell the contract at a higher price before it comes due. This form of market speculation is beyond the scope of this discussion.

The above are examples of financial hedges, but it is also possible to hedge costs through operational decisions. The most obvious example is the use of inventory. If you are buying a commodity with a fluctuating market price, you can choose to buy more when the price is low and less when it is high. To do this, you need to increase your inventory level above what you would normally choose. Your excess inventory becomes your hedge against fluctuating prices. There are many other ways to construct operational hedges, some of which belong more properly in the discussion of real options (below). A key point about operational hedges is to make sure that the left hand is talking to the right hand – meaning that you shouldn't make decisions about financial and operational hedges independently of each other.

The bottom line on this discussion is that there is no universally correct answer as to whether you should hedge your risks or not. Simulation models can help to inform the discussion, but ultimately it comes down to how averse you are to risk and how much you are willing to pay for its reduction.

Real Options

Making decisions in the face of uncertainty is not a passive game; you don't necessarily commit to a particular choice forever. Many times, you would like to change your mind at some point, but the initial decision may have left you with more or fewer options. The key point to note here is that when there is uncertainty, the option to make a change always has some positive value, which is why changeable airline tickets cost more than non-changeable ones. The option value may be small or large depending on the situation, but if we are comparing costs of different decision alternatives, we need to take that value into account. As with any situation involving uncertainty, calculating precise numbers is difficult, but some useful approximations can be made.

Many readers will have at least a passing familiarity with the basic financial options. These are based on *puts* and *calls*. A call is the option, but not the obligation, to buy something at a future date at an agreed price. A put is the reverse, the option to sell something at an agreed price at a future date. Since financial options involve buying or selling well-defined assets such as company shares, analyzing their value is reasonably straightforward, although not simple. The best-known analytical solution for the value of a call option is the Black-Scholes formula, which basically finds the probability that the option will be "in the money" at exercise time and multiplies this by the expected value of its worth if it is exercised. All of this is discounted back to the present period. At least, that is the simple explanation! Options, like all financial instruments, are priced in a market, and the evidence is mixed as to whether the Black-Scholes model accurately predicts their value. One of the weaknesses of the model is that is assumes the asset price to vary randomly with a constant trend and standard deviation (the "random walk"). This is not a particularly robust assumption, and the market often has other opinions about how the asset value will fluctuate. Nonetheless, the model is a useful indicator, and it reinforces the two key lessons about options, a) options always have non-negative value, and b) the greater the uncertainty about the future value of the asset, the more valuable an option becomes.

The complements to financial options are what we call real options, the word 'real' signifying that they are based on tangible assets, not financial instruments. These options are embedded in many of the operating decisions that we make and while we often have an instinctive sense of their value, it is rare that this is quantified. Let's take an example of a call option that we can create for ourselves. Suppose you buy a component from a foreign supplier. The supplier is high-quality and low-cost, but it insists on pricing its product in its own currency, which happens to vary considerably against your own. If you cultivate a domestic supplier, so that you can move production quantities to it when exchange rates dictate, you have created a call option. The domestic supplier may be higher-cost on average, but the presence of the option has some positive value to you. Whether that value offsets the higher costs of qualifying (and probably giving some share of the business to) the second supplier is something that can be simulated and evaluated. Supplement

18-1 shows the use of simulation for assessing uncertainty. Another way to create a call option is to invest in keeping up with a developing technology, so that if it takes off, you have the option to participate in that business sector. The option value inherent in new product development is often dismissed when evaluating these expenditures.

Similarly, you can create a put option by making it easier to exit a business if it proves unattractive. The most obvious way is to avoid investing in product-specific assets and instead use flexible automation or reusable equipment. Operating managers don't usually think in terms of puts and calls, so it may be useful to categorize the available real options as follows:

1. The ability to buy something at an agreed price in the future, that is potentially better than the default option (the classic call option).
2. The ability to abandon a project at a manageable cost, should it prove to be unprofitable (a version of the classic put option).
3. The ability to delay a major commitment such as a capital investment until more information is available to evaluate its profitability.
4. The flexibility to convert assets to different uses (and back again) to respond to changes in supply or demand.

Some of these situations can be modeled with the tools used for valuing financial options, but real options tend to be somewhat more complicated and, in many cases, you are better off building a simulation model. Supplement 18-2 shows how we might use simulation to evaluate the worth of an option that is embedded in a choice that might otherwise seem too costly. As always, our focus is on differential analysis, and in this case, we are looking for options that are present in one decision alternative, but not in another. If we can assign a value to that option, then we can better compare the TCOs of the choices.

Chapter 18 – Key Takeaways

1. Risk creates cost.

2. The general riskiness of a business sector is reflected in the discount rate (cost of capital) used for evaluating projects.

3. Most of the apparent profit in a supply chain is not economic profit; it is just the cost of assuming the risks of the business. As such, it is a legitimate cost that must be accounted for during pricing negotiations.

4. Project-specific risk cannot be reduced to a single number, but must be expressed in probabilistic terms, usually in the form of a mean and a standard deviation. It is often difficult to calculate these values, but they can be estimated with simulation techniques.

5. Actions can be taken to reduce the riskiness of business choices, although usually at some cost. Key examples are hedging, risk-pooling and the creation of real options.

6. The decisions about how much risk to accept, or how much cost to incur to mitigate them, are human decisions that have no single right answer.

Supplement 18-1 – Using Simulation to Determine Variance

When evaluating a change that has some uncertainty in its outcome, being given an expected value for the NPV is of limited value. To make an informed decision, you must know something about the range of values you might encounter. This can be expressed in several ways, the commonest being the standard deviation (σ). To arrive at this value, two things are necessary. First, you must know, or assume, the probability distributions of all the components of the change that are uncertain, and then you must use these to calculate the probability distribution of the outcome of interest. If using our differential analysis template, that outcome will be the NPV of the change.

Assigning probability distributions to the uncertain elements is one of those areas where it is better to be approximately right than to ignore the situation, so we do the best we can. In some cases, you may have historical data that you can project into the future, either by fitting the data to one of the common statistical distributions (normal, exponential, etc.), or by establishing a histogram of actual data with no reference to any particular distribution. Sometimes all you have is an estimate. You may ask your roofing contractor how long a job will take and get an answer like: "most likely six days, five if everything goes right, but maybe up to eight if there are any snags." That doesn't give you too much to work with, but there is clearly variability that you should account for.

Calculating the standard deviation of the output can get extremely complicated if multiple sources of variance are present, so for the most part we avoid an analytical approach. Instead, we use simulation, specifically Monte Carlo simulation. Monte Carlo simulation is a sampling technique. The way it works is that, for each of the uncertain elements, we take a random sample from the probability distributions that we assigned to them, and use these values to calculate our result. We then repeat this process a very large number of times until we have a histogram that approaches the true probability distribution of the output. From this histogram, we can easily calculate mean, standard deviation, and any other statistical property of interest.

There are specialized software packages that automate this process, and many companies use them. Generally, these packages are quite expensive, but some freeware options are available[1]. You can actually do quite a lot with the standard Excel tools, as we will show in this example.

We will use the same product that we used in Supplement 16-1, Case #2, but we will introduce a third process change option that has some uncertain elements in it and call it Case #3. As with case #2, we will make some product redesigns and change how we purchase parts to allow us to retire the automated assembly equipment. However, one of the new purchased components must be made from an exotic material that has very volatile pricing in global markets. Based on the average price of this material, we expect the cost of purchased parts to increase by $0.25, as before. However, based on the pricing history of this material, this value could be anywhere between $0.10 and $0.40. We could model this with different probability distributions, but for example purposes we will use a uniform distribution and assume that any value on this range is equally likely.

To process the new material, we have to buy some new equipment for the assembly line at a cost of $100,000. We will depreciate this on a ten-year, straight line basis and assume that its salvage value at the end of production is uncertain but will be in the range of its book value, plus or minus 50%. We will simulate this with a triangular distribution. Triangular distributions are not really an accurate representation of any natural process, but they are frequently used in simulation because they have some useful properties and are a simple way to capture rough estimates such as this one.

The upside of buying this new equipment is that processing speed can be increased, with a corresponding reduction in direct labor. The process engineers think a 10% increase in

---

1   Specifically, see: http://home.uchicago.edu/~rmyerson/addins.htm (at the time of writing).

standard can be expected, but aren't sure – it could run as much as 20% faster or not at all. We can simulate that with a triangular distribution as well.

We will make the same assumptions as we did in Supplement 16-1 about overheads and SG&A – that the total amounts don't change except for depreciation. If we do that, and put in the expected values or all of the changes, the comparative cost file looks like Figure 18-1.1:

Figure 18-1.1: Comparative Cost File

Product Cost File		
	NEW	OLD
Direct Costs:		
Net Purchases	$2.25	$2.00
Direct Labor: $20x5/(125*1.1)	$0.73	$0.80
Total Direct Cost	$2.98	$2.80
Overhead:		
Specific Depreciation ($100,000/10/500,000)	$0.02	$0.40
General Overhead (@250% of DL)	$1.82	$2.00
Total Overhead	$1.84	$2.40
Total Factory Cost:	$4.82	$5.20
SG&A (10% of Factory Cost)	$0.48	$0.52
Total Cost:	$5.30	$5.72
Target profit (10% of total cost)	$0.53	$0.57
Target Selling Price:	$5.83	$6.29

At a quick glance, this looks like a worthwhile cost reduction. To be sure, we can do a differential analysis, using the most likely values again, and we get the result in Figure 18-1.2:

Figure 18-1.2: Case #3 Differential Analysis

Case #3 Differential Analysis

	Now	Year 1	Year 2	Year 3	Year 4
Change in Net Revenue					
Price Effect	-	-	-	-	-
Volume Effect	-	-	-	-	-
Other Revenue (e.g.: scrap recovery)	-	-	-	-	-
Total	-	-	-	-	-
Changes in Cost of Goods Sold					
Purchased Materials	-	125,000	125,000	125,000	125,000
Shipping	-	-	-	-	-
Other Items (duties, storage, etc.)	-	-	-	-	-
Net Change in Purchased Goods	-	125,000	125,000	125,000	125,000
Changes in Direct Labor		(40,000)	(40,000)	(40,000)	(40,000)
Changes in Overhead					
Depreciation	-	(190,000)	(190,000)	(190,000)	(190,000)
Other Overhead	-	-	-	-	-
Volume Effect on Variable Overhead	-	-	-	-	-
Sales and administrative expenses	-	-	-	-	-
Total Overheads	-	(190,000)	(190,000)	(190,000)	(190,000)
Changes in Other Income					
Gain (Loss) on disposal of assets	(1,600,000)	-	-	-	-
Changes in Gross Income	(1,600,000)	105,000	105,000	105,000	105,000
Change in Taxes (at 35%)	(560,000)	36,750	36,750	36,750	36,750
Changes in Net Income	(1,040,000)	68,250	68,250	68,250	68,250
Plus Depreciation		- (190,000)	(190,000)	(190,000)	(190,000)
Less Gain (loss) on disposal of assets	(1,600,000)	-	-	-	-
Adjusted Net Income	560,000	(121,750)	(121,750)	(121,750)	(121,750)
Less capital expenditures	100,000	-	-	-	(60,000)
Less Increase in working capital	31,250	-	-	-	(31,250)
Changes to Net Cash Flow	428,750	(121,750)	(121,750)	(121,750)	(30,500)
NPV @12%	$116,944				
IRR	-3.6%				

Again, with a positive NPV of nearly $117,000, this looks like a worthwhile project. Notice also, that this is one of those examples mentioned in Chapter 2 where the IRR figure is not meaningful. Since the initial cash inflow more than offsets all of the future outflows, NPV will be positive for any positive value of r, so we have to use the NPV at a designated discount rate to tell the correct story.

However, when we take into account the uncertainties, we find that most-likely values only give us part of the story. Figure 18-1.3 shows the same differential analysis, but with randomized values inserted for all the items we listed above. These values are sampled from the distributions we assumed, so this figure shows just one possible outcome of the project, and is equally likely as any other sample outcome.

Figure 18-1.3: Case #3 Randomized Differential Analysis

Case #3 Differential Analysis with Randomness					
	Now	Year 1	Year 2	Year 3	Year 4
Change in Net Revenue					
Price Effect	-	-	-	-	-
Volume Effect	-	-	-	-	-
Other Revenue (e.g.: scrap recovery)	-	-	-	-	-
Total	-	-	-	-	-
Changes in Cost of Goods Sold					
Purchased Materials	-	152,598	102,770	149,635	131,472
Shipping	-	-	-	-	-
Other Items (duties, storage, etc.)	-				
Net Change in Purchased Goods	-	152,598	102,770	149,635	131,472
Changes in Direct Labor		-	-	-	-
Changes in Overhead					
Depreciation	-	(190,000)	(190,000)	(190,000)	(190,000)
Other Overhead	-	-	-	-	-
Volume Effect on Variable Overhead		-	-	-	-
Sales and administrative expenses		-	-	-	-
Total Overheads	-	(190,000)	(190,000)	(190,000)	(190,000)
Changes in Other Income					
Gain (Loss) on disposal of assets	(1,600,000)	-	-	-	-
Changes in Gross Income	(1,600,000)	37,402	87,230	40,365	58,528
Change in Taxes (at 35%)	(560,000)	13,091	30,531	14,128	20,485
Changes in Net Income	(1,040,000)	24,311	56,700	26,238	38,043
Plus Depreciation	-	(190,000)	(190,000)	(190,000)	(190,000)
Less Gain (loss) on disposal of assets	(1,600,000)	-	-	-	-
Adjusted Net Income	560,000	(165,689)	(133,300)	(163,762)	(151,957)
Less capital expenditures	100,000	-	-	-	-
Less Increase in working capital	38,150	-	-	-	(38,150)
Changes to Net Cash Flow	421,850	(165,689)	(133,300)	(163,762)	(113,807)
NPV @12%	($21,242)				
IRR	14.5%				

The NPV value from Figure 18-1.3 doesn't really tell us much of anything – it is just one possible outcome. To get a sense of the range of possible outcomes and their likelihoods, we used the Excel Data Table function to repeat this experiment 10,000 times, and while the results are approximate, they are good to within a couple of percent. The results are shown in Figure 18-1.4:

Figure 18-1.4: Case #3 Simulation Results

Data Table From Simulation				
Run #	$94,408		Mean:	$117,275
1	$215,622		Std. Dev.:	$56,566
2	$32,015		P<0:	1.85%
3	$53,067		Max:	$301,996
4	$164,235		Min:	-$89,039
9995	$180,334			
9996	$113,310			
9997	$44,804			
9998	$73,958			
9999	$120,715			
10000	$147,978			

This confirms the $117,000 figure as the expected value, but there is a lot of variance, and the actual outcome can be very good or very bad. The odds are still pretty good though: there is only a 2% chance that this change would actually make things worse. Would you still want to do it? There is no single right answer about how to make this decision, but if you go ahead, you should do it with full awareness of the possible outcomes.

The point of this example is that, when variance is present, it is dangerous to make decisions on the basis of single-point estimates – even if they represent the most likely outcomes. The probability distribution of possible outcomes needs to be considered in some way. To do this, Monte Carlo simulation is a powerful and widely-used tool.

Supplement 18-2 – Real Options: The Worth of Flexibility

One of the real options available to operating managers is the use of flexible equipment (and this could include people too, through cross-training) to respond to differing conditions. Typically, a flexible setup will cost more than a more dedicated one, and the challenge is to determine how much of a premium is worth paying. This can be very challenging, so here we will illustrate one approach, using a purely hypothetical example.

Suppose we have need for a large pump, and the choices available to us are to power it either a natural gas turbine or a large electric motor. We have done our analysis, and we find that although the electric option is initially cheaper (less capital investment), the cost of electricity used will be higher than the cost of gas and that the turbine option is preferred on an NPV basis. So far, so good, but it might occur to you to ask whether having both available (and the ability to switch between them as needed) might be better yet. Intuitively, we can see that this would only make sense if there were some non-zero probability that electricity might be cheaper than gas for at least some of the expected life of the equipment. We might also conclude (correctly) that the wider the price swings, the more this option would be worth. But how much is it worth? Analytical approaches can be applied to some of these situations, but simulation is often an easier approach. Let's consider an example.

In the above scenario, we are primarily interested in how much value is added by having the electric option on standby, and for that we need to know the probability distributions of the costs of gas and electricity. Forecasting future energy prices is problematic, but we can make some approximations.

Let's assume, in a purely hypothetical situation, that running our pumping equipment on electricity would cost $50,000/ mo. at current rates, and that gas would cost $40,000/mo. As long as those rates remain in that relationship to each other, gas is the clear winner. However, if their costs may vary in an uncorrelated way, and if the ranges overlap, there will be some option value to consider. For that we have to assign probability distributions to these two cost elements, and here, one guess may be as good as another. For simplicity we'll assign triangular distributions (popular in simulation models) to both, with the following properties:

Monthly Cost	Minimum	Most Likely	Maximum
Electricity	$40,000	$50,000	$60,000
Gas	$25,000	$40,000	$65,000

We'll further assume that we can know our costs for the coming month and can change over accordingly. We can then run a simulation for ten years (120 months) to see what our expected energy cost would be if we could switch on a month-to-month basis, and bring this back to an NPV value. The results of this simulation are shown in Figure 18-2.1.

The actual simulation is of a ten-year (120-month) period using randomized values for gas and electricity prices every month. The lower cost alternative was used for each month, and the end result is compared to the cost of using only gas (the baseline decision). The present value of the differences was collected. This ten-year period was then repeated 10,000 times using a data table and averages were taken of the key parameters. The main points are shown in the summary box at the lower right. The single most important takeaway is that, under all of these assumptions, having the option to use electricity has an NPV of about $98,000. Whether that is enough to pay for the equipment that constitutes the real option will depend on additional data and analysis.

We can also see that the option will lower our monthly expected energy costs by about $1,400, consistent with the NPV figure. What is interesting to note, although it doesn't have a cost figure attached to it, is that the option also lowers the variability of energy costs, reducing the standard deviation by about 20%.

Figure 18-2.1: Simulation of Option Value

Simulating an Option Value

	Monthly Cost					
	Minimum	Most Likely	Maximum		Expected NPV:	-$98,263
Electricity	$40,000	$50,000	$60,000		Gas-Only Cost	$43,331
Gas	$25,000	$40,000	$65,000		Std. Dev.	$8,239
					Cost w. Option	$41,956
	Per Year	Per Month			Std. Dev. W. Option	$6,585
r	12%	0.949%				

Month	Rand #	Electricity Cost	Rand #	Gas Cost	Actual Cost	Saving
1	0.098	$44,438	0.216	36,395	$36,395	$0
2	0.164	$45,732	0.746	49,051	$45,732	-$3,319
3	0.619	$51,273	0.177	35,306	$35,306	$0
4	0.322	$48,020	0.884	54,226	$48,020	-$6,206
115	0.228	$46,755	0.658	46,519	$46,519	$0
116	0.994	$58,891	0.001	25,826	$25,826	$0
117	0.879	$55,075	0.267	37,646	$37,646	$0
118	0.491	$49,908	0.354	39,570	$39,570	$0
119	0.824	$54,065	0.372	39,932	$39,932	$0
120	0.854	$54,596	0.518	43,034	$43,034	$0
	Mean	$49,508		$43,299	$41,695	(116,814.08)
	Std. Dev.	$3,967		$8,009	$5,971	

Data Table	NPV	Gas Cost	Std. Dev.	Actual	Std. Dev.
	-$116,814	$43,299	$8,009	$41,695	$5,971
1	-$124,625	$44,021	$9,059	$42,287	$6,926
2	-$107,009	$43,654	$8,463	$42,246	$6,954
3	-$93,034	$43,756	$8,073	$42,280	$6,547
9996	-$102,726	$43,764	$8,027	$42,325	$6,578
9997	-$112,395	$42,563	$9,032	$41,030	$6,870
9998	-$123,390	$44,111	$8,534	$42,313	$6,230
9999	-$63,079	$43,080	$7,722	$42,065	$6,343
10000	-$141,057	$44,459	$8,527	$42,538	$6,585

Chapter 19 – Cost Management as a Strategic Initiative

The theme of this book is cost *management*, and the general meaning of that is that we are trying to make the costs of what we do as low as they can feasibly be, consistent with our tolerance for risk. The foundation for management of costs is a comprehensive model for evaluating the consequences of our decisions, and that has been the core of this book. Once the core is in place, we can examine different avenues by which we can manage (reduce) our costs. What we discover in many cases is that our options are constrained by decisions previously made, or by structural factors in our organization. Correcting or overcoming these issues requires upper management awareness and involvement, and often doesn't look specifically like a cost reduction initiative. The goal of this chapter is to take a step back from day-to-day operations and view the organization, its customers and suppliers as an integrated whole.

Tactical vs Strategic

Actual cost management can take place at multiple levels and we can roughly segregate these into tactical and strategic. Working on the premise that reducing costs is always good, much can be done at a tactical level by giving incentives to operating-level employees to reduce the costs of what they do. We can see this in the various performance measures that are used for evaluation, most of which are some sort of productivity measures. Examples include purchased-price-variance (PPV) for purchasing staff, labor productivity for line supervisors, unit part cost for plant managers, and so on.

To a point, these are useful measures, but they focus on individual parts of the puzzle. This creates two main difficulties. The first, as we have seen, is that such performance measures don't capture the true TCO of the actions that might be taken, with the danger that it is possible to improve a specific measure but at the same time worsening true company performance[1]. This book provides a set of tools to analyze this, but there is still the need for some sort of management oversight that goes beyond the basic performance metrics. Someone has to analyze the consequences of actions and determine their acceptability. Most companies have some informal ways of doing this, but counter-productive actions still slip through.

The second difficulty is that cost management opportunities requiring coordinated action between multiple functions tend to be overlooked. Even when such coordination is attempted, reliance on simple performance metrics tends to create winners and losers. In other words, a total gain may be possible, but it will often look like a loss to one or more parties. The result is that resistance to implementation is the likely reaction.

This highlights the need to approach cost management on a more strategic level, giving proper attention (and incentives) to the various functions that need to be involved – and that includes both suppliers and customers. The enabler for a strategic approach is a comprehensive measurement tool that captures the true TCO of any situation or solution, and that is what this book attempts to provide.

Local vs Global

A corollary to the strategic/tactical divide is the nature of optimization. When we try to manage costs, we are implicitly trying to achieve the optimal, or best possible solution. When we give performance incentives to operating-level employees, that is what they will try to do, within their scope of control. However, students of system design and system thinking are well aware that while this sort of local optimization *may* lead to an improvement in performance overall, it does not result in global optimization. Global of course is a somewhat relative term; for our purposes it may mean the overall cost of a particular product or product line. Or, it may mean the performance of an operating facility, or an entire company.

1   See: Melnyk, S. A., et al. (2010). "Hitting the Target but Missing the Point: Resolving the Paradox of Strategic Transition." Long Range Planning 43(4).

However we define it, managing costs at that level becomes a strategic initiative requiring management intervention and oversight. Achieving optimization at this level requires performance measurements that all parties can agree are correct for evaluation of their results. This, ideally, is what a TCO analysis can provide.

Future Orientation

We noted that many cost management options are constrained by past decisions, suggesting that managing those decisions strategically is an important element of cost management. This shows up most clearly in the new product development phase where we have shown that there are options in how a product is designed, how it is specified, ownership of tooling and/or intellectual property, degree of early engagement with suppliers, and more. These choices should, but often don't, dovetail with the supplier relationship strategies described in Chapter 17. Getting the right alignment of these elements is one of the most critical factors in cost management, but requires a very strategic approach that we can describe as design for supply chain (DfSC). Integrating the new product development and supply management functions is a powerful way to achieve this, but it still requires a forward-looking mentality that can look beyond short-term performance measures.

TCO Mentality – What Really Is the Total Cost?

The term TCO has entered our vocabulary and is now widely-used, particularly in the purchasing function. This is encouraging as it signals an increasing awareness of costs that might previously have been ignored. However, the term is used rather loosely, and there is the danger that a TCO "analysis" may only include the items that the proponent wanted to include. Some companies have formal TCO worksheets, usually for purchasing of specific product lines. This is also good because it promotes the right way of thinking about our decisions, but the results are only as good as the templates. Some things might come up that were not considered when the templates were developed, and attempting to apply the template to even slightly different products or services may miss key factors. That is why, in this book, we tend to advocate a do-it-yourself approach, if for no other reason than it forces you to think through all of the implications of any action. This may seem like a lot of work, and it can be, but if you focus only on the differential aspects of the change it minimizes this. The template provided in this book is sufficiently comprehensive that it can be expanded to include almost any eventuality.

How You Convince Others

Unless you are the sole proprietor of your business, you don't usually get to make and implement decisions without getting the approval of others, or at least having to face scrutiny of your decisions after the fact. This means that you must not only do good analyses and make good decisions, you must also find a way to convince others that your conclusions are correct. This can be quite difficult in several situations; most commonly where achieving an overall gain requires giving up something on a measure that is important to someone. An example might be an outsourcing decision where the result is an apparent decrease in unit profitability that is offset by cash flow and tax considerations. There will also be situations where some of the stakeholders have strong preconceived opinions and will need a very solid analysis to gain their concurrence. The outsourcing example would be the sort of decision where there may be strong opinions for or against. Often, this is a measurement problem, as traditional measures may fail to capture the necessary detail. It is also a performance management problem caused by the use of local or otherwise inappropriate measures to motivate performance.

The differential analysis template presented in Chapters 10 & 11 is a very robust tool to use in these circumstances, for several reasons. First, the overall structure is based on standard financial accounting documents, so that anyone familiar with finances or accounting will recognize the flow and logic. Second, it is transparently comprehensive. Because it mimics financial accounting documents, every item that can be considered has a home. If anyone thinks an item is missing, it is possible to see where in the model it should go, and the results can be tested. To this last point, if the analysis is presented as a live spreadsheet, any differences of opinion can be tested on the spot. For example, if someone wants to disagree with your estimate of a residual, you can ask them for their number and plug it in. Finally, all of the data points on the template have an "owner" – someone you can go to and ask: "is this right?" If you have done that, it is unlikely that an analysis presented in this way will face any serious challenges.

What Problem Are You Trying to Solve?

When presenting an analysis in support of a decision or recommendation, it is important to understand the criteria by which it will be evaluated. Chapter 1 asked the question of why we care about cost and we showed that different stakeholders have different reasons for being concerned about cost. Consequently, they may react differently to proposed actions. The analysis tools we have covered will allow most of these concerns to be addressed, and more importantly, can show when some concerns are misplaced.

ROA

Our guiding principle throughout, is that the goal of business is to make economic profit, which is to say, earning the best return on the assets invested. It is possible to make a calculation of economic profit, or economic value-added, but this is not commonly done, and the results are subject to misinterpretation. Instead, it is more common to report return on assets, which is closely correlated with economic profit. There is an implicit understanding that a certain minimum value is necessary for ongoing viability and to satisfy shareholders. Assuming that ROA is really the concern, then you can use the strategic profit model (Supplement 3-1) to demonstrate how the proposed change will enhance it. The problem with using this model is that only large-scale improvements will show up in a total-company ROA, and many of the things we do will be no more than rounding errors. Instead, our emphasis has been on establishing the NPV of a proposed change to show whether it is positive or not and by how much. This is generally more impactful for decision-making purposes. The caveat is that any form of NPV or economic profit calculation requires that you choose a discount rate (cost of capital). Since this can be contentious, it is often preferable to present the IRR instead. However, not all cash flow patterns lend themselves to a meaningful calculation of IRR, so this cannot be a universal recommendation.

Profit Margin

Many stakeholders are interested in the apparent profitability of a product or a company, expressed as a percentage of sales or of costs. Product line managers are interested in the per-unit profitability of their products, as it tends to impact their compensation. We have seen how the standard cost information gives us a figure for that, but we have also shown that this standard cost is not only an incomplete picture, it may also be quite misleading when evaluating changes. The latter is most likely to be the case when the company's cost allocation methods are unsophisticated. It is possible to present standard cost file-type information as justification for a particular change, and that may be all that your stakeholders want to see, but we know by now that this is not full disclosure! It would be far better to complete the differential analysis worksheet as shown in the supplement to Chapter 16 and make reference to the line showing changes in net income. This will give a truer picture of the actual profit margin changes.

Cash Flow

While profit matters in the long-term, all operations need positive cash flow to survive in the short-term. A useful byproduct of the NPV calculation is that we generate year over year cash flow information that may be the most important part of the analysis for some constituents. What we are showing is cash flow from operations, so negative numbers are not necessarily bad, they just have to be offset by cash inflows from other parts of the organization, or by new cash from loans or share sales. What we are able to show is how cash flows differ between decision alternatives. How this information is evaluated depends on company specifics, so is beyond our scope, but we can at least provide the data.

Risk Abatement

Two things that the differential analysis worksheet does not show explicitly are the levels of risk inherent in the alternatives being compared, or the option values that may be embedded in them. There are a couple of ways that we can adjust for risk, as discussed in Chapter 10. We can add or remove buffer stocks of inventory (increasing or decreasing working capital) as a way to equalize situations with different risk levels. We can also use residuals, such as a reserve for excess warranty claims to accomplish the same thing. Since these are not very transparent in the overall calculation, explanatory notes should be provided. When these equalizing tactics are not appropriate, the fallback position is a simulation of the inherent risks as shown in Chapter 18. Simulation can also be used to show when there is an option value to consider. Just because a particular audience has not requested an evaluation of risk doesn't mean that they shouldn't be exposed to it! If they aren't, what will often happen is that they will start arbitrarily adjusting the discount rate as a subjective risk evaluation. Far better to make that discussion explicit.

PPV (Purchase Price Variance)

There are many function-level metrics that are affected by cost management activities, but one that comes up quite frequently is PPV. It does have value as a tracking metric, to see how you are doing, but it is dangerous to use it as the basis of an incentive plan. This is the performance management problem again. That said, it remains in wide usage and certain individuals will be vitally concerned by changes. The standard cost file, combined with a volume forecast usually provides all the data needed to estimate a change in PPV, but as we know, this may not be a complete picture. For one thing, PPV is calculated against a baseline that may not be accurate – something that we should have sorted out when doing a proper differential analysis. If done correctly, the line on the differential analysis worksheet for change in purchased materials should be an accurate representation of the effect. However, the main value of the differential analysis and bringing it down to an NPV, is to be able to make the case – where appropriate – that a change may be detrimental to PPV, but still be NPV-positive for the company. In other words, you may be able to use this sort of analysis to do the right thing and hopefully get rewarded for it rather than penalized.

Different way of thinking about profit

One of the consequences of thinking deeply about cost is that one develops a different conceptualization of profit. We quickly discover that most of what we typically call profit isn't really profit at all in the economic sense. Instead, it is actually a cost; specifically, the opportunity cost of using assets for a specific purpose. This insight is helpful in assessing the prices that our suppliers charge us, particularly in those cases where there is no clear market price or where prices have to be negotiated after the fact. Once we recognize that we are mostly talking about cost, not profit, it also makes for a more objective discussion.

The same thing applies to the accounting profits made by our own organization. If we recognize that these are mostly a cost, then it is a cost that can be managed like any other. There are two components of this cost: the assets involved, and the degree of risk they are exposed to. The first impulse is probably to try to reduce the assets employed, and the most obvious way to do that is to outsource various operations. Unfortunately, that represents single company thinking as opposed to system thinking – outsourcing, by and large, doesn't reduce the total asset base, it just transfers some of it from one company to another. Naturally, the opportunity cost of those assets has to be paid for, as discussed in Chapter 18 (Make vs. Buy). We have previously discussed approaches to reducing the asset requirements, primarily under process optimization and new product/process development, but here we want to explore reducing the risk exposure.

Thinking strategically about it, we can look at all of the risks associated with a line of business, and ask the question of who is best equipped to either manage them or to pool them. What we quickly conclude is that unless we have some comparative advantage over other companies in our ability to manage or pool specific risks, then we are going to come out ahead by paying the experts to do it for us. This is the outsourcing scenario discussed previously, where even though the apparent profit margin may go down, the effective reduction in the cost of capital causes economic profit to go up. This is a tough argument for most executives to accept, so perhaps we should turn to noted economist Robert Merton for a better explanation[1]!

Major Unresolved Problem – Cost of Risk

No field of study would be interesting if it didn't have some unanswered questions, and for cost management, that is the true cost of risk. Throughout this book, we have kept coming back to the idea that risk creates cost and that reduction of risk is effectively a reduction of cost. The problem of course, has been to quantify that effect. For one thing, risk tends to mean different things to academics and business people. The former generally consider risk as simple unpredictability of outcomes that is passively assumed, and can be measured with statistical parameters. The latter have a more subjective interpretation since they don't passively assume risk if they can help it. Therefore, they categorize risk by its degree of manageability, and tend only to be concerned about unpredictability on the down side.

Regardless of definition, certain risks can be priced in a market, and this shows up in our computations as a cost of capital. This market is imperfect because the information available is imperfect. Investors cannot look into every decision made by a company, they can only react to broad market averages, modified by scraps of company-specific information. Every so often, these market evaluations go through some gyrations as events cause investors to re-assess the market risks. Nonetheless, market pricing of

1   Merton, R. C. (2005). "You Have More Capital Than You Think." Harvard Business Review 83(11): 84-94.

risks does give us some broad guidelines that we can use for discounting future events.

What we still don't have, and probably never will, is any concrete way to compare two decision alternatives that are specific to our firm only and to quantify them in the sense that "all else being equal, alternative A costs X more than alternative B because of its inherent risks." What we can do, using the tools in this book, is to *price* that risk. We do that by quantifying everything that we can, including the costs of hedging those risks that can be hedged or insured against. Once we have done that, the differential that remains is the price that we would receive to take on the remaining risks. Whether or not we accept that price and go forward is a very subjective decision, meaning that the answer will depend on a set of circumstances that are unique to each decision-maker.

Chapter 19 – Key Takeaways

1. Cost reduction can be pursued at the local level or at a higher system level. Both can be beneficial, but system-level solutions offer many more opportunities.

2. System level cost reduction can take place across company functions or across buyer/supplier boundaries. Both require management oversight, and rely on comprehensive cost analysis tools.

3. The most effective cost management is achieved by configuring, designing and specifying new product in a manner consistent with supply chain strategy. To be strategic in this process frequently requires top management involvement.

4. Comprehensive cost analysis is required to evaluate proposed initiatives and is critically important for achieving approval or buy-in from stakeholders.

5. No cost analysis can attach a definitive cost to risk, but can put a price on it, allowing human decision-makers to make an informed choice.

Appendix – Spreadsheet For Differential Cost Analysis

The central theme of this book is the need to conduct differential analysis when comparing cost scenarios. Several spreadsheet examples were introduced to show how this can be done, with the main point being that you must build the model to suit your particular situation. The important thing is to keep the headings intact so that you have a checklist of sorts to ensure that your analysis is comprehensive. Below those headings you can expand or contract the level of detail as needed.

Although the basic template was developed in Chapter 10, a more generalized version is used in the supplement to Chapter 16 (Figure 16-1.7) to show how to analyze the effects of a process change.

To make this into an even more general template, it needs to be cleaned up a bit. Specifically, there are three data points that were hidden in that example to improve readability. These are: the tax rate, the average payment period on payables and receivables, and the discount rate used for evaluation. Good spreadsheet design practice requires that these be given their own labeled cells. This is done in the example below (Figure A.1) that also shows all of the formulas used to build the model.

As is always the case with such models, there are multiple ways that some of the formulas could have been written, so feel free to modify as long as you observe the sign conventions. Some people prefer to use named cells and ranges as it makes the formulas easier to read and understand. Unfortunately, doing this makes it much harder to modify the spreadsheet, so it is best not to do that until you have an absolutely final version to release to the world.

The model can be simplified if certain elements are not present. For example, if there is no volume change involved, you don't need rows 5 or 20. Similarly, if there is no capital acquisition or disposal involved, you don't need rows 25 or

35. What you will do however, is to add rows to itemize the specific details of your situation. Basically, this means that any of the rows in the model that have numbers in them (including ones with zeros in this example) could be subdivided to show more detail.

Figure A.1- Spreadsheet Model

	A	B	C	D	E
1		Version of Figure 16-1.7: Case #2 Differential Analysis			
2				Now	Year 1
3	Change in Net Revenue				
4		Price Effect		0	0
5		Volume Effect		0	0
6		Other Revenue (scrap recovery)		0	0
7		Total		0	=SUM(E4:E6)
8					
9	Changes in Cost of Goods Sold				
10		Purchased Materials		0	125,000.00
11		Shipping		0	0
12		Other Items (duties, storage, etc.)		0	0
13		Net Change in Purchased Goods			=SUM(E10:E12)
14					
15		Changes in Direct Labor			0
16					
17	Changes in Overhead				
18		Depreciation		0	-200000
19		Other Overhead Categories		0	0
20		Volume Effect on Var. Overhead		0	0
21		SG&A		0	0
22		Total Overheads		=SUM(D18:D21)	=SUM(E18:E21)
23					
24	Changes in Other Income				
25		Gain (Loss) on disposal of assets		-1600000	0
26					
27	Changes in Gross Income			=D7-D13-D15-D22+D25	=E7-E13-E15-E22+E25
28		Change in Taxes (at 35%)	0.35	=D27*C28	=E27*C28
29	Changes in Net Income			=D27-D28	=E27-E28
30					
31		Plus Depreciation		=D18	=E18
32		Less Gain on disposal of assets		=D25	=E25
33	Adjusted Net Income			=D29+D31-D32	=E29+E31-E32
34					
35		Less capital expenditures		0	0
36		Less Increase in working capital		=E10*C39	0
37	Changes to Net Cash Flow			=D33-D35-D36	=E33-E35-E36
38					
39		Payment terms (yrs.)	0.25		
40		Discount rate (r) in % per year:	0.12		
41		NPV @ r		=NPV(C40,E37:H37)+D37	
42		IRR		=IRR(D37:H37,C40)	

Figure A.1- Spreadsheet Model (Cont'd.)

	F	G	H
1	**Differential Analysis - Page 2**		
2	Year 2	Year 3	Year 4
3			
4	0	0	0
5	0	0	0
6	0	0	0
7	=SUM(F4:F6)	=SUM(G4:G6)	=SUM(H4:H6)
8			
9			
10	125,000.00	125,000.00	125,000.00
11	0	0	0
12	0	0	0
13	=SUM(F10:F12)	=SUM(G10:G12)	=SUM(H10:H12)
14			
15	0	0	0
16			
17			
18	-200000	-200000	-200000
19	0	0	0
20	0	0	0
21	0	0	0
22	=SUM(F18:F21)	=SUM(G18:G21)	=SUM(H18:H21)
23			
24			
25	0	0	0
26			
27	=F7-F13-F15-F22+F25	=G7-G13-G15-G22+G25	=H7-H13-H15-H22+H25
28	=F27*C28	=G27*C28	=H27*C28
29	=F27-F28	=G27-G28	=H27-H28
30			
31	=F18	=G18	=H18
32	=F25	=G25	=H25
33	=F29+F31-F32	=G29+G31-G32	=H29+H31-H32
34			
35	0	0	0
36	0	0	=-D36
37	=F33-F35-F36	=G33-G35-G36	=H33-H35-H36
38			
39			
40			
41			
42			

Glossary

Accounting Profit – this is the official value of a company's profitability as defined by accounting rules. For our purposes, this is the value of net income from continuing operations as given on the income statement. It does not reflect actual cash flows, and does not include the opportunity cost of the assets employed.

Activity-Based Costing (ABC) – essentially, a method of allocating indirect costs to specific products. The idea is that all the indirect costs are created by activities, and that if you dig deeply enough you can discern the linkage between each activity type and specific products. This information can be valuable for price-setting and for evaluating managerial decisions.

Average Cost – the term applies to something that is made or done in multiple units. The total cost to produce all of the units is divided by the number produced to give an average cost figure. The total cost often contains a significant amount of sunk cost that is incurred at the beginning of production and must be amortized over total production. As a result, average costs are very sensitive to the quantity produced – or the assumptions about that quantity.

Balance Sheet – a formal accounting document that lists all of the firm's assets and all of its liabilities to effectively establish its net worth. Not all assets are listed, for example, intellectual property is mostly ignored. The valuation of assets is also governed by accounting rules and may not be current.

BOM – Bill of Materials – a list of all the components that go into a finished product. An indented BOM breaks up components into their own lists of materials – usually only used when there is in-house assembly or manufacturing of components. The BOM does not typically list the labor operations needed to complete the assembly unless these are outsourced activities. That information is usually found in a document called the Routing.

Clockspeed – A term coined by Charles Fine in a book by the same name as a descriptor of the frequency with which an industry segment undergoes significant technological or structural change.

Cost of Capital – a complex subject, but for our purposes it means the rate of return that we must earn on our assets to satisfy our investors. This would be expressed as a discount rate used to calculate comparative present values of alternatives.

Depreciation – in a general sense, depreciation is the value that an asset loses with use. For accounting purposes, and to comply with tax rules, this is normally figured on a time basis according to preset schedules. This value loss per period then finds its way into the standard cost calculation as a period cost, needing to be divided by the expected level of usage.

Diffusion Curve – when a new product or service is introduced to a market, it starts with zero market share and increases until it reaches a saturation level. The plot of this progression is roughly S-shaped and is called the diffusion curve. Several different variants of these curves have been proposed to model different categories of products.

Discount Rate – a measure of the degree to which a future unit of cost or revenue is lower in value than the same unit in the present. Typically expressed in units of percent per year and represented in equations as r.

DuPont Model – a graphical model that combines the income statement and the balance sheet to show how the components of a business interact to result in a ROA. So named for its first use by the DuPont Corp.

Economic Profit – a rather conceptual term meaning the excess of revenue over all of the costs incurred – specifically including the opportunity costs of using assets that are missing from accounting profit.

Economic Value-Added – essentially the same concept as economic profit, but in a structured accounting-like format.

Frequently known by its three-letter acronym, which is actually a trademark, so is not used here.

Expected Value – a statistical term meaning the weighted average of the possible outcomes of some sort of experiment.

Hurdle Rate – in the presence of multiple opportunities for investment of finite funds, firms often establish a minimum rate of return that is required for a proposal to be approved. This rate is usually considerably higher that the firm's cost of capital and can be expressed either as the discount rate to be applied to a present value calculation, or the IRR value that must be exceeded.

Income Statement – a formal accounting document that captures all of the revenues and expenses of a company in a given time period. This document does not reflect the actual cash flows in and out – that is handled by a separate document.

Intangible Costs – this term applies to cost impacts that cannot be usefully expressed in currency terms. This means that they cannot be measured directly, nor can they be reliably priced in a market. The term is also used somewhat loosely to describe costs that are conceptually quantifiable, but only with great difficulty.

Lean Production – a very widely used and misused term meaning really nothing more than operations without waste. Intuitively this seems to align with a low-cost operation, but what makes it a somewhat complex concept is that waste must be defined from a customer perspective. Inventory is almost always waste from that viewpoint.

Learning Curve – an empirical tool to model the observation that the cost of performing a task can and should decline over time as mistakes are eliminated and new methods are discovered. Unfortunately, there is no theoretical basis for establishing the coefficients of the curve, so rules of thumb are commonly used.

Life Cycle Costing (LCC) – the process of accounting for all of the costs of a product or action that occur over its total lifespan, including initial acquisition or setup costs, ongoing costs of operation and maintenance, and end-of-life costs such as disposal or warranty liabilities. These costs may or may not be discounted back to a present value, but if they are, a discount rate must be stated.

Lumpy – We say that costs are lumpy when they can only be incurred or eliminated in relatively large increments. "Relatively large" in this case means large with respect to the marginal increase or decrease in capability required for whatever decision is under evaluation.

Marginal Cost – This is the incremental cost to make or do one more unit of whatever is in question. Marginal cost contains only the cost items that will change with this additional unit, and disregards any costs that would have been incurred anyway. Marginal costs tend to be constant over ranges of production quantity, but can take large jumps when capacity limits are reached.

Monopolistic Competition – a seeming oxymoron, this means competition in a marketplace where products are potentially substitutable, but not fully interchangeable, hence there will be a sloping demand curve for a particular company's products.

Net Present Value (NPV) – present value is the current value of all future cash flows, in or out, expressed in present day currency value using a defined discount rate. The term *net* present value implies that there are cash flows in the present that need to be added or subtracted to get the full (net) picture.

Opportunity Cost – this is the measure of what you forgo by doing something. All costs are really opportunity costs in a sense, but the term is usually reserved for non-monetary considerations, as in: launching product A would mean forgoing the opportunity to launch product B. It is not really necessary to identify this as a separate line item if a proper differential analysis between alternatives is done.

Purchase Price Variance (PPV) – When a standard cost for a product is established, it is based on assumed purchase prices for the materials and components. The variance is the difference between the total of these prices at the actual production level and the amount that was actually spent to procure them. Often used as a measure of performance for the purchasing staff on the assumption that if the buyers are doing a good job, they should be able to get better pricing than was initially established. The flaws in this assumption are discussed in the text.

Relevant Cost – simply put, a cost is relevant to a particular decision if it can change in response to that decision.

Residual – for the purposes of this book, a residual value is an entry we place in the last period of a multi-period cost analysis to reflect the value at that time of any effects that continue beyond the analysis range. An example might be warranty or liability issues that could last for years – we come up with a single lumped value as a way to account for these.

RFx – "Request for x." The most common usage is RFQ; a request for a formal quotation that can be used as the basis of a purchase order or contract. The same general format can be used to request information about a supplier's capabilities (RFI) or a proposal (RFP), in which a supplier is asked to outline how it would approach a certain job.

"Right" Price – broadly speaking, a price that is acceptable to both buyer and seller. From a buying perspective, a right price is one that is no higher than it should be.

ROA – Return on Assets, normally net income divided by the book value of a company's assets.

ROI – Return on Investment; similar in concept to ROA, but from an investor's perspective. Internal to a company, ROI is the increase in net income divided by the investment needed to realize it. Externally, investors will think in terms of net income divided by their investment, which summed up is the market capitalization of the company.

Salvage Value – the value that can be recovered through the sale of an asset after the analysis period in question. This value can be negative if there are decommissioning expenses.

SG&A – Sales, General and Administrative expenses. These are generally separated from Factory Cost because they are not directly related to production and have to be added on as a sort of corporate "tax." Engineering costs (sometimes called R&D) are often included in this category as they relate to future, not current, product.

"Should" Cost - similar in concept to a "right" price; an evaluation of what it would cost to buy or make something if all best practices were followed. The value has two uses: one is as a target in negotiating purchase prices, and the other is as a basis for establishing selling prices. The latter are frequently based on what something actually does cost, but if this is different from the "should" cost figure, the result may be uncompetitive pricing in a competitive marketplace.

Shrinkage – Typically applied to inventory assets, the amount by which the value of the asset declines over time. The main causes are theft and spoilage.

Sticky – in Finance, dividends are said to be sticky in the sense that once one has been declared, the market expects that it will continue in future periods and will react negatively if that is not true. In a similar fashion, we say that costs are sticky if, once taken on, they are hard to get rid of. Employees are a prime example.

Strategic Profit Model – see "DuPont Model"

Sunk Cost – a cost is sunk if it has already been spent or committed and cannot be retrieved. If that is the case, the amount of the cost should be irrelevant to any future decision.

Supply Chain Finance - a blanket term with multiple meanings, but most commonly applied to the working capital tied up in accounts receivable, or not tied up, as in accounts payable. Current usage is typically applied to the idea that if you increase your accounts payable (by extending payment terms to your suppliers) you achieve a reduction in working capital and a one-time cash inflow. This looks good from a single-company perspective, but is clearly a zero-sum game when the entire supply chain is considered.

Switching Costs - literally, the cost to switch from one alternative to another - usually meaning from one supplier to another. Typically only one-time costs are included under this heading and might include the cost to qualify a new supplier, and any tooling or design changes required.

Tangible Costs – less commonly used than its complementary term – intangible costs – we use this to describe any cost impact that is quantifiable by some method and can be expressed in currency terms.

Tooling - a generic term for unique items required to create a certain product or family of products. Examples would include molds, dies, fixtures, jigs, etc. Accounting may treat these as capital equipment and apply standard depreciation, but since their lifespan depends on the product, a different calculation may be needed for pricing purposes. For that reason it is often billed separately from the unit price.

Total Cost of Ownership (TCO) – this is a widely-used term meaning the collection of all the costs relevant to a particular decision alternative. In many ways this is similar to LCC, but explicitly adds the cross-sectional dimension, looking at cost impacts across all facets of the operation. As discussed in detail in the text, the determination of what costs are relevant can only be made with reference to a specific alternative or baseline. In many ways the term defines a philosophy more than a specific calculation.

Triple Bottom Line - a conceptual more than a calculable number. The traditional "bottom line" is the net income after deduction of all relevant private costs. The TBL concept recognizes that businesses incur public costs by operating, specifically: social and environmental costs, and that a "true" net income figure would be what is left after suitable deductions for these.

WIP (Work in Process) - The amount, or value, of material that has been withdrawn from raw material but is not yet at the finished goods stage. This is part of working capital, and requires as much attention as other classes of inventory.

References and Additional Reading

Anklesaria, J. (2008). Supply Chain Cost Management. New York, AMACOM.

Blocher, E. J., et al. (2010). Cost Management. New York, McGraw-Hill/Irwin.

Bragg, S. M. (2010). Cost Reduction Analysis. Hoboken, NJ, John Wiley & Sons.

Burt, D. N., et al. (1990). Zero Base Pricing, Byline Publishing.

Burt, D. N., et al. (2010). Supply Management. New York, NY, McGraw-Hill Irwin.

Eisenhardt, K. M. and B. N. Tabrizi (1995). "Accelerating adaptive processes: product innovation in the global computer industry." Administrative Sciences Quarterly **40**(1): 84-110.

Fine, C. H. (1998) Clockspeed. Reading, MA, Perseus Books

Garrison, R. H., et al. (2010). Managerial Accounting. New York, NY, McGraw-Hill Irwin.

Hanson, J. D. (2011). "Cost Modelling Based on Experience; Do We Have It Backwards? " International Journal of Procurement Management **4**(5)

Hanson, J. D. (2011). "Differential Method for TCO Modelling: An Analysis and Tutorial," International Journal of Procurement Management **4**(6).

Hanson, J. D. and J. Henkel (2020). "Collaborative Innovation: Weak Commitments and Unenforceable Contracts." International Journal of Procurement Management **13**(1): 63-82.

Harbuck, R. H. (2009). "Life Cycle Cost Analysis for Transportation Projects." AACE International Transactions, AACE International.

Hilton, R. W., et al. (2008). Cost Management. Boston, McGraw-Hill/Irwin.

Horngren, C. T., et al. (2009). Cost Accounting: A Managerial Emphasis. Upper Saddle River, NJ, Pearson Prentice Hall.

http://home.uchicago.edu/~rmyerson/addins.htm

https://money.cnn.com/2012/10/17/technology/apple-china-jobs/

https://www.itl.nist.gov/div898/handbook/pmc/section1/pmc16.htm

Jackson, D. W. and L. L. Ostrom (1980). "Life Cycle Costing in Industrial Purchasing." Journal of Purchasing and Materials Management **16**(4): 8-12.

Kraljic, P., "Purchasing Must Become Supply Management," Harvard Business Review, Sept. – Oct. 1983

Kros, J. F. (2008). Spreadsheet Modeling for Business Decisions. New York, NY, McGraw-Hill/Irwin.

Melnyk, S. A., et al. (2010). "Hitting the Target but Missing the Point: Resolving the Paradox of Strategic Transition." Long Range Planning **43**(4).

Merton, R. C. (2005). "You Have More Capital Than You Think." Harvard Business Review **83**(11): 84-94.

Monczka, R., et al. (2009). Purchasing and Supply Chain Management. Mason, OH, South-Western.

R. Cooper, R. Kaplan (1988) "Measure Costs Right, Make the Right Decisions," Harvard Business Review, September-October, 1988

Shank, J. K. and V. Govindarajan (1993). Strategic Cost Management. New York, The Free Press.

Terweisch, C., et al. (2002). "Exchanging Preliminary Information in Concurrent Engineering: Alternative Coordination Strategies." Organization Science **13**(4): 402-419.

Wileman, A. (2008). Driving Down Cost. London, Nicholas Brealey Publishing.

Index

A

Activity-Based Costing (ABC) 62, 81, 95, 99, 166, 225

B

Balance Sheet 43, 50, 53, 133
Baseline 41, 71, 102, 185, 192
Bill of Materials (BOM) 70, 165

C

Cash Flow 3, 24, 64, 114, 123, 137
Clockspeed 105, 196
CMA (Certified Management Accountant) 55
Commitment 164, 188, 211, 243, 245
Concurrent Engineering 188, 190, 193, 202, 211, 215
Cost
  Allocation 53, 54, 55, 62, 75, 76, 95, 278
  As Measure of Performance 4, 276, 279
  Average 17, 52, 98, 118
  Avoidance 41, 102, 185, 218
  Driver 78, 95, 225
  Factory 69, 82, 136
  Fixed 19, 78, 87, 88, 106, 219
  Intangible 3, 6, 12, 29, 41, 148
  Lumpy 84, 90, 119
  Marginal 17, 98, 118
  Opportunity 20, 33, 38, 56
  Relevant 5, 15, 65, 116
  Standard 67, 127, 278
  Sticky 84, 93
  Sunk 15, 18, 106, 219
  Unquantifiable 11, 40
  Variable 41, 87, 88, 135, 141, 156
Cost File 67, 68, 278
Cost of Capital 34, 170, 244, 251
Cross-Sectional Analysis 6, 62

D

Demand Elasticity 46
Depreciation 54, 64, 114, 122, 132, 135, 219
Differential Analysis 27, 39, 113, 116, 129, 256, 262, 264, 266,
    276, 278, 280, 284

Profit
  Accounting 3, 33, 280
  Economic 3, 56, 170, 255, 277, 280
Purchased Materials 70, 135, 165
Purchase Price Variance (PPV) 72, 279

Q

Quality 98, 115, 187, 202, 223, 246

R

R & D 69, 81, 168, 169, 215
Residual 13, 115, 139, 144, 279
Residual Income 57
Return on Assets (ROA) 34, 43, 53, 277
"Right" Price 9, 152, 154, 155, 156, 157, 158, 159, 161, 171, 187
Risk 8, 22, 32, 40, 103, 146, 167, 174, 180, 250, 251, 279, 281

S

Salvage Value 24, 114
Service Level Agreement (SLA) 186
S, G & A 81, 136, 168
"Should Cost" 157, 162, 170, 183
Simulation (Monte Carlo Simulation) 147, 222, 253, 261, 264,
    279
Six Sigma 202, 223
Specification 152, 160, 178, 186, 194, 199, 202, 211
Statement of Work (SOW) 186
Supply Chain Finance 138

T

Time & Materials Contract (T & M) 175, 177, 183, 188
Tooling 115, 169
Total Cost of Ownership (TCO) 7, 61, 113, 275
Trust 164, 181, 243

W

Working Capital 7, 56, 64, 97, 125, 137, 138